ARSON

ARSON

A HANDBOOK OF DETECTION
AND INVESTIGATION

by

Brendan P. Battle

and

Paul B. Weston

ARCO PUBLISHING COMPANY, INC.

NEW YORK

PUBLISHED BY ARCO PUBLISHING COMPANY, INC.

219 PARK AVENUE SOUTH, NEW YORK CITY 10003

COPYRIGHT MCMLIV BY GREENBERG : PUBLISHER, A CORPORATION

Fifth Arco Printing, 1972

ALL RIGHTS RESERVED UNDER INTERNATIONAL AND PAN AMERICAN
COPYRIGHT CONVENTIONS

Library of Congress Catalog Card Number: 54–7113

ISBN 0–668–00665–X

MANUFACTURED IN THE UNITED STATES OF AMERICA

ACKNOWLEDGMENTS

The authors gratefully acknowledge the valuable assistance of the following persons in preparing this volume:

A Bruce Bielaski, Ass't. General Mgr., National Board of Fire Underwriters

Charles L. Haggerty, President, International Ass'n. of Arson Investigators

William A. Kirwan, Director, New York State Police Scientific Laboratory, Albany, New York

Michael F. Nealis, Ed.D., Director of Voc. and Adult Educ., Mt. Vernon, New York

Albert H. Pike, National Board of Fire Underwriters

CONTENTS

INTRODUCTION
by
A. Bruce Bielaski

*Assistant General Manager of the National
Board of Fire Underwriters, in Charge of
the Arson Department.*

ARSON, a major felony, is one of the most heinous crimes.
At one time in England it was punishable by death by burning. It is rarely, if ever, committed on the spur of the moment,
but always with premeditation and much planning. It may
—and occasionally does—involve not only the loss of property, sometimes irreplaceable, but of lives, as well, and usually the lives of completely innocent people, including firemen.

Twenty-five years ago arson was much more prevalent
than it is today and its perpetrators then included professional arsonists, available for hire, and organized arson rings
operating for their own profit. Most of the cases then, however, as at the present time, were the acts of individuals
without previous conflict with the criminal law. Greed, financial reverses, seemingly easy means of profit, revenge,
and jealousy all have been and still are motives which
prompt individuals to crimes of this kind. Criminals, both
professional and amateur, have resorted to arson as a means
of preventing the discovery of other crimes.

Today, it seems unlikely that any organized rings or any
important professional arsonists are to be found.

Over the years there has come about great improvement in the laws under which arsonists may be dealt with, so that many of the artificial loopholes have been eliminated. A model arson law is now in effect in forty-two states and substantially comparable laws in the rest of the country. The greatest improvement, however, has come about in the increased number of law enforcement officers available for the detection and prosecution of these crimes and the greatly increased skill and knowledge which such law enforcement officers today possess in contrast with those of earlier years. Nothing has added more to this cause of good law enforcement than the arson schools of various types held for the benefit of officers of the law and the manuals and instructive articles on different phases of this work.

There have been, however, too few efforts made to make available an all-embracing book covering this field and Messrs. Battle and Weston, the authors of this book, are to be commended on the thorough and interesting manner in which they have covered all phases of arson investigation. This book can be read with profit by the most experienced investigator of this type of crime and with even greater profit by those who are beginning the work or have occasion infrequently to undertake something of this sort. It is so interestingly written that the layman may get pleasure and profit from it. The authors are to be congratulated on this contribution to the cause of good law enforcement.

ARSON

CHAPTER ONE

SUSPICIOUS FIRES

AN ARSONIST is a potential killer. The fire-bug who crumples a newspaper under a baby carriage in a tenement hallway and then lights it is handling a murder weapon as dangerous as a gun, and a weapon that is inherently capable of far greater damage than any single firearm. A murderer with a gun is almost clean compared to the furtive fire-setter whose match turns the dark night into a hell of smoke and flame.

No one will ever know the exact number of fires which have been set for one reason or another. All fires which occur during the summer are not due to lightning, and all fires which occur in the winter are not due to over-heated stoves.

Invariably a serious fire is regarded as an unfortunate accident rather than as a possible arson case. This belief may result from the fact that fire has been a constant menace to man over the centuries and is rightfully looked upon as a fearsome element that may leap out of control at any time and create great havoc. Another fact may be that most people are normal, law-abiding individuals who have never had any urge to set fire to a building.

Such thinking builds up a tremendous total of fires classified as of accidental origin even though some of them resulted from the acts of arsonists.

In addition to all the incendiary fires whose origin is

erroneously listed as accidental must be added those fires whose origin could not be determined.

DIFFICULTY OF DETECTING ARSON

The frightening thing about the fire-setting picture in the United States is the impossibility of creating a valid statistical picture of the extent of fire-setting. We do know the total number of all fires and we can ascertain the number of accidental, cause unknown, origin undetermined, suspicious, or incendiary fires, but because arson is so difficult to detect such classifications cannot be relied upon. And, of course, some jurisdictions are unfortunate in that their classification of fires may be by untrained personnel, lazy or incompetent persons, or individuals with a heavy work load.

Some idea of the tremendous number of fires which *might* be arson as against those officially recorded as arson can be gathered from a recent annual report of the New York City Fire Department. Slightly over *twenty thousand* fires were investigated but only 231 were classified as incendiary in origin.

Since the New York City Fire Department has one of the top investigating units in the arson field, these figures highlight the difficulty of detecting incendiary fires.

The number of possible arson cases when compared to the number of persons actually arrested for arson also presents a disproportionate picture. The possibility of arson in any local community is pin-pointed in the local press with some frequency. Daily, weekly, or monthly a local news story is concerned with the possibility of arson. Pointing up the possibility of arson on a nationwide scale are the press reports received each day at the headquarters of the International Association of Arson Investigators in Chicago. These reports span the entire country and encompass both urban and rural areas. The following rundown of one day's headlines reveals the nationwide incidence of suspected incendiarism:

San Diego, California—STATE ATTEMPTS TO LINK COWBOY TO FOREST FIRE.

Magnolia, Arkansas　—ARSON BLAMED FOR FIRE LOSSES AT TWO RURAL COUNTY CHURCHES.

Spokane, Washington —ELEVEN-YEAR-OLD BOY ARSON SUSPECT.

Carbondale, Illinois　—FIRE GUTS HOME—COUPLE HELD ON ARSON CHARGE.

Covington, Kentucky —HALLOWEEN VANDALS BLAMED FOR BRIDGE FIRE.

Rochester, New York —THREE FIRES IN THREE DAYS ON NORTH-WEST SIDE LAID TO PYROMANIAC.

However, against this nationwide incidence of suspected arson the total of those arrested is almost ridiculous. An analysis of all arrests reported to the Federal Bureau of Investigation by law enforcement agencies in the United States since 1936 reveals the amazing fact that the yearly average of arson arrests numbers less than nine hundred throughout the entire United States.

In view of such figures it is easy to understand why arson has been termed the easiest crime to commit and the most difficult to detect—tougher to solve than a homicide. The arsonist arms himself with a match, a common item possessed by thousands of people. The arsonist cannot be arrested and charged with possession of a common match because it is an arson weapon. The arsonist has the "edge" before the fire, and he holds it after the blaze. Physical evidence which normally aids in convicting criminals may have been wholly destroyed by the fire itself. At least in a homicide there is some kind of a weapon: a gun, poison, or the like, and there is always the body—good physical evidence.

One of the difficulties in detecting the incendiary origin of fires rests squarely upon fire-setters as a group. Only in rare instances is a true professional criminal, a "torch," encountered. Fire-setters as a group are amateur criminals. The great frequency of crimes committed by professionals—men

and women who make their living from such acts—offers
the police numerous opportunities to identify and apprehend them. The majority of arsonists only offer the police
one opportunity to detect their fire-setting.

A businessman decides that the only manner in which he
can avoid bankruptcy is to have a "successful" fire. A girl
takes another lover and possibly establishes the motive for
a revenge fire. A dishonest employee seeks to conceal his pilferage by setting his employer's store on fire, or a racketeer
toys with his newly discovered weapon of intimidation. A
businessman, a disappointed lover, a thief, and a racketeer
—all of them potential fire-setters.

Among the amateur fire-setters only the "pyros" set fires
with marked frequency. While the frequency of their acts
affords an excellent opportunity for identification and apprehension the lack of rational motivation is a major obstacle
in the investigation of such cases.

However, the greatest handicap to the detection of arson
is in the determination of a fire's origin. *Unless all accidental
causes of a fire can be eliminated, the blaze cannot be classified as an incendiary fire.*

EXCLUSION OF ACCIDENTAL CAUSES

Therefore the first step in recognizing arson is the exclusion of all accidental causes. Possibly the best method is to
cast out the obviously impossible causes and thus narrow the
field of probability. The investigator should be familiar with
the generally accepted causes of accidental fire and should
inquire into the following:

The Electric System—fuses, bridged with wire or foil or in
which pennies have been inserted; broken or rotted insulation; over-loading of circuits; defective switches or fixtures; or wiring not installed in accordance with the local
code or the National Electric Code.

Electric Equipment—not of approved type; defective; fire originated close to equipment such as iron or other heating element; or traceable to paper shades on electric bulbs.

Gas—leaks in pipes or defective stoves or heating unit.

Pets—presence of dog or cat and its possible contribution to cause of fire.

Painting Equipment—carelessness with paint, paint rags, linseed oil, turpentine, etc.

Heating Units—overheated stoves; clothing being dried too close to fireplaces or open flames; overheated steam pipes; faulty chimneys or flues; explosions resulting from kerosene stoves; stoves overturned in dark by pets, during fight, etc.

Sun—concentration of sun's rays by bubbles in glass window panes, convex shaving mirrors, odd-shaped bottles, etc.

Lightning—check on duration of storm.

Children—accidentally, while at play.

Smoking—careless disposal of cigars and cigarettes, pipe ashes; falling asleep while smoking in chair, auto, bed, etc.

Storage of Hay—date stored and condition.

There are other less common causes, but any possibility should be thoroughly explored. Some of the less common causes are sparks from electric motors or friction caused by running machinery; rubbish and brush fires spreading to a nearby building; ignition of hot grease, tar, oil, or like substance; explosion of natural or artificial gases; fireworks; sparks from an outdoor fire or a passing locomotive; or improperly combining chemical solutions.

A good rule for an investigator to remember is that no listing of possible accidental causes can be considered as all-inclusive. It must be remembered that some fires are the result of odd and unusual accidental ignition, but that in order for a fire to start it is necessary to combine combustible material with a source of ignition. These ignition sources are fairly well established: i.e. open flames, electric arcs, heating and cooking devices, moving machinery, chemical processes, and spontaneous ignition. Each one of these sources of ignition can be located in a specific section of a building, and if present, then it should be determined whether or not it was possible for such ignition source to combine with a combustible material and result in a fire.

COOPERATION OF FIREMEN

All too often fire personnel are satisfied with extinguishing a fire and leaving the determination of suspicious origin to their superior officers. Of course a fireman's first duty is to fight fire and this attitude is readily understandable, but the active cooperation of all firemen would be a tremendous aid in alerting arson investigators to fires of suspicious origin.

The attitude of a few fire-fighters can be summed up in the story of an arson investigator who visited the scene of a fire a few minutes after the arrival of apparatus. Since he was known to the fire officer in charge, he borrowed a helmet and coat and went in with a hose company. It was quite a blaze and as he tells it, "I helped on the hose until things settled down a little. When we secured control I relaxed, and as soon as I did I realized that there was a strong odor of kerosene. Turning to the fireman alongside me on the hose I asked him, 'You smell that?' He gave me a long look, then queried me, 'You a boss?' When I denied being a superior officer he growled, 'Tend to your own business and don't go smelling around.'"

Firemen can help in the discovery of suspicious fires. Seek their active cooperation, talk to them, and listen to their stories. After all, fire and fire prevention is their business. Every day they risk their lives to fight fire, and aiding the arson investigation is just another means of fighting fire.

TELL-TALE SIGNS

One of the explanations for the great activity of the professional torches during the business depression era of the 1930's was the commonly held belief that a fire could be set and in burning obliterate all evidence of incendiarism. The smart criminal today realizes that this is far from true. The development of laboratory facilities and techniques such as the spectrograph, the ultra-violet light, the infra-red ray and the vacuum distillation process, the high level of training among arson investigators, and the alertness of firemen are all increasing the likelihood of detection.

Set fires leave tell-tale signs. These signs may be so obvious that the first fireman on the scene will suspect arson, or they may be so well concealed that months of patient investigation will be required to show that the fire was set. However, the sign is always present. It may not scream out, "THIS IS ARSON!" but it will whisper, *"This is a suspicious fire."*

As the superior officer on the first fire truck to near the scene comes into view of the fire he'll size-up the fire and the building. If he notes two or more separate fires it is a definite indication of arson. So is it if the first firemen to enter the building detect a strong odor of kerosene or other petroleum products—unless their presence is accounted for by the occupancy of the building. An unaccountably rapid spread or intensity of a fire is also suspicious.

There are many of these signs which are encountered again and again at fire scenes; some point directly to arson, while others serve to alert the firemen and officers at the scene. Ranging from a study of the burned building to a search of the debris, the tell-tale signs most encountered are listed in the following paragraphs:

The Burned Building—The type of building in which the fire occurs may indicate a set fire under some circumstances. A fire of considerable size at the time the first apparatus arrives on the scene is suspicious if it is in a modern fireproof building. In addition, modern type loft and warehouse construction has eliminated many of the accidental causes of fire as well as providing means for preventing fire travel.

Separate Fires—Perhaps the most conclusive sign of firesetting is a number of separate fires. When two or three separate fires break out within a building or group of buildings or even in one room or store, it is certain that accident or misfortune can be ruled out and arson definitely suspected. Today's top efficiency in most fire-fighting units has been a tremendous aid to arson investigators. In one recent case in New York City the first firemen to enter a bar and grill in response to an early morning alarm counted over six separate fires; some claimed to have noted eleven separate blazes, ranging from the front booth to the kitchen and rest rooms. Their prompt arrival resulted in definite and direct evidence of arson. A few minutes' delay and there would have been one big fire involving the entire tavern.

Years ago professional torches would touch-off a building in three or four places, from the basement to the attic. By the time the fire equipment arrived it would be one mass of flames. Today the men and equipment arrive a great deal faster and discover the three or four separate fires and thus uncover the work of the torch.

An outstanding example of this was furnished as recently as April 27, 1953, when the Monticello, N. Y., Volunteer Fire Department responded to an alarm in a resort bungalow colony. They found one building completely demolished, two other buildings with fires burning in closets, and a fourth building with the "fire-trap" (a lighted candle set in a cardboard carton holder amidst paper and kindling) just ready to go off. The intelligent manner in which the volunteer chief and his assistants handled this situation resulted in the intact preservation of these tell-tale signs as evidence and the obtaining of extremely valuable photographs.

Color of Smoke and Flames—Some fires burn with little or no smoke, but they are the exception rather than the rule. Combustion of the materials burning is usually incomplete and there is some smoke. The characteristics of smoke very often assist in identifying the substances which started or boosted the fire.

As H. Rethoret notes in his fine book *Fire Investigations,* the observation of smoke must be made at the start of a fire. Once a fire has assumed major proportions the value of an observation of the smoke is lost, for the fire is then consuming the building itself, and the smoke will not indicate the materials used by the arsonist. It is therefore extremely important to locate and question the first person who saw the fire and the first firemen on the scene.

When white smoke appears before the water from the fire hoses comes into contact with the fire, it indicates humid materials burning. Burning hay and vegetable matter in stable and barn fires give off a white or light gray smoke. Phosphorus—an incendiary agent—also gives off a heavy white smoke but with a distinct garlic odor and a noxious effect upon those inhaling quantities of it. (Phosphorus is used in the preparation of war-time chemical agents.)

Biting smoke, irritating the nose and throat and causing lacrymation and coughing, indicates the presence of chlorine—another war-time chemical agent. The inhalation of smoke containing chlorine gas is also dangerous.

Black smoke indicates a lack of air; but if accompanied by large flames, it generally indicates the burning of a material with a petroleum base. Unless petroleum, tar, coal, rub-

ber, or like compounds are stored within the burning building, it is possible that some fire-setter utilized a petroleum
product to accelerate the blaze.

Reddish-brown, thick yellow, or brownish-yellow smoke
is an indication that films, or substances containing nitro-
cellulose fibre, sulphur, or sulphuric, nitric, or hydrochloric
acid are burning. If later investigation fails to reveal that
any quantity of such substances are normally stored in
the building, then incendiarism can be suspected.

To a great extent the appearance of smoke is also governed
by the supply of oxygen available to the fire. This also gov-
erns the flames. No flames, or comparatively small flames, indicate a lack of air. More flames than smoke indicate the
burning of dry substances. Large flames indicate a good
supply of oxygen, while erratic flames shooting out at odd and
unusual intervals indicate the presence of an accumulation
of some gases. When the flames swirl around in a sort of
pattern and are accompanied by clouds of dust and fine
ash, it indicates better-than-average ventilation at the fire.
Sparks in large quantities indicate powdery substances are
burning in a well ventilated fire.

The color of the flames is a good indication of the intensity
of the fire, an important factor in determining incendiarism.
A reddish glow indicates a heat of about 500 degrees
Centigrade, a real light-red about 1000 degrees Centigrade.
Red flames also indicate the presence of petroleum, as does
the appearance of tongues of flame on the water running off
from the fire. A fire temperature of close to 1100 degrees is
indicated by a yellow glow, and a blinding white fire usually
reaches a temperature of 1500 degrees Centigrade.

Though large quantities of alcohol will burn with an orange
flame, a blue flame reveals the use of alcohol as a fire accelerant, and although not used too frequently because the color
of the flames readily identify it, there is a possibility an
investigatior may encounter its use someday.

· *Size of Fire*—This is important when correlated with the type of alarm, the time received, and the time of arrival of the first apparatus. Fires make what might be termed normal progress. Such progress can be estimated after an examination of the materials burned, the building, and the normal ventilation offered to the fire.

Thus the time element and the degree of headway made by the flames become important factors to anyone probing into possible incendiarism. For instance, a drug-store fire a a few years ago was immediately labeled as suspicious by the fire chief because of the following circumstances:

a. His department received the alarm at 9:31 P.M., responded promptly, and found the entire interior of the detached one-story brick building involved, with flames shooting through the roof.
b. The owner had closed the store between 9:20 and 9:25 P.M. and had boarded a suburban bus directly in front of his building.
c. The bus driver had left his terminal at 9:20 P.M. and had arrived in front of the drug store on schedule at 9:26 P.M. Nothing unusual was noticed about the building at that time.
d. Within a minute or two the next-door neighbors were attracted by a red glare—looked out the window and saw flames shooting out through the windows of the pharmacy above the roof level. They fixed the time at 9:27 P.M. as they were watching a favorite TV program that ended at 9:30 P.M., and the commercial had not as yet broken into the program.
e. The telephone company received this alarm at 9:29 P.M. (three minutes after the owner had boarded the bus directly in front of the premises involved).

Investigators who developed this information learned that the business was in poor financial condition and was steadily deteriorating, thus giving a motive for a touch-off. Their findings corroborated the suspicions of the fire chief when he first noticed the unusual size of the fire. The report in this case, pointing out the time element involved, the great rapidity with which the fire spread, and the fact that the entire store was involved in a very few minutes, sums up the importance of the size of a fire as a tell-tale sign of arson.

Direction of Travel—While it is acknowledged that no two fires in buildings burn in identical fashion, it is also necessary to point out that fires can be expected to make normal progress through various types of buildings. Experienced firemen can usually determine whether a fire has spread abnormally fast when they take into consideration the type of construction, the channels of ventilation, the combustibility of the contents of the building, and the circumstances surrounding the sending of the alarm.

It is known that hot gases rise and fire tends to sweep upward until its progress in this direction is blocked by some obstacle. It then seeks holes, cracks, or outlets through which it can escape. If none is present, the flames mushroom out horizontally until the fire can bend around the obstruction or find some break through which to continue its progress. Dumbwaiter shafts in tenement houses and elevator shafts in hotels and apartment houses have furnished tragic examples of the speedy progress of a fire and then the mushrooming of the smoke and flames horizontally into hallways when the fire meets the dead-end at the top of the shaft.

A fire does not spread nearly so rapidly in a horizontal direction unless favorable ventilation conditions are present, or possibly the wall surfaces have been treated with a flammable substance.

When a fire has spread in a direction which normally would not be expected, it might be suspected, as was the case a short time ago when a large, frame hotel building was gutted by fire shortly after the owner had left the premises entirely unprotected. At that time the volunteer fire chief observed in his report: "There were a large number of windows open about five or six inches from the top and bottom in the main building, which seemed to be somewhat peculiar for the time of the year and the fact that there were no occupants on the premises at the time. . . . In the main building there was a hallway on the second floor, which ran from the front to the rear, and at the end of this hallway there was a door which led out on a balcony. . . . This door was open at the time I first observed it shortly after coming on the scene."

This attempt to speed the spread of the fire was later to prove in court the possibility of an incendiary origin and prevent the owner of this hotel from profiting financially from the fire.

Another point to be borne in mind when seeking to determine the direction of the burning is the depth of the charring at various points on the studding or beams in a building and the pattern of burning as indicated by the charring, scorching, blistering, and soot deposits in a room or about a building.

Sometimes a fire-setter will seek to better ventilate a building by cutting holes between rooms or floors, opening windows, tying back doors, or blocking up fire doors. Sprinkler systems have also been made inoperative to permit a fire to spread. In most cases the means used to ventilate a building or damage a sprinkler system are readily visible if the fire is quickly extinguished. Unless the structure is burned to the ground, a close inspection may reveal the arsonist's techniques; and even when it is burned to the ground, the unusual speed of travel may tend to cast suspicion on the fire.

Intensity—The degree of heat given off by a fire and the color of its flames oftentimes indicate that some accelerant has been added to the materials normally present in a building and alert the firemen or the investigators to look for further evidence of the use of flammable liquids or compounds. Possibly some difficulty in extinguishment will lead firemen to suspect the presence of such fluids as gasoline and kerosene. Fires react to a stream of water in various fashions. If a flame burns brighter when hit with a hose stream or if the flames change color when the water strikes them, any experienced fireman is alerted.

Odors—There's little question that the odor of such flammable substances as gasoline, kerosene, and alcohol has trapped more arsonists than any other tell-tale sign. It must be remembered that most fire setters are not too bright or they would not believe they could escape detection in their arson attempts. They seek a substance which will make the blaze certain and which will burn up any evidence of arson. Kerosene and alcohol spring to the minds of the amateur, gasoline to the twisted mental equipment of the professional. All three will burn, but in burning up the evidence of arson, a readily identifiable odor is given off and it is this odor which points to a fire-setter.

Investigators can quickly learn to recognize the odors of various flammable liquids by placing small amounts in wide-mouthed glass jars. By shutting their eyes, opening a jar, and guessing as to its contents they'll soon build up an experience which will permit them to make prompt identification.

Condition of Contents—Persons intending to touch off a fire frequently remove objects of value or items to which they are sentimentally attached. Clothing, personal papers— particularly bank books and insurance policies—such articles as typewriters, television sets, and objects associated with the arsonist's hobby are likely to be removed before household fires are set. Pets are frequently left with relatives before the fire is set. Stores and other business establishments sometimes remove the major portion of their inventory, or replace

CHAPTER TWO

"TOUCH-OFFS"

WHEN a fire is classified as suspicious, it is then the task of the arson investigator to determine if it is in fact a "touch-off" —a set fire. At this point all plausible accidental causes have been excluded and observation at the fire scene has pointed either to the possible use of some fire accelerant, or to the setting of a fire without the use of a recognizable accelerant. It is now up to the arson investigator to determine the *modus operandi* of the fire-setter.

POINT OF ORIGIN

Initially the important point to be established at any fire is at what point in the building did the fire originate?

This point of origin frequently may be established by an examination of witnesses, by an inspection of the debris at the fire scene, or by both such methods.

The first person to be questioned is the discoverer of the fire, the second is the person who turned in the alarm, and lastly, any other witnesses that can be found. Each of these witnesses should be interrogated as to his identity, his business in the area of the fire, what attracted his attention to it, time of observation, and his position in relation to the fire at such time. When it has been ascertained that he was in a position to view the fire (time and place of observation), then the investigator seeks to learn the exact location of the blaze, its size, its intensity, and the rapidity of its spread.

Witnesses will also be questioned as to other persons in the vicinity. Did they observe one of the other witnesses? Did they observe anyone in or about the premises just before or immediately following the fire?

In many cases this happens to be a single witness; one man discovered the fire and turned in the alarm, and diligent inquiry fails to uncover any other witnesses.

The person who turned in the alarm will also be questioned as to whether he used a fire box, telephone, or other means. Is is also important that an attempt be made to learn the length of time that elapsed between the discovery of the fire and the time the alarm was dispatched.

All experienced arson investigators know that the identity of these witnesses, their business in the area at the time of the fire, and what attracted their attention to it are three vital questions in any investigation of fire-setting.

It is astonishing the number of times, year after year, that investigators have come across the fire-setter among the small number of persons who "discovered" the fire, who turned in the alarm, or who were on hand before the fire apparatus and were helpful in directing the firemen to the scene. It might not be out of place at this point to mention that individuals who have come to the attention of police and fire departments as chronic "false alarm ringers" have, in many instances, later blossomed out as thrill-seeking fire-setters.

An inspection of the debris must always be made, first to determine the point of origin and secondly to attempt to uncover the arsonist's technique.

Charring of wood occurs as a fire burns, the "alligatoring" of the surface varying as the wood is consumed. When a fire is extinguished quickly, the charring is only slightly below the surface and the alligatoring shows large segments or squares. As the fire continues the charring goes deeper into the wood and the segments of the alligatoring become smaller. "Alligatoring" will not only help locate the point of origin but may also reveal the existence of two or more separate fires.

Tracing liquid accelerants to the place of spillage aids in definitely locating the point of origin of any fire in which such fluids were used.

Any fluid will flow downward to a lower level and in such movement will flow around any fixed object in its path. Therefore fluid fire accelerants such as gasoline, kerosene, turpentine, and alcohol may be traceable from the point of spillage to its lowest point. Quite frequently unburned quantities of such liquids are found in rooms below the fire, in cellars, or in portions of a foundation, as a considerable quantity of such fluid sometimes runs down to a low point out of the range of the fire.

In burning, these fluid accelerants will sometimes pool on a large level floor and burn from the outside of the pool toward the center, leaving a distinctive mark upon a floor. These accelerants also cause deep charring, and this deep charring sometimes neatly charts the flow of the flammable fluid used by the fire-setter. Cases have been encountered in which charring traced the path of the accelerant into cracks of the floor to the underside of the floorboards. In addition these fluids will mar furniture and painted surfaces upon which they have been splashed and which may be found untouched by the fire.

The point of origin itself points to many suspicious fires. Arsonists place their fire-setting devices where the flames will take hold, while many accidental fires occur in locations where they burn out instead of gaining headway. Thus the location of the point of origin may be of great help in excluding accidental causes.

FIRE-SETTING MECHANISMS

It is the duty of an arson investigator to search the debris of a suspicious fire, particularly around the point of origin, to gather evidence pointing to the mechanism used by the fire-setter in his effort at arson.

An arsonist may use the simplest of methods, a match and some paper; or he may use elaborate mechanical or chemical means to start and accelerate his fire.

An incendiary mechanism may be mechanical or chemical. It consists of an ignition device, possibly a timing mechanism, one or more "plants" to feed or accelerate the initial flame, and frequently "trailers" to spread the fire about the building—sometimes from plant to plant.

IGNITION AND TIMING MECHANISMS

An ignition device may be a simple one (a match, for instance), or it may be a complex mechanical or chemical device which can be timed to go off hours or even days after it is set. This latter type provides a time lag between the time of setting and the outbreak of the fire, and gives the fire-setter an opportunity to leave the scene and possibly establish an alibi for the time of the actual fire.

Matches—Frequently a match is struck by the arsonist, but only the juvenile arsonists and the pyros—the mental cases —seem to favor this method. Other fire-setters want some delay, so they adapt the ordinary match to some timing mechanism.

Several matches may be affixed to a lighted cigarette with a rubber band or scotch tape, with the heads of the matches about half-way down the cigarette from its glowing end. In some cases the matches are just laid alongside the cigarette. Books of paper matches have also enjoyed popularity. Since cigarettes will continue to burn when laid on their sides, they are effective ignition devices; the slow-burning cigarette allows the fire-setter a few minutes to get away from the scene before the fire makes any headway.

Matches are also used in conjunction with numerous mechanical devices. One misguided arsonist hooked them up with his telephone, strapping them to the ringing mechanism in a wall box and inserting a piece of abrasive board in place of the bell. This "brain" thought he could set a fire from miles away by calling his home. However, his estranged wife had a change of heart and came home unexpectedly.

She settled down to await the amateur fire-setter's return. It wasn't long before she noticed a wisp of smoke from a pile of old clothing on the floor of the living room. Frightened, she called the fire department. The ignition device had been actuated but had fizzled out. The firemen carefully preserved the rags (wet down with lighter fluid), the matches, and the abrasive board, and arranged a warm reception for the husband who had planned "the perfect crime."

Unburned or partially burned matches about the point of origin of a fire should be carefully preserved for examination and comparison. A suspect may have similar matches in his pocket or the book from which paper matches have been torn.

Candles—As a timed ignition device, candles have been in use by arsonists for over a century. A candle will burn at various rates, depending upon its composition and size. Thick candles burn slowly and long candles naturally burn for a longer period than short candles.

Some years ago Dr. Richard Steinmetz established a table of the burning time of candles of various compositions and sizes in his fine text *Arson Investigator's Manual*. This table can be summed up as follows:

COMPOSITION	DIAMETER	TIME TO BURN 1"
Tallow	3/4"	61 minutes
Wax	7/8"	57 minutes
Paraffin	13/16"	63 minutes

Arson investigators sometimes work on a rule of thumb of an hour's burning time for each inch of candle of above diameters. Of course this is only guesswork and the investigator must arrive at a more definite time when he secures a

little more information about the candle used in the fire
under investigation. The fire-setter makes his experiments
prior to a fire in order that the burning time will fit in with
his plans. Once he knows the average burning time of the
candle, the arsonist can adjust to a desired time lag merely
by cutting the candle to the desired length. The candle is
therefore not only an ignition unit, but also a device which
can be adjusted within certain limits to set a fire hours after
the arsonist has departed from the scene of the crime.

Candles are mostly used in conjunction with containers of
easily combustible materials, which are sometimes set within,
or close to, other containers of inflammable liquids or in an
area sprinkled with such accelerants.

However, candles leave a deposit of wax as their tell-tale
sign. It may have soaked into the wood of a floor or it may
be found in a pool at the low point of a floor or table top.
Anther sign is the protection afforded the floor or table top
by such wax—the spot upon which the candle rested will
show less charring than the surrounding area. In many cases
a part of the candle, and possibly the container in which the
candle was placed, may be found upon a search of the fire
scene.

Chemicals—Various chemical combustions have been used
to set fires. Saboteurs have used such means for years. Units
which provide for an acid to be released upon some combination of chemicals is a favorite device, with the acid re-
leasing itself by eating its way through the cork or even the
metal of its container. The time lag from setting to ignition
can be estimated with some certainty by an arsonist with a
little knowledge of chemistry.

Various rubber receptacles, such as hot water and ice bags
or contraceptives, have been used for a phosphorus and
water ignition device. A pinhole is made in the rubber container, allowing the water to seep out. Once it drains below
the level of the phosphorus, ignition takes place. As this

chemical ignites upon contact with air, a time lag is secured by controlling the amount of water and the size of the hole in the container.

Even the ordinary fire-setter sometimes utilizes a chemical which ignites upon contact with water, setting up a device actuated by the next rainstorm. Holes in the roof or some connection to the gutter system have been used to "trigger" this device. So also a diversion of the sewage line in a building, the device being set up at night but planned to trigger off the next morning when the toilet is flushed for the first time.

Another chemical combination which can be used to produce a fire is Potassium Chlorate, sugar, and sulphuric acid. Potassium Chlorate is used in various industrial processes such as manufacturing textiles, medicines, dyes, and paper. Table sugar is obtainable anywhere, and sulphuric acid is a well-known and easily obtainable substance. Potassium Permanganate and Glycerine are easily obtainable and start a nice fire. Metallic Potassium and carbide is another combination which can be used for spreading a fire, but is not easily used in setting a fire.

However, most chemical ignition units leave some residue or have a distinctive odor, or both. Naturally, the debris must be analyzed at a laboratory when it is suspected that chemicals have been employed as an ignition device.

Fortunately, most arsonists are not equipped with the knowledge required for the use of chemical ignition or timing devices, nor are the machinery and tools necessary for the construction of some of these devices readily available. Unless prepared by a saboteur, the device will probably be a fairly simple one. The more complex units are encountered as a rule only in time of war, and usually in the possession of a frustrated enemy agent who has not had the opportunity to use them.

Gas—Not commonly encountered, but always a possibility,

is the combination of gas and the pilot light on the kitchen stoves of many residences. Illuminating gas rises to the ceiling, being lighter than air, and then slowly moves down to floor level as it continues to escape. When it reaches a combustion build-up, it is close to the pilot light level and an explosion, usually followed by fire, takes place. A candle placed in a room adjoining the kitchen has also been utilized as a means of ignition. Therefore arson investigators must remember that while such explosions normally follow suicide attempts, or stem from accidental causes, it is possible that an incendiary may utilize an ordinary gas range as an arson tool.

Mr. John J. Ahern, Director of the Department of Fire Protection and Safety Engineering of the Illinois Institute of Technology, pointed out the possibility of the use of gas as an arson tool during a lecture at the University of Purdue Arson School in 1949 when he said: "From an arsonist's standpoint, utility gas is a perfect working tool. It has a built-in time fuse since it must build up to an explosive concentration before it lets go. It will even furnish its own source of ignition by means of a pilot light. Let's not fool ourselves. There are cases occurring using gas and if they go off as planned they are extremely difficult to discover and pin down since they introduce no mechanical gadgets nor new materials to the premises."

In such cases the investigator should get help from an engineer of the local public utility. An estimate of the time lag between the initial release of the gas and the explosion can be estimated from the size of the room involved, number of openings, type of gas, and related data.

For example, a normal kitchen of about 10 x 15 with a ceiling of 9 feet equals a total volume of 1350 cubic feet. When 71 cubic feet of gas is introduced into the room, the lowest limit of the explosive range will have been reached. In a well-ventilated room it is almost impossible to build up to this limit, but an arsonist will seal off the room or rooms concerned so that the gas volume will build up. In a fairly well-sealed room a single burner left open on a kitchen gas stove will deliver sufficient gas to reach the above explosive range in about five hours. The oven jets will build up the same volume of gas in two hours, and if the stove has an oven and four burners and all of them are left open, the lower explosive limit of gas volume can be reached in from thirty minutes to one hour.

The thing which has prevented the widespread use of gas as an arson tool, and which has thwarted some attempts to use it, is its smell. Neighbors detect the gas odor and call police or firemen, or break in themselves, and thus ruin a carefully planned arson attempt.

Electrical Systems—Any wiring system, including doorbell and telephone circuits, can be used as a fire-setting tool. Ignition devices hooked to the wiring system of a building have been used throughout the country as an arson tool. The time lag can be established by a study of the habits of the persons using the premises in which the fire is to be set. Possibly a watchman may switch on the lights every hour as he inspects the various portions of the building on his rounds of inspection; employees turn on the lights at the time of opening; etc.

One case hinged on the defendant's knowledge that no one in his office turned on the electricity until a coffee-pot was plugged in for the morning coffee about 9:00 A.M. Accordingly he had set his electric heating coil in a bag of waste in the basement of the building. It went off a little behind schedule, the fire department recording the alarm at 9:41 A.M. Something had delayed the morning coffee.

Investigation disclosed an electric plug inserted in a wall outlet about ten feet from the point of the fire's origin, the wire from this plug ended in two blobs of copper a few inches from the outlet. A routine questioning of employees revealed that their employer had been home sick when the fire was discovered. More questions revealed it was his first absence due to illness in two years, and he had telephoned twice that morning, once at 9:15 A.M. and again at 9:25 A.M., both times asking for some inconsequential information. Alerted, the investigators soon discovered that the coffee pot had been plugged in only about five minutes before the discovery of the fire. The delay had resulted from an unexpected shortage of coffee; an office boy had to be sent out to a nearby store for a new supply.

Upset by an unexpected flaw in his timing device, and worried about why it had not been actuated, this arsonist gave himself away by the two telephone calls, both made in a frantic search for information.

While doorbell systems can be used in the same manner to trigger an ignition device, the possibility of flaws in the timing obviates any widespread use. The bell may be rung by some chance visitor and upset the carefully laid plans of the fire-setter.

Telephone timing devices have the same fault, a "wrong number" or an unexpected call and the fire is under way, possibly days ahead of schedule.

Electrical appliances have also been used to set off fires. An open heater is placed close to a flimsy set of curtains and an apparently accidental fire results. An iron can be set in its usual position; overheating serves to ignite the ironing board cover; and again an apparently accidental fire results. Or perhaps an electrical circuit is deliberately overloaded with several appliances until some portion of it heats up. Sometimes an accelerant or "booster" such as kerosene is dropped into a switch box, and there have been a few cases in which a length of normal wiring was removed and a lighter wire substituted so that it would overheat and, without blowing the fuses, serve as an ignition device.

Investigators will generally find that some physical trace

of an electrical ignition device can be discovered after a fire. Some portion will not be completely destroyed by fire.

Sun's Rays—Utilization of the sun's energy is not often encountered, but it cannot be discounted entirely. Magnifying glasses, shaving mirrors, bottles, and the like, which concentrate the sun's rays, have been used by arsonists as ignition devices. Grass, grain, and forest fires were once set by this method quite frequently. Failure to function, except under ideal conditions, has proved this method to be extremely unreliable and, since most fire-setters seek guaranteed performance, this method has not been popular in recent years.

Animals—Sometimes a family pet, usually a dog or a cat, will be pressed into service as part of an ignition device. Tied to portable kerosene stoves or lamps, they serve as effective agents for the arsonist. It is a vicious method because the animal is almost certain to be burned. At first glance such fires may appear accidental.

Fortunately, modern living with its electric systems now installed even in remote farmhouses has somewhat curtailed this *modus operandi;* the presence of a kerosene lamp may be difficult to explain. However, portable kerosene stoves are still used extensively in cold weather in both urban and rural areas, so the possibility still exists.

Mechanical—Alarm clocks were once a favored weapon of arsonists. A simple alarm clock, some wire, a small battery, and a fire-setter was "in business," but after a search of the fire debris disclosed the remains of an alarm clock, the arsonist was in trouble and usually on his way to prison.

The arsonist utilizes the lead hammer which normally hammers away at the alarm bell as his tool: to break a glass tube which will then feed inflammable matter to a fixed flame; to push over a container of chemicals into a container of other chemicals; to close an open electrical circuit; or by attaching matches to the hammer so that they will be pressed back and forth against an abrasive surface, to ignite a previously prepared "set" of inflammable material. The clock is actuated by simply setting the alarm for a certain time; when that time arrives the alarm "goes off" and the lead hammer starts to swing. The weights in a grandfather's clock have also been utilized in a similar manner.

Mechanical devices which the minds of fire-setters have dreamed up beggar description. Some are childish, some are worthy of master craftsmen, and others are truly fiendish.

Unfortunately for most of these ingenious incendiaries, the major portion of their infernal machines will not burn and can later be hung like a millstone around their necks.

PLANTS

Any preparation for the unlawful setting of fires is termed a "plant." It is the material placed about the ignition device to feed the initial flame. Newspapers, wood shavings, excelsior, rags, clothing, curtains, blankets, and cotton waste are some of the materials used in plants. Newspapers and excelsior seem to be the most frequently used material, with cotton waste being used extensively in factory or industrial fires.

Accelerants or "boosters" to speed the progress of the fire are also part of the plant. Kerosene and gasoline are favored boosters, with alcohol, lighter fluid, paint thinners, and other solvents enjoying some popularity. However, any flammable fluid or compound may be used to accelerate the blaze.

TRAILERS

Trailers are used to spread the fire. A trailer is ignited as a result of the blaze kindled in the primary plant by the ignition device, and it carries the fire to other parts of a room or building. Sometimes the trailer will simply carry the fire to these other locations, the arsonist depending upon the flames from the trailer to spread the fire, but usually a trailer will end in a secondary plant, *i.e.*, another pile of papers or excelsior sprinkled with gasoline, kerosene or some other booster.

From the primary plant a fire-setter may lay four trailers to an equal number of secondary plants, thus securing four separate fires from the one ignition device.

Rope or toilet paper soaked in alcohol or like fluid, motion picture film, dynamite fuses, gun powder, and other such substances have been used as trailers. Sometimes rags or newspapers are soaked in some fire accelerant and twisted into a rope. On other occasions an arsonist will use a fluid fire accelerant such as kerosene as a trailer by pouring a liberal quantity on the floor in a desired path.

Incendiary Fires

When any fire-setting device, any components of the various ignition and timing units, or any of the materials used in plants or trailers as described in this chapter are found in premises in which a suspicious fire has occurred, then the classification of such fire can be made. Unless the presence of materials used by fire-setters bears some relation to the occupancy of the premises, the blaze should be classified as an incendiary fire.

When kerosene, gasoline, excelsior, candles, and like substances are discovered about the point of origin of a suspicious fire, it is evidence of arson, and if the investigator can prove such material had no right to be in such premises, then he has established the corpus delicti; that is, he has overcome the presumption of accident as established by law and has proved the body of the crime—that the fire occurred from some criminal agency.

CHAPTER THREE

ALIBIS, MOTIVES, AND THE CORPUS DELICTI

THE establishment of an alibi is a normal defense mechanism in the minds of the majority of fire-setters. "I'll prove I was somewhere else at the time of the fire. How could they suspect me?"

Arsonists viewing their possible involvement in a planned fire in a more realistic light will add, "They'll probably suspect me, but if my alibi stands up, how can they prove I was involved?"

Members of this second group realize that they may be numbered among the suspects because of the benefits or profits they stand to derive from the fire. These alluring prospects are what motivated them to scheme and plan and finally set the fire. Thus a close relationship between alibis and motives often is built up. Both breed in the mind of the fire-setter during his period of planning. One can be broken down or overcome, and the other can usually be discovered.

ALIBIS

The purpose of timing devices—sometimes termed "long-range" ignition units—is to give the fire-setter a chance to establish an alibi. So also is the employment of accomplices. Both permit the establishing of an alibi, a claim of being at some other location at or about the time of the fire. It is one of the most frequently encountered defenses to suspicion of arson.

Long-range Timing Devices—When an arsonist employs a timing device which precludes the possibility of some witness placing him at the fire scene shortly before the fire, it is more than likely that he'll claim an alibi as his defense in the event the finger of suspicion points to him. The purpose of all timing devices is to give the incendiary time to get away from the scene; those which give an extended period of time from the actual setting of the device until the outbreak of the fire are commonly termed "long-range" units. And it is these units which give the arsonist time to establish an alibi.

The exact length of this time lag is important as it pinpoints the specific time at which the guilty person was actually at the scene of his crime. In all arson cases the investigator must seek information as to the ignition device. If the stub of a candle is found, a time period may be estimated (see page 21). When other methods of ignition and timing are discovered, partially identified, or even just suspected, the investigator can initiate experiments with similar materials and oftentimes determine the time of the actual fire-setting within an hour.

When the investigator knows the timing device and the time lag, he is in an advantageous position. He can now talk to the arsonist on better terms. "You told me where you were from an hour before the discovery of the fire until about an hour after; now tell me where you were five hours before the fire?" Or the investigator can secure a resumé of the suspect's activities for a day or even several days before the fire and thus not reveal to the suspect that his time lag has been pinpointed.

This method is highly desirable because it can become a routine part of every investigator's interrogation of owners, occupants, policy holders, employees, and all others concerned with the fire. If this line of questioning is habitual with an investigating officer, it is unlikely that he will "tip his hand" when talking to a suspect. Furthermore, it forces the arsonist either to admit his presence at the scene around the time of the setting of the ignition unit or to tell a poorly prepared story as an alibi. Such hastily fabricated alibis are easily broken.

No investigator can expect to break a prepared alibi in relation to a suspect's presence at a fire scene at the time of the alarm because, if a timing device was employed, the suspect is telling the truth. He was not at the scene when the fire broke out.

However, unless an accomplice set the fire, good investigators can break a "spur of the moment" alibi relating to the actual time of the fire-setting, because the suspect is lying. He must have been at the fire scene at such time to set his timing unit.

Employment of Accomplices—When an accomplice is employed, it is difficult to establish the actual time of the fire setting until the accomplice is located and identified. However, witnesses sometimes aid in fingering these tools of the arsonist. Full development of the investigation usually leads to their identification as the result of some contact with the suspected arsonist. These accomplices may range from the professional torch to some friend of the fire-setter. Their identity may be determined through the use of surveillances, or possibly through information furnished by a confidential informant.

When an arsonist employs an accomplice to actually set the fire, he will have a ready alibi for his whereabouts at the time of the fire, and possibly for days or even weeks previously. Failure to break the alibi of a suspect with a strong motive for fire-setting as well as failure to discover a long-range timing device may indicate either that an accomplice actually set the fire or possibly that the investigator is "barking up the wrong tree."

When two or more persons enter into a conspiracy to commit arson, it must be remembered that any member of the group can set the fire, or still another accomplice may be added for the purpose of actually setting the fire. Even if five or six individuals conspired together to set a fire, it doesn't necessarily follow that one of this group did the actual fire-setting. Frequently they all feel that the finger of suspicion will point to them because of their reasons for wanting a fire and each will try to push the task of setting the fire to others in the group. This usually leads to the hiring of an outsider, a "mechanic," to set the fire.

Overcoming Alibi Defense—When an alibi cannot be broken down or the employment of an accomplice determined, the investigator may feel that the most desirable course is to close out the investigation and attempt to overcome the defense of alibi upon trial.

This step, of course, must be discussed with the prosecuting attorney who is to try the case, and with whom the investigating officer should be in constant touch during the course of the investigation. The district attorney will usually inform the police officer or fire marshal of the additional evidence he believes necessary to make a successful case.

In overcoming an alibi defense, the prosecution seeks to prove the time of the actual fire-setting when a timing device was used. Then an attempt is made to prove that the fire-setter was present at the scene at such time.

When one or more accomplices are concerned in the crime, the presence of only one defendant at the fire scene need be proved so long as the remaining defendants are connected with the common scheme or plan.

Evidence that a person was at a location other than the scene of a fire at the time of its ignition raises a reasonable doubt of guilt, but when the prosecution develops substantial evidence of guilt, the jury is not required to credit the testimony concerned with the alibi defense. Fortunately, testimony concerning the defendant's alibi is evaluated in the same manner as other evidence.

Briefly, when an alibi defense is encountered, it is necessary to overcome it and place the suspect at the fire scene at or about the time of its outbreak unless:

1. The use of a timing device can be shown, its time lag pin-pointed, and the suspect placed at the scene at the time of the actual fire-setting, or
2. The employment of an accomplice can be proved.

MOTIVE

The question of motive or lack of motive is always a question deserving the serious consideration of all investigators; the guilt or innocence of a suspect may sometimes hinge upon the discovery and proof of motive.

Fires are set by two types of fire-setters, persons with a motive to set a fire and those without any rational motive. In the first group are those individuals who desire fires either for profit, for revenge, to conceal evidence of other crimes, or for the purpose of intimidation. In the second group we have the mental cases, the pathological fire-setters, the pyros or psychos. They range from imbeciles to apparently well-adjusted persons possessed of a compulsive neurosis. This second group must also include the thrill-seekers, the "heroes," the vandals, and the juveniles. No rational motive activates any of the pyros.

It must be remembered, however, that a pyro may also set a revenge fire. Being unduly interested in fire, such an individual naturally seizes upon it as a weapon of revenge. In fact, Lewis and Yarnell (*Pathological Fire-setting*) estimate that 25 percent of the more typical pyromaniacs set at least one direct hate fire in the course of their fire-setting activities.

Motivation may also be of an odd and unusual nature, the

result of twisted thinking. A good example of this type of case occurred in a central New York city a short time ago. A grammar school building was remodelled into a veterans' housing project containing forty-seven apartments. Since only a few of the apartments had private baths, large community baths for each sex were located in the basement and on the first and second floors. These rooms contained rows of tubs and showers. Fires broke out in September, October, November, and December, 1946. The first fire involved shower curtains in the ladies' showers on the first floor; the second totally consumed curtains in the ladies' showers in the basement; the third consumed curtains in the ladies' showers on the first floor; and in the last fire the recently replaced curtains in the ladies' showers in the basement were again totally consumed and the fire spread to the walls before discovery.

As a result of diligent investigative efforts a twenty-seven-year-old veteran, employed as assistant engineer in the building, was taken into custody on February 22, 1947. He admitted that he had bored holes in the walls of both the basement and the first floor bathrooms so that he might be able to watch the women take shower baths. He had set fire to the curtains because he believed that if he burned enough of them they would not be replaced and he would have a better view.

In determining motive, an investigator concentrates on three major factors: the point of origin of the fire, the modus operandi of the arsonist, and the identity of persons who might benefit from the fire.

The first two factors aid in discovering if the fire was set by an arsonist with a rational motive or by a pyro. The mental case arsonist uses those portions of buildings accessible to the public as the point of origin for his fires. Fire-bugs don't set fire to their own homes or places of business; they set fires in places where they can make ready entry and hurried exit.

Hallways, easily accessible basements, roofs, spaces under porches or garages, and public toilets are the scenes of their efforts.

Nor is the preparation of a fire-bug's plant as extensive as that of an arsonist with a normal motive. The pathological fire-setter uses a few twists of newspaper, rubbish, and possibly a baby carriage found in a hallway as his plant and a match as his ignition device. The arsonist with a rational motive employs more elaborate preparations, usually marked by accelerants or fire boosters.

Once the investigator has determined which type of arsonist he is looking for, he can move along in his investigation. If he has found that a pyro was not responsible for the fire, then he can seek out all the persons with possible motives— Someone who benefitted from the fire, who "got even" as a result of it, who may have attempted to conceal a larceny or other crime, or someone who may be using it as a tool of extortion.

Motive alone is not sufficient to classify a blaze as an incendiary fire, but in fraud fire cases a motive may be strong enough for it to be termed a tell-tale sign and permit classification of a fire as suspicious.

Motive is not an essential element of the crime of arson, but evidence of strong motive helps to eliminate accident or misfortune as probable causes. Proof of motive also serves to bolster evidence tending to prove criminal intent on the part of the arsonist.

While it is not absolutely necessary to establish a positive motive on the part of the accused in the trial of an arson case, it is extremely helpful. Curtis in his *Law of Arson* admits that when the prosecution fails to show a motive which might lead the accused to set a fire, the evidence is more carefully scrutinized to determine its worth, and without proof of motive the courts often hold that the prosecution has not supplied the required burden of proof. Several New York courts have held that, while motive may not be an essential element of the crime of arson, proof of motive is considered essential to secure a conviction based solely on circumstantial evidence.

Since arson is a crime of stealth, committed with great secrecy, it is not usually possible to produce witnesses who'll be able to give direct evidence of a suspect's guilt. Most cases are based on circumstantial evidence; therefore the importance of discovering motive cannot be over-emphasized.

Of course, a defendant cannot be convicted merely upon a showing that the fire was of incendiary origin and that he had a motive for committing arson. This is little more than mere suspicion and requires evidence to support it which will definitely connect the defendant with the fire.

However, once the corpus delicti of an arson case is established, then every circumstance tending to shed light upon the case is generally admissible as evidence against the defendant. On the question of motive, evidence is admissible which tends to prove that the accused set the fire for gain, to secure employment, to conceal murder, or for similar reasons.

Most arson investigators align their investigations along two broad lines; each case as it develops will be placed either in the pyro—without rational motive—class, or among those committed by persons having a rational motive for the fire-setting. Once classified as a pyro blaze, the phase of the investigation dealing with motive can be forgotten. If classified as one with a possible rational motive, then the prompt ascertaining of the motive becomes of paramount importance.

It is only by first exploring the avenues of both opportunity and probability that an investigator can picture possible motives. Who had the opportunity to set the fire? Who would have a reason to set it? Would any of the possible reasons for desiring the fire be sufficient motivation for the persons under suspicion?

Quite a few suspects may be in the group of those having the opportunity to set the blaze, but the field will narrow when possible reasons are explored, and it will be further reduced when the motivation is considered in respect to the background, personal characteristics, past activities, and financial status of each suspect. Ten individuals may have had an opportunity to set a fire, but only four or five had good reasons for wanting a blaze. And of this number only one or two would risk possible disclosure as fire-setters for the anticipated profit or satisfaction to be secured as a result of the fire.

When a profit motive exists, it is usually fairly simple to determine those with possible motives; it's a case of who will benefit from the damage wrought by the blaze.

Fires motivated by revenge, to conceal crime, or to intimidate are more difficult of analysis. It is difficult to ascertain either the "who" or the "why." The identity of the suspects as well as their reasons for wanting the fire will be the major portion of the investigation. However, once this information is secured the remaining facts are usually discovered and the case brought to a successful conclusion.

In some arson cases the discovery of motive leads to a full confession. The individual responsible for a fraud fire is least likely to break down. He is fully aware that he will be suspected, because he is the one who will profit from insurance or like benefit. Reasonably, he has steeled himself for questioning. The revenge fire-setter breaks down more easily when the fact that his carefully guarded secret is known to the investigator is fully exploited. Lastly, discovery that the motivation for fire was due to an attempt to conceal a crime, or to assist in a crime such as extortion, will in itself lead to other data of almost as much evidentiary value as a full confession.

Techniques for the exploration of possible motives will be detailed in succeeding chapters, each dealing with one of the major motives for arson.

INTENT

Intent is an essential element of the crime of arson.

If a person intentionally sets a fire, he does so willfully, and such act implies knowledge and purpose. A willful burning is a malicious one, the malice of the fire-setter being inferred from his intent. When a person intentionally performs a wrongful act it is safe to term it a malicious one, and setting a fire under circumstances which permit it to be termed arson is certainly a wrongful act.

The intent may be inferred from the act itself, if the inevitable consequence of the act is the burning of the building, or if the particular purpose cannot be effected without such burning. Every person is held responsible for the necessary and natural consequences of his acts and is held to intend to produce such consequences.

It has also been held that it is arson when a person sets fire to or burns a building while engaged in the commission of some felony such as burglary, even though there be no specific intent in the mind of the accused to set fire to or to burn the building. (People vs. Fanshawe 137 N.Y. 68, 32 N.E. 1102)

Malice, like intent, is a mental element and when it is shown that a fire did not result from accidental or natural causes, then malice can be reasonably presumed from the intent of a fire-setter. Sometimes intoxication is used as a defense, but even an intoxicated man knows it is wrong to set a fire.

It must be remembered that the forming of an intent to set

a fire is a secret and silent operation of the mind, and possibly its only physical manifestation is in the accomplishment of the act of arson.

The fire-setter may remain silent when questioned as to his intent, or he may answer untruthfully. Therefore it is almost a necessity to revert to the actual physical sign of intent, the resultant fire, as the safest and perhaps the only real proof of intent.

NEGLIGENCE RESULTING IN FIRES

Alleged negligence which causes fires resulting in property damage or personal injury should receive greater attention than at the present time from police and other authorities.

After all, when some clown exhibits what amounts to culpable negligence there is no reason to excuse his act because he may have lacked specific intent. It is something more than slight negligence that causes many fires; a goodly number of them result from an indifference to the rights of others and a complete disregard of the consequences of acts.

This negligent rather than willful setting of fires has only infrequently been punished in a criminal court. Yet many years ago Roman law recognized the possible criminality in a careless act resulting in a fire and an early English law cited careless servants who set fire to property. In the United States the only legal action against carelessness as a cause of fires seems to be when it affects forests and woodlands.

Quite frequently a clever fire-setter will set a fraud fire and claim carelessness to mask its incendiary nature. In cases of this type the arsonist often points out the obvious point of origin of the fire and bitterly blames himself for his carelessness. The lack of appropriate laws in such cases handicaps investigators, but fortunately most of these cases are resolved by a background investigation of the insured, a little delving into possible "needs" for the fire, and possibly an un-covering of some pre-planning in anticipation of the fire.

ATTEMPT AT ARSON

After conceiving a plan to set a fire, a person may change his mind. However, he must abandon his plan voluntarily and not because he is baffled by an unexpected obstacle or condition.

Unless the intent to set a fire progresses to an overt act of some kind, no crime is committed. An overt act is one done to carry out the intention and it must lead toward the con-summation of the intent. It should be an act such as would normally effect the desired result, a fire. It does not have to be the final act of igniting the blaze, but should be one of a natural series of acts which would generally result in a fire.

An attempt is complete when an opportunity occurs and the intending perpetrator has performed some act tending to accomplish his purpose.

When two or more persons conspire together to commit an act of arson, the initiation of the conspiracy is complete at the time of the agreement between the conspirators, but the actual attempt at arson must wait upon opportunity and an overt act.

Essential ingredients of an attempt at arson are:

1. An intent to set a fire under circumstances constituting arson if carried out.
2. An overt act in furtherance of such intent.
3. A failure to burn.

CORPUS DELICTI

It is a rule of law in regard to arson that every fire is presumed to be of accidental origin. This presumption has to be overcome before an arson charge can be established.

Therefore a prime fact to be established by competent evidence is that the building was burned by someone with a criminal design. It is necessary to prove that the burning was the willful act of some person and not the result of some accidental or natural causes.

In proving the corpus delicti it is essential that all accidental causes of fire be eliminated. Unless direct evidence of fire-setting can be secured, it is a fundamental rule of all arson investigations that every possible cause except incendiarism be eliminated. It is then the task of the arson investigator to detail the suspicious circumstances surrounding the fire which indicates the work of an arsonist. Since direct evidence of fire-setting by the defendant is not frequently encountered, this is the usual manner of establishing the corpus delicti.

The investigator of arson must keep in mind the order of proof upon a trial for arson. While some judges believe the order of proof in arson cases is at the discretion of the court, it is safer to assume that the court will require evidence of the corpus delicti before the admission of other evidence.

When the major evidence in a case will be the confession of the defendant, it is necessary to secure other evidence to show the incendiary nature of the fire. While such evidence may appear to be weak when first viewed by the investigator, it can be deemed sufficient if it tends to show the fire was of incendiary origin and thus corroborates the confession of the defendant.

A corpus delicti is established when the investigator has secured enough facts to prove upon presentation in court that the building in question burned and that such burning resulted from the intentional criminal act of some person.

CHAPTER FOUR

FIRES FOR PROFIT

ARSON for profit is the first motive to be considered. It accounts for many more fires than the public, or many police officers, realize. However, there is always sufficient time to investigate crimes of this type. Unless the aid of a professional torch has been secured, there is no hurry, no need to apprehend the perpetrator before he sets another blaze. The profit motivated fire-setter is not going to run away; he must stay in order to collect his insurance or otherwise profit from the fire. And no fire insurance firm is in a hurry to pay off on suspicious fires.

FRAUD FIRES

Even otherwise honest persons have been known to set fires for the purpose of defrauding an insurance company. A man who is at heart law-abiding, who would run from robbery or burglary, who becomes upset at a reprimand from a traffic policeman, and who carefully guards his children from minor transgressions, may become an arsonist for profit without a twinge of conscience.

It is indeed strange to burn and steal and then rationalize the arson and larceny. The fire itself is not to hurt anyone, just to conceal the evidence of fire-setting and to make possible the fraudulent claim by damaging the stock or gutting the building. And most of them console themselves with the thought that it is not really larceny; they are not stealing; the insurance company honors their proof of loss claim and pays them. Few of them will admit to themselves that they are thieves and possible murderers of firemen and others who might be around the burning building. It is badly twisted thinking—to put it mildly.

The prevalency of fraudulent fires and this type of thinking can be estimated from the fact that the term "a successful fire" has crept into the American language. Only recently it was used on a nationwide television show. The comic on the show was queried as to a friend's business. "Did he fail?" was the query. "No," the comic replied, "he had a successful fire."

This is a basic handicap in the investigation of fires to defraud the insurer: normally honest people often commit the crime.

An investigator must be careful in establishing a motive of fraud. A large number of business men operate on little or no capital, some are in debt, others seem to be directing their business solely for the benefit of the landlord and their employees. It would appear obvious that an operator of any well-insured business would profit from an extensive fire if he is operating at a loss, but was he responsible for the fire-setting? Was this his motivation?

It is only by studying the circumstances of each case that an investigator can safely arrive at any conclusion. Business difficulties mean nothing to some people, while others become extremely worried and sometimes conclude that it's either suicide or arson.

Fortunately for the investigator, the more desperate the need the less the attempt to conceal the arson, and there is little likelihood of successfully concealing motive when a business enterprise is in real financial difficulty.

"Business" Fires—Sometimes termed "commercial" fires, "business" fires result from the acts of business men. Busi-

ness fires occur more frequently in times of general business depression. The years 1930 to 1935 were marked by a tremendous number of these fires. In times of general prosperity, when business is "good," there is little need for such fires.

However, general prosperity sometimes by-passes a few enterprises. A ready market for some product may suddenly tighten up and result in a large inventory at the factory. Unexpected sales resistance may result in a failure to receive orders which had been counted on in stock-piling a supply of the necessary raw materials. Possibly a seasonal business will face several "dead" months with a large inventory on hand and the probability that new styles will make their present models "trash" merchandise by the next season.

In any event great losses can be anticipated; the stock on hand cannot be moved through normal channels. The sale of such "distress" merchandise brings very little cash. Some shady merchants have a saying to fit such situations—sell it to the insurance company!

Sometimes manufacturers are faced with the problem of re-tooling to produce new models; some radical changes in manufacturing methods may require the scrapping of valuable machinery. Possibly an inability to get raw materials will idle machines in a normally busy plant. Or there may be some other urgent need for ready cash. Such situations breed arson.

Possibly an estate is tied up in some heavily-insured business. Five or six heirs must await liquidation before they can realize on their inheritance. The idea of converting the insurance into cash may occur to one or more of them, and a fire results.

Sometimes land is more valuable without the buildings; other times a business may outgrow its quarters. A few persons may seize upon such instances as a golden opportunity for profit, or to secure funds for larger quarters.

Possibly a building may be condemned for occupancy because of building or fire code violations. Rather than lay out the money to rehabilitate it or pay for the cost of demolishing it, and unwilling to let it stand idle and become a tax burden, the owner may have it burned down and attempt to collect from the insurance companies. (In New York City only a short time ago it was not unusual for schemers to buy up dilapidated, unoccupied, old tenements for a nominal sum, place insurance on them, depart from the city, and arrange to have a fire break out in the building during their absence at a safe "alibi" distance from New York.)

Many buildings in rural areas are erected on land that does not belong to the building owner. When notified by the land owner to remove the structure from the property for any one of a number of reasons, building owners have been known to set fire to the building and then submit a claim for an accidental fire loss.

Partnerships—Partners disagree: one may think the firm can weather a financial crisis; the other may think only of bankruptcy. Possibly one partner would like to buy out the firm, but may not have the cash, or the other partner may refuse to sell. One partner may be satisfied with small profits while the other may be unhappy at the limited success of their enterprise. It's a fertile ground for fraud fires based on complex motivations.

The Insured—The most logical suspect in such cases is the policy holder, the individual who'll profit most from the fire. In some cases it is the occupant of rented premises, while at other times it is the building owner who expects to profit from damage to the structure rather than from damage to stock and fixtures. However, in recent years landlords have found rentals a very profitable item and unless an urgent need for cash exists will not burn a building bringing in a profit.

The initial investigation of a policy holder suspected of

setting a fire to defraud the insurer is a brief financial worth and personal background study. What is his equity in the property? How much cash on hand? What is the value of other assets? An analysis of his debts is made and the nature of the debts thoroughly explored. If a business enterprise is concerned, a like audit is made. If a partnership, each partner will be thoroughly checked. Income tax, sales tax, and other tax records are of particular value in such studies.

Questioning in these cases is along the following lines:

How long have you been operating this business at this locality?
How long have you been in this line?
Where did you come from and where did you operate previously?
Under what trade name, corporation name, or partnership did you operate previously?
Have you had any previous fire losses?
What are the names of officers of corporation?
What are the names of members of your immediate family?
Home address?
Previous addresses?
Where do you bank?
Have you had any bankruptcies?

A partially truthful answer that he, the insured, has never suffered a previous fire loss may boil down to the fact that a loss was incurred in his wife's name, or his son's name, or a corporation name.

A check of the records of a reliable credit agency frequently shows discrepancies in the suspect's story concerning his personal or business background. The more information that can be uncovered about the subject without his volunteering it, the more likely he is to credit the investigator with knowing a good deal about the fire, and cultivation

of this belief is a vital factor in breaking down fraud fire
suspects.

To implement such financial reviews the arson investigator
present at the scene of a suspicious or incendiary fire will
seize any bills, letters requesting payment of overdue debts,
account books, inventory or other bookkeeping records which
would shed light upon the financial condition of the business.
Such physical evidence can be evaluated by the investigator, aided by skilled accountants when necessary. If such
evidence indicates a desperate financial plight, it will
greatly aid in the successful prosecution of the case when
produced in court.

The following confession of a fraud fire-setter reveals the
typical motive and *modus operandi* in such cases and highlights motive and opportunity as the most profitable basic
lines of inquiry in such cases:

Q. What is your full name and address?
A. Albert J. R........, Black Lake, New York.
Q. What is your age and date of birth?
A. I was born March 10, 1930.
Q. Do you own a feed storage building in the Town of Athol,
   on the property of Lillian B.........?
A. Yes.
Q. I am going to ask you a few questions concerning a fire
   which occurred in that building this morning. Are you will-
   ing to answer these questions truthfully?
A. Yes.
Q. Do you have insurance on that building?
A. Yes.
Q. What is the amount of the insurance?
A. $1200.00 on the building and $1800.00 on the merchandise.
Q. Whom did you obtain this insurance from?
A. Art G......., Mongan Valley, New York.
Q. Tell us in your own words what you know of the fire which
   broke out there this morning.

A Dallas, Texas, woman first removed all her linens, clothing, and silver-ware from her home, then set it afire. Her multiple fire "plants" illustrate the insane ingenuity of a frantic fire-setter.

In the west bedroom two large boxes were filled with newspapers. One of the boxes contained a fruit jar full of gasoline with coal oil on top of it. The other box had papers and a pan full of gasoline in it. An electric iron was set on an improvised ironing board above the box containing the pan of gasoline, and the current was turned on. As can be seen, the iron burned through but did not set off a blaze.

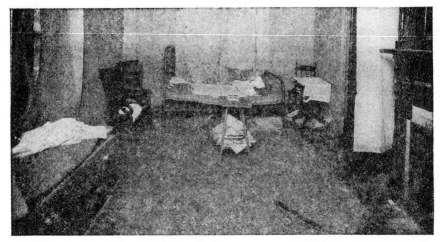

In the front bedroom a burning candle was stuck in a match box on a table in the center of the room. The gas jet in the room was turned on and the gas was flowing through a rubber tube to the center of the room. When the gas built up in sufficient quantities the candle or candle and matches would set it off.

In the dining room a pan full of gasoline was placed in an old trunk and the trunk filled with papers. A candle was used as an ignition device and gas fed in by a rubber tube as another fire booster. Picture shows that in spite of the damage from fire, the white enameled pan which contained the gasoline and the gas tube leading into trunk are clearly visible.

A. I owe quite a bit of money and my wife has been sick. I figured that if my place burned down I could collect 80 per-cent, or $2,400.00, and that would help me out of my finan-cial difficulties. This morning I left my home about three-thirty or a quarter of four to go to Liberty to get my truck. I was driving my Pontiac Catalina. I drove down Route 17 and turned into a shale road which runs near the rear of my building. I parked my car and went over and into the build-ing through the front door. A few days ago I had thought about setting fire to the building and had put excelsior in different places behind the feed bags and between the studs. When I got in the building this morning, I picked up a gal-lon jug of kerosene that I had bought for the purpose and poured it on the excelsior and sprinkled some of it on the floor. Then I lit the excelsior in three places with wooden matches. I went out of the building and locked the door and got back in my car and drove to Liberty. I think it was just about four o'clock in the morning when I set the fire.

Q. Do you remember soaking a piece of rolled up newspaper with the kerosene?

A. That was used for a cork on the kerosene jug.

Q. Where did you buy the kerosene?

A. At a Shell gas station on upper Avon Street in Liberty.

Q. Are all these answers the truth?

A. Yes.

Q. Have you been mistreated in any way since you have been in this substation?

A. No.

Q. Are you willing to sign this statement and swear that all your answers are true?

A. Yes.

The usual defense of a guilty policy holder is that he was not in debt, that his business was not on the brink of bank-ruptcy, and that he had no motive for an attempt to secure money through fire-setting and fraud. When an investigator can show a very urgent need for ready money with no income in prospect, then he is on his way to a "break" in the case.

Another essential part of the initial investigation is a study of the personal habits of a fraud fire suspect. Extensive gambling and heavy drinking can rapidly develop a need for cash greater than a recorded debt. Extra-marital affairs are sometimes very expensive during their course and sometimes lead to demands for money upon threat of exposure. Homosexuality is another possibility for an attempt to extort money. Some "homos" would risk a fraud fire rather than exposure.

When a large inventory of stock has been allegedly destroyed, a check should be made with manufacturers, or jobbers and wholesalers, as to the exact amounts shipped to the insured. Talk to the policy holder's landlord, to customers, competitors, and employees as to the extent of business activity. Office employees, particularly the bookkeeper, are worthwhile persons for some "cultivation" and questioning.

An interesting case of this nature was investigated several years ago in a textile center in a Southern state. A small clothing factory was totally destroyed by a fire of unknown origin. No evidence of incendiarism could be found. The stock loss, in coats and suits, ran to many thousands of dollars according to the claim submitted.

Some debris remained, unidentifiable, but said to represent the stock of clothing destroyed in the fire. The investigator didn't like the "feel" of the case—he couldn't put his finger on anything specific, but he sensed there was something wrong. Perhaps it was the appearance of the debris, possibly the attitude of the insured. At any rate he obtained from the factory operator detailed descriptions of the clothing items involved—textures, models, quantities, etc., even the type and composition of the buttons on the coats.

In discussing the case with a research chemist, this investigator learned that the particular type of button used on

many of the garments could not be consumed by fire. Armed
with this piece of information, he set about determining the
number of coats actually burned in the fire. He arranged to
have the debris sifted in a search for buttons which should be
intact in the ruins of the building. A tedious operation, but
a button count should help establish the number of coats
involved in the fire.

The sifting operation was performed painstakingly under
the investigator's direction. The search turned up not a single
button! The investigator confronted the operators with this
development and in very strong terms suggested that a fraud
had been perpetrated. And he was right: the stock of clothing had been removed, the fire touched off; and the false
claim submitted. A very fine case to break after starting
out with nothing but a vague suspicion because of a swollen
inventory.

In the course of such initial investigation it must be remembered that not all men in debt, nor all men whose personal habits may be open to criticism, set fraud fires. Many
business firms are operated close to bankruptcy for years and
many persons never get out of debt, and such concerns or
individuals sometimes suffer perfectly legitimate fires.

However, disclosure of poor financial status or questionable habits is an asset to the investigator when he interrogates
the suspect. Properly exploited, such knowledge can result
in a full confession.

There are certain clauses contained in most standard fire
insurance policies that can be utilized to great advantage
by a diligent arson investigator. One of these, captioned
"Requirements in Case Loss Occurs," reads:

> The insured shall give immediate written notice to this com-
> pany of any loss, protect the property from further damage,
> forthwith separate the damaged and undamaged personal prop-
> erty, put it in the best possible order, furnish a complete inven-
> tory of the destroyed, damaged and undamaged property, show-

ing in detail quantities, costs, actual cash value and amount of loss claimed; AND WITHIN SIXTY DAYS AFTER THE LOSS, UNLESS SUCH TIME IS EXTENDED IN WRITING BY THIS COMPANY, THE INSURED SHALL RENDER TO THIS COMPANY A PROOF OF LOSS, signed and sworn to by the insured, stating the knowledge and belief of the insured as to the following: the time and origin of the loss, the interest of the insured and of all others in the property, the actual cash value of each item thereof and the amount of loss thereto, all encumbrances thereon, all other contracts of insurance, whether valid or not, covering any of said property, any changes in the title, use, occupation, location, possession or exposures of said property since the issuing of this policy, by whom and for what purpose, any building herein described and the several parts thereof were occupied at the time of the loss and whether or not it then stood on leased ground, and shall furnish a copy of all the descriptions and schedules in all policies and, if required, verified plans and specifications of any building, fixtures or machinery destroyed or damaged. The insured, as often as may reasonably be required, shall exhibit to any person designated by this company all that remains of any property herein described, and submit to examinations under oath by any person named by this company, and subscribe the same; and as often as may be reasonably required, shall produce for examination all books of account, bills, invoices, and other vouchers, or certified copies thereof if originals be lost, at such reasonable time and place as may be designated by this company, or its representative, and shall permit extracts and copies thereof to be made.

These provisions are not familiar to most police investigators, but demanding compliance can be very helpful. False statements in a proof of loss, or when being examined under oath, frequently result in a charge of "false swearing."

Household Fires—Each year in America there are more household fires than nearly all other types of fires combined. Many of these are very minor and most of them are due to accident or negligence. However, in every twelve-month period, scores of household fires are incendiary. Of course, not all of these deliberately set fires are motivated by a desire for gain—many of them are attributable to spite, revenge, jealousy, and other outgrowths of domestic friction or mental instability.

A fire in a private residence is closely aligned to the commercial or "business" fire. Financial embarrassment may point to an attempt to defraud the insurer of a sizable amount of money through the destruction of an entire house and its contents. Such fires usually point to the head of a household as the person most likely to gain from the blaze.

Such gain may be in terms other than cash profit. A home owner may be moving away from a locality and find himself unable to dispose of his dwelling at a profit. He may decide to "sell it to the insurance company." A home-owner who is in financial difficulty may find himself too pinched to pay off on the mortgage. Rather than let the property go by default he may burn the building down, planning to have the insurance company pay off the balance of the mortgage, as per the clause in the policy, and then collect the remainder of the loss payment himself. In this way he will still retain the land, mortgage free, and possibly realize enough from the fire to start anew.

Household fires frequently take place in apartments occupied by a woman tenant or a married couple. The point of origin is often in a closet, and it is generally the wife or the woman tenant who sets the fire. The motivation in these cases is either a desire to redecorate the apartment, purchase new furniture, or to replace an out-of-style wardrobe. The fire-setting device is generally not too elaborate; neither is the alibi. A small fire is set with a match as an ignition unit and the arsonist hastily takes her leave. Later, she'll claim she was at the store or at the movies at the time.

An odd factor about such household fires is that in many

instances the fire-setters do not actually need money; they just think they can secure something new for something old without spending any of their money, or without fighting with friend husband for the money.

From the above it can be seen that fraud motives for household fires may be as varied as are those for fraudulent business fires. The illustrations set out are, of course, not all-encompassing, but serve to alert the investigator that he must be ever watchful for unexpected angles when pursuing a possible motive for fire-setting.

Mortgaged Property—As mentioned earlier, mortgage payments may enter the picture as possible motives. The imminent foreclosure of a mortgage, or a chattel mortgage, should not be overlooked by the investigator. Has the interest been paid promptly? Is a satisfaction of the mortgage overdue? Has an extension of the mortgage been requested? All too often, property in danger of foreclosure burns, and frequently the circumstances of its burning should be viewed with some suspicion.

And it is not beyond the realm of possibility for two men to conspire together and attempt to "guarantee" a profit from their fire-setting by the preparation of a false mortgage. The Number One man in the conspiracy owns a building; he mortgages it heavily to the second man. If the insurance is paid without question, they split the proceeds. If payment is questioned, the mortgage holder screams that he had no part in any suspected arson and wants to be paid. Even if the Number One conspirator goes to jail for arson, the holder of the mortgage will continue to sound off, and unless the conspiracy can be proved, he and the actual arsonist will still split the proceeds.

Suspicious Acts Prior to Fire—It is the exceptional fire-setter who can refrain from removing some object of real or sentimental value from his office or home when he intends to have a fire. Arson investigators develop a knack for "smelling out" the signs which point to removal of pictures, clothing, important private papers such as school diplomas, birth certificates, etc., and sometimes even stock and fixtures or household furniture.

Only last year in Sullivan County, New York, a dwelling and barn fire occurred that immediately drew the suspicion of the local volunteer chief despite the fact that by the time the fire apparatus arrived the buildings were totally destroyed and it was impossible to fix either the point of origin or the possible cause.

The barn was located thirty feet from the house. There was very little wind at the time and the chief wondered how the fire could have spread from one building to the other. There was no electricity in either building.

The fire was discovered at 4:00 P.M. The owner had left early that morning for New York City, traveling by plane, and had arrived in New York at 8:45 A.M. No one else was known to have been around the premises.

The fire chief didn't like the looks of the entire set-up, so he notified the state police that this was a suspicious fire. The police investigators inspected the scene and noted that the debris did not reflect the presence of normal household furnishings.

Alerted, the state troopers scanned the area and noticed a number of small shacks and old unoccupied buildings about a half-mile down the road from the insured's premises. On a hunch they decided to search these places. They were nicely rewarded. In one of the unlocked buildings they found the rooms piled high with furniture, bedding, tools, kitchenware, and all manner of household furnishings. The old four-room shack was literally jammed with all of the personal belongings of the air-borne defrauder. A glance through some of the drawers resulted in finding a life insurance policy in the name of the owner of the burned dwelling. A further search unearthed a ledger which contained a pencil sketch of the burned house and barn with notations on the size of each room and an itemized list of the property which was supposed to have been in each room at the time the fire occurred.

Investigation revealed that a nephew had recently gone to live with the owner of the destroyed property. The nephew was picked up, questioned, and confessed that he had set fire to both the house and barn at his uncle's instigation, after the uncle had safely departed for New York City.

Both the fire chief and the state police had also been alerted to the possibility of arson by the fact that less than ten months before this fire the owner had suffered (?) a fire loss for which he had been paid $4175.00. That fire had destroyed a barn on the property and, in like manner, the cause of the fire could not be determined. Apparently his earlier success had made him overstep the bounds of caution.

It's an odd fact, but true, that even though many individuals seek money from destroying property, they hate to think of certain articles being destroyed. Sometimes it's sentiment, but at other times they are motivated by the greedy thought that they can still profit further by hiding things of some value and selling or using them later.

In numerous cases it has been proven that the fire-setter removed his fire insurance policy just before the fire. A policy holder in one case had kept his policy in his office safe for years, but just two weeks before the fire the insured brought it home and "forgot" to return it to the office.

In another case the insured failed to pay a great number of bills but paid his fire insurance premiums in person, asking his agent at the time whether anything was wrong with the policy. Such acts or any increase in the coverage of the policy just prior to a fire of undetermined or incendiary origin can justly be viewed with suspicion.

In fairness, it must be pointed out that since World War II real estate and property values have increased at such a tremendous rate that many insurance companies and agencies have conducted campaigns to educate the property owner to increase his insurance coverage to keep pace and be properly protected. In this period there is no doubt that some accidental fires have coincided with the honest and innocent increase of insurance coverage by conscientious home owners. A superficial check of such an increase might reflect doubt as to the validity of the fire, but any "digging in" for facts will quickly resolve such doubts.

Acts performed before a fire are of top importance to an investigator. When a guilty suspect finds out that the investigator knows about these acts, he is very likely to panic. Such knowledge is good evidence in court, but an even better instrument when skillfully used during the initial phase of the investigation.

Records of Previous Fires—An investigator must keep his own records of all those concerned in fraud fires, and seek the use of records maintained by insurance organizations and law enforcement agencies. It need not be much, just the basic details as to location, date and time, suspect's business, insurance total, amount of loss and cause of fire, if determined.

Fire investigators find that many persons attempting arson in fraud fire cases have a previous history of a small fire loss. Possibly the insured collected only a little more than the actual loss, but such fact may have whetted his appetite and may have given birth to the motive for arson. On the other hand it may show a previous history of fraud fires in another locality.

Someday there'll be a national file of such information for the use of arson investigators, and, on receipt of a form request, this central unit will be able to issue a review of records covering the entire country. However, today the arson files and loss information files of the National Board of Fire Underwriters provide a great deal of information.

Common Fraud Fire-setting Techniques—Fraud fires are sometimes the result of direct ignition. A dishonest factory owner may return to his plant at night and touch a match to a pile of waste material. One employer ignited his fire-setting "plant" with a match, locked the front door of his store, and walked down the street in view of several employees still loitering on the sidewalk. Fifteen minutes later the fire was discovered.

However, delayed ignition is the more common technique encountered in fires to defraud the insurer. The selection of delayed ignition is an indication that the arsonist expects to be accused and therefore must prepare an alibi as to his whereabouts.

Typical of the technique used is the case of the California masseur. A two-story frame building contained on the ground floor a shoe repair shop, a physiotherapy and massage parlor, and some vacant rooms. The second floor was ostensibly a rooming house operated by the building owner, but official reports described it as a house of prostitution.

A fire originated in the massage parlor and the firemen were able to confine it to this parlor. While fighting the fire, firemen noticed a buzzing sound and saw sparks coming from an electric extension cord. It developed that the buzzing sound came from an electric timing clock and that the sparks came from a short circuit in the cord where the insulation had been destroyed. The short circuit was on the floor under a mattress-covered massage table and the end of the cord was plugged into a connection on a large broiler cover, the underside of which was equipped with exposed electric heating elements. A piece of cheesecloth was attached to the heating elements. Adjacent to the cover were the broken remains of two one-gallon glass jugs which gave off the odor of paint thinner. Nearby was a one-gallon metal can containing paint thinner.

All of this evidence except the electric clock and some of

the extension cord was taken to fire department headquarters. Police and insurance investigators were notified. Working together, they went to the premises to inspect the scene and pick up the massage parlor operator for questioning. They discovered that the electric clock and the extension cord had been removed from the premises. They located the shop operator and brought him in for interrogation. At the outset his answers were evasive and misleading. However, he admitted that he got his room rent free and a commission from the operator of the second floor house of prostitution whenever he sent up customers.

After a time, this arsonist and "pimp" agreed to tell the truth and he outlined how he had set the fire, using the time clock and the plant as described. He claimed his motive for setting the fire was his fear that his wife might learn of his association with the building owner, but it also developed that he had $6500 of insurance on meager equipment of only fair quality. He likewise admitted removing the electric clock and the balance of the extension cord from the unguarded fire scene after the fire. It developed that five years earlier he had collected $15,000 as a result of a fire in which paint thinner and electric wires were involved. The repeat performance by a previously successful perpetrator is quite common. The sentence in this case was for a term of two to ten years in San Quentin.

Civil Action as a Deterrent—The need for proof beyond a reasonable doubt upon a criminal charge of arson sometimes places the investigator of fraud fires in a strange position. He may be certain that it is arson, but the utmost diligence may have failed to secure proof which will convict the accused under the law. Sometimes the rules of evidence handicap a prosecution. Other times a small link may be missing from a substantial chain of evidence. Even though it is obviously arson, it cannot be proved to a moral certainty in court.

However, when an investigator can prove his allegation of

deliberate fire-setting by a fair preponderance of evidence, he can take the case to the civil courts of most states. In a civil action it is not necessary to prove a fact beyond a reasonable doubt, but only to prove it by a fair preponderance of evidence. The simple method is for the insurance company concerned to refuse to honor the proof of loss submitted by the insured, *i.e.*, to deny liability, setting forth their reasons for so doing. In turn the insured commences a civil action to recover his alleged loss, and the investigator can have his day in court.

The best deterrent to fraud fires is arrest, conviction, and imprisonment, but, failing that, anything that eliminates the profit from such fires will also serve as a deterrent. Perhaps we cannot put an arsonist for profit in jail, but at least we can withhold his profits by this technique of forcing a civil action.

Over-Insurance—A great number of responsible fire and police officials believe the careless writing of fire insurance policies is partly to blame for fraud fires. A strong inducement is present when policies are issued in amounts far in excess of the true value of the insured property, or when due care is not exercised at renewal periods. Possibly the value of the premises concerned may have depreciated during the life of the original policy, or perhaps some other circumstances which point to the insured as a poor risk may have developed.

This practice of over-insuring has been recognized even in a far country. The proposed criminal code for the Philippine Republic includes a presumption that the existence of "insurance at least twice the amount of actual value at the time of the issuance of the policy" is *prima facie* evidence of guilt if the policy is dated within ninety days of the fire.

Fraud fires usually cannot be blamed on agents for the careless writing of policies. Insurance is a highly competitive business and many policies are handled daily by the great majority of agents. A poor risk who is determined to get insurance coverage can invariably "shop around" and obtain insurance, frequently through an agency located at some distance from the premises covered.

The Problem of Automobile Fires—Mr. Dennis N. Key, Manager of the National Automobile Theft Bureau, highlighted the existence of fraud fires in automobiles during an Arson Detection and Investigation Seminar at Purdue University in Lafayette, Indiana, on April 28, 1952.

Mr. Key first scotched the belief that automobiles are highly inflammable and likely to burn entirely of their own accord without outside assistance. "Let me remind you," he said, "that just prior to World War II in certain sections of this country automobiles were burning up every night by the hundreds. Arson investigators were swamped in making investigations covering these fires. Immediately after Pearl Harbor, when automobiles were frozen and their manufacture ceased, these automobile fires suddenly stopped. They did not start burning again in large proportions until after the war was over and automobiles became more plentiful."

Investigation of such fires follows the same general pattern as that of any fire. Why the fire? Who will benefit? Is the car over-insured? Can a faster return of cash be secured by a fraud fire than through selling the car? These are some of the questions which should be explored in these cases. In addition a thorough examination of the car should be made to determine any reason for a fraud fire rather than an attempt to sell the car. Burned out main bearings, cracked blocks, front ends in need of repair, and so forth, are all "good" reasons in the minds of some owners to attempt a fraud fire.

FIRES FOR INDIRECT PROFIT

Fraud fires are not the only blazes motivated by profit. A fraud fire is an effort to swindle an insurance company by a

policy holder. The basic motive pin-points the prime suspect
—the insured.

In fires for an indirect profit the motive is more obscure,
and, naturally, so is the suspect. Possibly it was set by a competitor in business. A contractor may have ignited the fire in
order to secure a lucrative rebuilding contract. Or perhaps
some individual seeking a position as a guard or watchman
may have lighted the blaze to firmly establish the need for
his services. Whatever the motive in any single case, it can
be safely assumed that because of its remoteness it will be
far from evident. The arson investigator must really "dig"
into cases that are suspected of being fires for indirect profit.

In cases of indirect profit, three of the most likely motives
and types of suspect are: to stifle competition—competitors;
to stimulate "new business"—builders, insurance agents or
adjusters, salvage contractors, etc.; to secure employment—
watchmen, firemen, and policemen.

Burning Out Competitors—In recent years such fires have
not been of frequent occurrence. However, the cases on
record reveal such motivation as an ever-present possibility.
Through personal magnetism, a better location, or more
skilled merchandising techniques, one business man may
move far ahead of another in a like business.

Only last year in a highly populated Eastern Seaboard
state several fires occurred in an unoccupied store building
which were rather puzzling until prolonged probing turned
up all the elements of fires set by a business competitor to
stifle competition.

A tavern had been operating very lucratively for a number
of years in a rather quiet, suburban area when a building
boom (apartment houses, garden apartment developments,
etc.) descended on the area. The store building next to the
tavern, approximately fifty yards distant, had been idle and
unrented for several months. As soon as the construction
work on the apartments was started, it became known that a

liquor store operator in a near-by town had applied for a transfer of his license and at the same time had approached the owner of the vacant store building and was negotiating a long-term lease with him. Obviously the newcomer intended to move his business into the section so as to take advantage of the anticipated increase in population and customers. Shortly thereafter the store building was rented by the liquor dealer, renovations were commenced, and the bustle of activity indicated that very soon an up-to-date business would be dispensing the same type of refreshments as the tavern had been doing so successfully for so many years. Lo and behold, a night or two after alterations had been started, a fire of serious proportions was discovered burning in the cellar of the soon-to-be liquor store and firemen found that a rear cellar window had been broken and some rags and other combustibles ignited and thrown inside.

For lack of a better motive, this fire was written off as vandalism by neighborhood rowdies or possibly drunks from the nearby tavern. The fire debris was cleared up and work recommenced, but within a week's time another fire of serious proportions was found burning inside the store proper. This blaze also occurred in the night time and also after a break-in had been effected. Now the authorities were definitely faced with deliberate, malicious arson. No insurance fraud, obviously; no concealment of another crime; too late at night for the average juvenile to be about; a pyromaniac? It could have been the work of a pyro, but the breaking into the premises would pretty well discount this possibility. Since the same premises had been victimized twice within a few days and just after a rental to a new business, it seemed to indicate the existence of a tangible motive with a planned attack directed against the newcomer—an attack planned very probably to scare the newcomer out of the neighborhood.

Investigation tended to support this latter theory and the

investigators developed sufficient information to satisfy them that they had the answer to the crimes, but in view of the lack of evidence, admissions, or witnesses, no prosecution was undertaken. In this particular case considerable surveillance work was done, most of it in the tavern, but no great amount of evidence was uncovered.

"New Business" Fires—One series of what at first appeared to be pyro fires was found to be the work of a local building contractor seeking new business. And as "good fortune" turned his way, he prospered. In one fire in which seven stores burned down he secured the rebuilding contracts for five of the seven firms burned out. In fact he became a sort of specialist, wasting no time in submitting a bid and offering a completing date in his proffered contract—only possible when employees and equipment are readily available and not tied up on other contracts. One of his fellow contractors mentioned this point to an arson investigator and an arrest was effected after a great deal of corroborating testimony was obtained.

An insurance agent or broker is not normally a fire-setter. But now and then one of them turns to arson as a device to awaken the interest of a community in fire insurance or to effect a more immediate monetary return.

The notorious Brooklyn arson ring which operated with such disastrous effect in the depression years of the 1930's included one fire insurance broker (unlicensed). His efforts to please his customers were so eminently satisfactory that he gained the reputation of being able "to guarantee a fire with every policy he wrote." He was later convicted of arson in the first degree and testified for the state against some of his former colleagues.

The torch of this arson ring, who had touched off more fires than he could recollect, also testified for the people. During the trial he was asked about a conversation with a public adjuster, also a member of the ring. The torch testified that the adjuster introduced him to the conniving broker with the recommendation, "He's an insurance broker and he believes he can give us a lot of business."

Another possibility in the field of "new business" is a fire set so that some salvage contractor may profit. Whenever insured property is destroyed, the insurer seeks to minimize his loss by disposing of the partially burned goods as salvage. It's not beyond the realm of possibility that such contractors might attempt an indirect profit. However, while some cases did occur many years ago, modern methods of awarding salvage contracts have curtailed this type of arson.

Fires for Employment—Sometimes men who fear the loss of their jobs will set a fire to highlight their alertness, loyalty, and fidelity to duty. Non-skilled labor such as guards, watchmen, elevator starters and operators, laborers, and cleaners are most likely to look for job security through arson. But now and then a clerical employee will resort to fire-setting, and a few occasions are on record in which minor "management" personnel holding positions close to the top reached down for arson as a technique to make their positions more secure.

Fires set by individuals seeking employment as guards or night watchmen are quite prevalent. Fortunately, they are also easy to solve. Either before or after the fire some individual applies for a job. The fire, coming as it does at an "opportune" moment, emphasizes the need for guard or watchmen services. All persons who seek to capitalize on such need are naturally suspect.

During the latter part of World War II a young man organized an upstate New York fire department and, with himself as chief, enlisted twenty-seven young men to serve in the department. Under the Office of Civilian Defense, he was very active in getting neighboring volunteer fire units into a single organization. After the war's end the county chiefs wished to continue this organization and suggested that the position of supervisor of fire protection for the county be created with a salary, expenses, and the use of a car. The young chief in question started an active campaign for this job, but he was opposed by other fire chiefs because of his lack of experience.

Within three weeks three fires occurred, all of which the young chief helped to extinguish. In one of these fires a school house was a total loss, and in another a barn was damaged considerably. The young chief stressed his unit's efficiency and requested an investigation into these fires. However, in the course of the investigation it was learned that the chief had telephoned a neighbor living near the school house and asked if it were on fire *before any evidence of fire was apparent*. He confessed, pleaded guilty, and has been sentenced to from four to eight years in prison.

Another "fire for employment" had its locale in a small town in Connecticut. A volunteer fireman set three fires in a local tavern. His motive was to secure promotion in the volunteer department to the position of night driver. He had made several attempts to get the appointment, but had failed. He explained his fire-setting by expressing his belief that if he could show the selectmen what a good job he could do in extinguishing a fire, they might promote him. He pleaded guilty and was sentenced to a year and a half in the county jail.

The Boston Post Road Case

A case that fairly well typifies all fires for profit and which also pin-points the amazing amount of evidence which can be secured by an alert investigator in these cases was a fire that occurred mainly because of a sudden need to liquidate a business and be relieved from an undesirable lease.

The operator of a restaurant in Connecticut on the old Boston Post Road was examined for military service in May, 1943, when he was thirty-four years of age. He was classified

1-A during the second week of June. Since he'd be in the Army he could no longer operate the restaurant. He tried to sell his lease and get out with some profit, but he couldn't. Ten days after he received his draft classification, an early morning motorist noticed flames shooting from the restaurant and notified the state police, whose barracks were about five hundred yards away.

Immediate investigation developed that there were *seven* separate and distinct fires in the involved building, the entire interior of which was saturated with kerosene.

When the fire chief arrived, the restaurant operator and his chef were standing in the rear of the building, fully dressed. Both claimed that they had been asleep on the second floor when they were awakened by smoke and had fled from the building. However, two suitcases neatly packed with their belongings were found in the tall grass at the rear of the building and the soles of the shoes worn by the operator had a strong odor of kerosene. The liquor license and two framed souvenir bills were found in one of the suitcases. The restaurant operator was found to have his insurance policy in his pocket.

The fire chief and investigators found no stock and fixtures, except two tables and forty-eight chairs. The restaurant operator claimed that, if any stock or fixtures were missing, they must have been stolen while he slept. Investigators finally learned of a moving van which had been at the premises early on the day before the fire. This led the investigators to an apartment on the upper East Side of New York City, where they found a large stock of canned foods, liquor, kitchen utensils, and equipment. The chef was identified as the man who had rented the apartment.

On September 29, 1943, the operator and the chef pleaded guilty and were sentenced to the Connecticut State Prison for not less than three nor more than six years, and not less than two nor more than five years, respectively.

This case also highlights the fact that need of some kind precipitates fires for profit—usually the need for money. It's economically impossible to remove this cause, but we can curtail its effect by greater success in the investigation of such fires. More fraud fires particularly must be detected, a greater number of such fire-setters have to be convicted, and a higher percentage of them actually sentenced to prison before fires for profit can be held to an absolute minimum.

CHAPTER FIVE

HATE AS A BASIC MOTIVE

IF AN incendiary fire has not been set for gain or promotion of some sort; if it has not been set to conceal evidence of a separate crime; if it cannot be suspected as the work of racketeers or saboteurs, then very possibly its setting stems from revenge, or anger, or spite. Otherwise it is a pyro or juvenile fire.

Of course, there is a little of the pyro in every individual who seeks to right some real or imagined wrong by fire, but in many cases it is a very small part of the fire-setter's make-up. The common hate fire is just another means of "getting even." The wronged person might have resorted to assault or to some destructive act such as slashing automobile tires or poisoning a dog.

During the initial investigation of a fire which apparently has not been set for gain, the victim must be asked if he has had any quarrels with any individuals who might set a fire as a means of retaliation. Is there any person who may wish to injure the victim? Have any threats ever been made? Who among the victim's business acquaintances, friends, relatives, or neighbors might harbor some grudge, some ill will?

Once a person with a possible motive—some reason to dislike or hate the victim—is discovered, then the investigator can check as to whether or not the suspect had an opportunity to set the fire. Motive and opportunity are the necessary ingredients to move an individual into the prime suspect class in a hate fire case.

Records of hate fires indicate that the individual with a motive usually sets the fire himself; hardly ever is an accomplice employed. Hardly ever is there more than one person concerned except among the juvenile fire-setters. Apparently the major satisfaction gained from a hate fire is in setting it personally.

MOTIVES

Hate fires can be divided roughly into three major groups: those that occur in a fit of passion, commonly termed "anger" fires; blazes set to spite another person; and fires resulting from a deep-seated desire for revenge. The motive is basically hatred, often spurred by jealousy, but this is a practical, working breakdown for arson investigators because such classifications aid in identifying the fire-setter by his *modus operandi*.

An anger fire is set within minutes or hours of the incident which has inflamed a person to such fury that he wants to hurt his "enemy" by burning him out. The arsonist is generally well-known to the victim.

A spite fire is usually set within hours or days; otherwise the desire to "get even" fades under the more pressing demands of daily life. However, the fire-setter (and in many cases his grievance) may not be known to the person against whom he is venting his hate.

A revenge fire is so termed because it is set by a person who may have harbored a "grudge" for years. This arsonist may be well-known to and even feared by the fire victim in many cases, but in some instances the incident which bred the hatred fostering the fire may have faded from the mind of the victim because of the passage of time. Diligent probing by an investigator is frequently necessary to recall possible motives to the mind of a revenge fire victim.

Anger Fires—Fires set in the heat of passion during the course of an argument or disagreement, or shortly thereafter, stem directly from a desire to retaliate without delay. The trouble may have been a business dispute, a quarrel between neighbors, or a fight between husband and wife. However, the desire to hurt the other party to the dispute is so great that some drastic action must be taken immediately, regardless of the consequences.

A husband may come home drunk and find that his wife has barred the door and refuses to let him in. After some pleading and continued refusal by the wife, the alcohol befogged mind of the husband may turn to arson—"I'll burn my way in." In a few minutes he may have a fire going against the door of the apartment. Some trash or old newspapers and a match often constitute the only fire-setting device of these individuals. In the majority of cases the fire dies out or a neighbor extinguishes it, but at times it may get out of control and spread rapidly, thus developing into another newspaper headline tragedy.

One case in recent years concerned a neighbors' quarrel. One asked the other not to race the motor of his car in the driveway and received a definite "I'll do as I please" answer. Within an hour the garage of the noisy neighbor was a mass of flames. It burned almost to the ground before the arrival of the apparatus. Because of its rapid spread and intensity the fire seemed to be of incendiary origin. Questioning of other neighbors resulted in locating one who had witnessed another neighbor walking away from the garage just as a mass of black smoke and flame leaped from its rear door. When this neighbor was identified as the one who had complained of the noise of the victim's automobile in the driveway, the investigator at the scene was in possession of evidence of both motive and opportunity.

A rather unusual demonstration of fire-setting in anger or during the heat of passion was given in Nassau County,

New York, a few months ago. An automobile mechanic attended a Christmas party with fellow employees, became intoxicated, but arrived home safely. He then decided that he needed a few more drinks and told his wife he was going to a nearby bar and grill.

His car stalled as he backed it out of the garage. He became enraged, smashed the windshield, poured motor oil all over the car, and tried to set it on fire by dropping lighted matches into the feed-pipe to the gas tank. His wife summoned several neighbors, but they were unable to restrain her husband. The mechanic, after tearing the window boxes from the front of the house, ran to the garage, poured the contents of an oil can on the floor and set it on fire. He then drove off in his other car while his neighbors extinguished the fire.

A Washington, D. C., case contained a bit of an O. Henry twist in the apparent clue that pointed to the fire-setter, and it serves to point up the maxim that poor leads sometimes develop into worthwhile results. Briefly, on February 21, 1953, an incendiary fire occurred in a large three-story brick building occupied by a department store for storage purposes. Shortly after the fire department arrived at the scene of the fire, a uniformed officer who was engaged in preventing spectators from getting too near the fire lines was questioned by one of the spectators regarding the fire and its possible origin. This man informed the officer that he could be of help to the firemen because he was employed in the building and had a key to the front door.

The officer noted that this man had a scorched spot on the shoulder of his coat and, because of this, accompanied him to the fire marshal, who suggested that he be taken to police headquarters for questioning.

The suspect, it was learned, was twenty-two years of age, married, living with his wife, and had received a medical discharge from the Marine Corps in June, 1952. He stated that he was one of four employees assigned to the warehouse and that the "boss" or foreman on occasion removed and witheld money from his pay envelope, telling him if he did not like it he could quit the job. He stated that other employees and station attendants at the next-door service station knew of this loss of funds and "kidded" him about it.

Shortly before the fire, one of these attendants had poked fun at him because of the shortage of money in his pay envelope. He said he could stand the kidding no longer and suddenly decided to burn the building in order to throw his "boss" out of a job. He unlocked the front door, tossed a lighted match into a pile of packing paper, which readily ignited, and then realizing that he had done wrong, attempted unsuccessfully to stamp out the fire. He left the building, however, locked the door, and went to his apartment. He returned to the scene when he heard the fire engines.

A peculiar feature of this case is that the scorched spot on his coat, which first directed suspicion toward him, was not caused by the fire but was the result of his having hung the coat too near an electric light bulb some weeks earlier. It later developed that this youth had a very low IQ and might be committed to a mental institution.

As will be noted, in all these anger fires there is definite evidence pointing to some one person as the fire-setter. These arsonists know that such is the case. They know, or should realize, that both opportunity and motive will point to them. However, they are in the grip of passion and think little of later arrest.

It is for this reason that fires set in a fit of anger are relatively easy to solve. Another factor in favor of the investigator is that these fire-setters invariably give way to anger again after a short questioning. "Sure, I did it," is often their prompt reply, sometimes followed by expressions of satisfaction about the success of the fire. Once an admission is secured, a full confession usually follows; in fact this type of arsonist seems relieved at the opportunity of blurting out all the facts and near-facts leading to the fire.

Spite Fires—These blazes are generally the result of opportunity and "sneak thief" thinking. The fire-setter's feelings have been hurt; he's resentful but not the type to attack directly the subject of his hatred. The opportunity to set a fire must be a convenient one. Any sizeable obstacle to the attempt to set a fire usually results in its prompt abandonment. However, their preparations may be extensive. Unlike the man who sets an anger fire, these arsonists for spite utilize great care to avoid discovery at the scene. The man who fires the home or business of another because of a real or fancied grievance is an individual marked by guile and stealth. He hates, but he makes little public expression of his feelings. And the trivial nature of the grievance is truly amazing when the scope of damage wrought by the fire is considered.

A chance remark about a neighbor's daughter resulted in the burning of a barn. . . . An arrest for drunkenness and attempted assault led to a fire in a bar and grill totalling close to $20,000 damage. The fire-setter *thought* the bartender had sent for the police. . . . An auto accessory store was badly damaged by fire as a result of the discharge of a clerk who was employed for only two weeks before his dismissal. . . . The home of a divorcee was set afire by a disgruntled suitor solely because he'd been refused a date.

These blazes, and many others of similar motivation, pinpoint the needlessness of a spite fire. And it is this fact that handicaps the investigator in such cases. The fire seems to be without reason.

Because the grievance is so slight the injured individual may not fully comprehend why he was burned out and cannot point to any suspect, the fire-setter's opportunity to set the blaze is often the factor that leads to the first break in spite fires. The investigator is then faced with the thankless task of determining the number of persons who might have had the opportunity of setting the fire and then attempting to narrow this field down to include only those who might have possible reasons, no matter how far-fetched, for desiring to hurt the victim. In other words, *who* could have done it, then *why* would he or she want to do it.

Another handicap in such cases is the continued denial of guilt made by these incendiaries, even when they are confronted with damaging evidence. They have given such care and attention to the preparation and planning of the deed that they are vain enough to feel they have committed the "perfect crime." However, when such an individual is brought up short and abruptly faced with evidence of his involvement in the fire-setting, his artificial defense mechanism is oftentimes not equal to the task and, in panic, the true story is blurted out with the culprit often attempting to justify his actions.

Not long ago a series of spite fires was set in West Riverside, California, by an ex-fireman. This man had resigned from the department only a short time earlier. Within a month after his resignation, three fires occurred in the district, each of incendiary origin. Investigation pointed to the former fireman as a likely suspect. He was picked up and questioned. Strangely enough, he promptly admitted setting all three fires, but would give no motive for his arson.

The fire chief, however, was convinced that these blazes were spite fires set to harass him because of differences between him and the fire-setter in previous years when both had served together in the department.

Revenge Fires—The desire to kill, maim, or damage irreparably predominates in real revenge fires. Of course, all fire-setters are potential murderers, but the arsonist who burns for the purpose of revenge has a definite desire to harm some person. The harboring of the grudge which served to trigger the fire may have wrecked the thinking of a previously normal individual. Indicative of murderous intent is the burning of the domicile of the victim rather than the business quarters. Of course, in rural areas barns may be the targets of revenge fires because loss of a barn creates a very real hardship for any farmer.

The strange thing about a revenge motivation is that hatred lasts for so many years. In Astoria, New York, two years, six months, and two days after being left at the altar, a jilted suitor entered the hallway of his former fiancee's mother, emptied a five-gallon can of gasoline around the stairs, lit a match, and threw it into the hallway as he fled.

In upstate New York, almost twenty years after winning a bitterly contested law suit on a legal technicality, a farmer awoke and found his barn ablaze. He never thought of the law suit, even when a state trooper asked about his neighbors. It was only when questioned about a mysterious shot fired into his living room eighteen years earlier that he thought of his suspicions at that time and named a neighbor.

Another case concerned two separate fires in the same building, one at the front door and one at the rear door of a second-floor apartment. The woman occupant was at the movies at the time. But the neighbors furnished the information that her former husband, divorced two years earlier, had been in the immediate vicinity that evening shortly before the fires were discovered.

A revenge fire is characterized by its direct attack against another person. It is far closer to an anger fire than those blazes set for spite. Persons who seek revenge have permitted their anger to smoulder before breaking out. Under questioning, these fire-setters are more akin to those individuals who set anger fires than they are to the spite arsonist. When confronted with some evidence tending to implicate them, a welling-up of the previously dormant anger seems to occur and they readily admit they set the fire, state they are glad they did, and then detail their "justification" for it.

In a small town in New Jersey a fire occurred in a dwelling on November 19, 1952. The chief of police summoned an insurance arson investigator and an immediate search uncovered a gallon glass jug in the debris of a bedroom. On-the-spot questioning revealed that the owner-occupant and his wife did not get along well together. Since the wife spoke little English, an Italian-speaking agent was called in by the arson investigator.

The second agent visited the premises under a pretext and succeeded in engaging the wife in a lengthy conversation in her native tongue. The woman told the agent that she had spread kerosene around with a dish and the kerosene had come from the jug found in the bedroom. The Italian agent left. The woman was shortly thereafter picked up and taken to police headquarters where she denied all knowledge of the fire. The Italian-speaking agent was brought in to confront her, whereupon she made a full confession, explaining that she had been mistreated by her husband and had meant to burn him up in the fire. She was arrested and held for action of the grand jury a little more than twenty-four hours after the fire.

An extremely malicious revenge fire against property was set by a person whom the victim did not even recall. In October, 1946, a fire in eastern Pennsylvania destroyed a large barn, a horse barn, a mill house, and a large silo, along with 200 tons of hay, 1,000 bushels of oats, a tractor, a corn planter, and many farm tools. The owner believed the trouble was due to electricity.

Two or three days later a local timber-cutter admitted to the postmaster that he had set the fire because the owner had brought in an outsider to cut timber in his wood lot. "Twenty years ago I offered him a fair price," he said. "And each year or two I'd make him an offer. Yet he brought in an outsider."

He waited until all the crops were in, then he slipped into the barn, emptied the contents of two bottles of gasoline on the floor and around the tractor, lit a match, and started the fire.

This aged arsonist believed that because the fire was set, the insurance companies would not pay and the owner would suffer the entire loss. When arraigned in court, he pleaded not guilty and made the following statement: "I set the fire all right, but what about those fellows who stole the timber?" He was found insane and sent to a state hospital for the criminal insane.

Both of these cases are typical, and both serve to highlight how little events lead to big fires when revenge is a factor in fire-setting.

Racial or Religious Antagonisms—Not as readily classified as hatred directed at individuals is hatred for those of another race or another faith.

Racial antagonisms are generally directed against a member of one of the minority groups in our population by one or more members of the majority. Negroes are burned out, so also Japanese, Mexicans, Chinese, and Puerto Ricans.

During the last war, hostility toward Americans of Japanese blood was quite marked in certain sections, and many thoroughly loyal Japanese-Americans were made the innocent victims of violence perpetrated by individuals of warped judgment or unstable behavior. In Los Angeles a thirty-nine-year-old man was arrested on six counts of arson after he admitted setting about two hundred fires in the Japanese quarters of that city. Practically all of these fires were small ones, but one of the peculiarities in his case is that he apparently set as many as *twenty* such fires in one night. He was found guilty on all counts and sentenced to the state penitentiary.

Religious intolerance may be directed against any group by a member of an opposing group or by one not believing in any conventional religion. Sometimes it is directed against Catholics, frequently against Jews, and sometimes against a congregation of which the fire-setter was formerly a member.

Churches, synagogues, and homes have been blasted by dynamite and damaged by fire. The racial or religious fire requires vigorous investigation. Deaths have frequently resulted from such bombings and burnings, and the persons killed are the innocent victims of a fanatical, unreasonable hate that may lead to a series of fires if not promptly exposed by the investigator of the initial fire.

Such investigations must be handled with great care, for any premature disclosure of the identity of witnesses may lead to determined efforts to dissuade them from cooperating with the investigator. Certainly any person capable of deliberately committing the crime of arson will not hesitate to use threats and coercion to prevent exposure of his activities by possible witnesses.

Such cases must also be prepared with great care for court presentation. Sometimes there is a marked feeling of sympathy for the defendant or defendants among the residents of the neighborhood, and some of these sympathizers may get on the jury trying the case.

OPPORTUNITY

Unlike the arsonist whose intent is to defraud the insurer of property, the hate fire-setter does not always have ready access to the premises concerned. The points of origin of these fires may be found on the outside of buildings, in hallways, under stairs, in cellars, or against entrance doors. When the point of origin is not accessible to an outsider, a check must be made of the possibility of forcible entrance or of the likelihood that the incendiary is a person with access to the point of origin because of employment, or some existing or former relationship to the victim.

Generally, fire-setting as a form of revenge, spite, or maliciously "evening-up" is preferred to other forms of violence because better opportunities exist to set a fire than to commit most any other destructive act. These fire-setters gravitate to arson in the mistaken belief that it offers the best opportunity to commit a retaliatory act without risking discovery. Only those individuals who burn in the heat of passion do so without contemplating the risk factor.

REPEATERS

When an individual repeats his act of arson time after time, pyromania is definitely indicated. True, an investigation may disclose the fire to be one resulting from anger or jealousy, but a check of the suspect's background sometimes discloses a whole series of such fires. No clear-cut mental deficiency may be evident, but the very fact of using arson as a device for retaliation rather than a variety of devices indicates twisted thinking.

A "grudge" fire repeater who did extensive damage was a borderline mental case. He was active in a large town in Illinois a few years ago and was not apprehended until he branched out into the sideline of selling information about the fires.

Shortly after a large commercial plant was involved in a fire, the company received a letter which stated that if $75.00 were sent to a certain address, the sender of the letter would divulge the name of the person who had set the fire. The authorities found that the address was the home of a bed-ridden woman and that a young boy, 18 years of age, had access to her mail box for the purpose of bringing her mail in to her. When the boy was picked up, he confessed that he had set the fire in question.

He had formerly worked for the company and had been

discharged because he had been annoying several of the girl employees. He claimed that he entered the building and searched through the drawers and boxes in the safe, but was unable to find any money. This made him angry and he therefore set the fire.

In the course of his confession he admitted that he had set six lumber yard fires in which the loss had totalled approximately $120,000. He was indicted and then sent to a mental hospital. The doctors were unable to agree as to his sanity, and after he entered a plea of guilty, he was sentenced to one to five years on two charges of arson and one of burglary.

A striking case of a "repeater" who was "getting even" is afforded in the case history of a forty-seven-year-old unmarried Syracuse man who confessed to starting nineteen fires in that city during 1944-1946. Included in these fires was the largest fire the city of Syracuse had had for many years. This particular fire involved a bicycle and hardware manufacturing plant, where the loss was reported to approach $1,000,000, and the insurance involved was approximately $750,000. The confessed fire-setter was a former employee of the concern who had been discharged two weeks before the fire. However, he claimed to have no ill-feeling but to have set the fire for the thrill involved.

Perhaps the series of fires will be in hotels, small restaurants, hospitals, and so forth, but they do set a recognizable pattern either because of locale or type of premises. In both of the above examples the series resulted from friction over discharge from employment and were solved when an alert investigator reviewed all recent fires in factories and recently discharged employees. Whenever a disgruntled employee is suspected, an investigator asks for a list of recently discharged employees from the firm having the fire.

Regardless of the apparently valid reasons for fire-setting, it is safe to assume a fire-setter is in the pyro class when he

sets more than two hate fires. A series of fires should term the
incendiary responsible a real "fire-bug"—some kind of a mental case—who seizes upon petty grievances merely as an
excuse to set fires, but since the identification and prompt
apprehension of these fire-setters rest in discovering persons
with even the most minute grievance, then it is good practice to continue to classify them as hate fire-setters rather
than as pyros.

LANDLORD-TENANT CASES

Bred no doubt by the housing shortage, the "fear fire"
to drive out a tenant paying low rent is always a possibility.
Warped thinking or emotional instability characterizes this
type of landlord-arsonist. Since such fires would usually follow repeated pleas to move or attempts to dispossess a tenant—possibly even threats—the victim would undoubtedly
draw the investigator's attention to the landlord as a possible
suspect.

Fires set in landlord-tenant cases have a basic profit motive, a desire to rent the premises at a higher rental than
that paid by the present tenant, but because of the hard
feelings developed in such cases they are classified with the
other hate fires.

Experienced investigators have noted that when a landlord sets a fire to scare out a tenant, the fire is so arranged
as to do little, if any, damage to the building.

A typical case has just occurred in New York State at this
writing. A charge of arson is pending against a 59-year-old
woman who owns a dwelling in an up-state county which
was rented to a family of seven. For several months during
the winter and spring of this year the landlady attempted
to force this family out of their home. All her efforts were
met with adamant refusal as no other quarters could be
found.

Finally the property owner instituted eviction proceedings against the tenants. One Saturday afternoon in May the owner visited the premises armed with legal documents and the ultimatum that if the tenants did not vacate the building at once they would be forcibly evicted, but the occupants said they could not move because all five of their children were ill with the measles.

Under such circumstances it seems incredible that any property owner or court officer could be so heartless as to remove a family from its lodgings. Yet the State Police charge that the elderly landlady deliberately started a fire in the building to force the tenants to leave. The charge is based on the fact that on the afternoon of her last visit the owner became involved in a heated dispute with her tenants. When it appeared that she was stymied in her attempt to evict them immediately because of the children's illness, she told the occupants that she wanted to go to an old storeroom in the building to get some articles out of a trunk.

She was permitted to enter, went to the storeroom, and soon thereafter left the dwelling. Within a few minutes of her leave-taking, smoke was observed seeping out from the storeroom. The man of the house gathered his family together and then investigated. He found that a bundle of rags had been ignited, creating a great deal of smoke but little flame.

Investigators felt there was little doubt that the landlady had resorted to setting a "little fire" to scare the tenants from the building. She succeeded to a degree, since the five sick children had to be removed from the house. However, the landlady was also removed from her home—and brought before a judge and charged with arson.

EXPLOSIONS

Many fires result from explosions; dynamite bombings usually start an intense fire complicated by broken water lines, damaged gas and electric lines, ruptured fuel oil tanks, and similar handicaps to putting out the fire. Even though an explosion may not result in fire, it is not unusual for an arson investigator to be called in and assigned to investigate a case involving blast damage.

Explosions may be encountered in any one of the following: real or fancied personal grievances, during the course of labor disputes, as a means of intimidation in racial or religious strife.

"Infernal machines" or "suspicious packages" mailed with the intent of killing or maiming the receiver are motivated by the same hate that sets anger and spite fires. However, the sending of a bomb to a person implies a little more of the psycho than ordinary fire-setting because of the utter disregard for the lives of others who might possibly open the package or be in the company of the recipient when he opened it.

Automobile bombs, once the favorites of gangsters, are now being used by individuals who do not have the normal repugnance to killing. Hate fire-setters, check-mated in their fire-setting efforts or in an attempt to do greater damage, have also utilized World War II "booby trap" techniques.

Bombings have occurred during labor disputes, but today they are almost always an act of a particularly disgruntled individual rather than a planned demonstration of force by official union representatives. Invariably, dynamite tied together and hand fused is the weapon in such cases.

Since explosives may be encountered by arson investigators, they must learn the action of both high and low explosives by visiting the scene of accidental explosions whenever possible. The following information on the different types of explosives, the numerous methods of ignition or detonation, and the various instances in which explosives may be encountered should be of assistance, but must be supplemented by active research on the part of the investigator.

High vs. Low Explosives—Low power explosives are those whose explosive velocity does not range beyond 3000 feet per second. High explosives are those whose velocities range from 3000 to 25,000 feet per second. Low explosives include natural or manufactured gas, black powder, and the more modern "smokeless" gunpowder. The sound of an explosion resulting from the ignition of a low explosive is of low frequency and some duration, a sort of "whooooom."

Dynamite, T.N.T., and nitroglycerine (in that order) are the most frequently encountered high explosives. Very few cases involve so-called "nitro" bombs. T.N.T. is also rarely used, but since it is used for demolition work by Infantry and Engineer units, it may be encountered around Army camps or in cases involving Army or ex-Army personnel. Dynamite is relatively easy to secure. It can be readily purchased by many types of business concerns and is handled by employees daily in building construction, mining, and road building. It is frequently stolen from places where it is sold or stored. The sound of a blast resulting from the detonation of high explosives is of high frequency but short duration, a sharp, cracking "WHOOM."

Low explosives are ignited by any spark or flame, while high explosives require shock as well as heat, such as a detonating cap, to set them off.

Examination of the Scene—In any explosion case the scene must be examined as soon as possible, preferably before rescue work or fire extinguishment is attempted. During the initial survey of the scene the investigator must determine how the explosion occurred and the extent of the damage. Photographs should be taken to show the effect of the blast for later study and use as evidence if the case goes to trial. Examination of the scene usually reveals whether the case involves a high or low explosive. Low explosives have a "pushing" effect, with little or no really violent damage about the immediate site of the explosion. High explosives, on the other hand, produce a tremendous shattering effect in the immediate vicinity of the explosion and there's a "blast" effect rather than the "push" of low explosives.

Interrogation of witnesses as to the sound accompanying the blast helps to determine which explosive is involved. Medical examination of victims may also aid: marked concussion results from the blast effect of high explosives.

Debris at the scene must be searched as carefully as the debris at the scene of a suspicious fire. *Anything unusual or foreign to the scene* may be of great value. Fragments of pipe, wire, clocks, burned fuses, and blasting caps will all aid in determining the type of bomb, possibly the method of ignition, and will sometimes aid in identifying the person responsible for the explosion.

Methods of Ignition—Explosions are set off by one of two methods: delayed or direct action.

Delayed action involves a timing unit which is set for the bomb to go off at a certain time. It has always been suspected that the "World's Fair" bomb which killed two of the top men of New York's Bomb Squad was a delayed ignition bomb. Detective Joe Lynch and his partner, Fred Soccha, rode on a "suspected package" alarm in 1940 at the British Pavilion in the World's Fair exhibition area. Quite a crowd had collected because of police activity and the two detectives had a difficult time reaching the scene, but it took them only a moment to examine the "package"—a small suitcase—and note the ticking of a clock of some kind from within the suitcase. The two bomb squad men risked their lives to move the package to an open area, protecting the curious assembled outside the building.

Lynch, a six-foot former professor of pharmacy at Fordham University, who joined the police force because he couldn't support a large family on his instructor's salary, noted that the clock mechanism was still ticking as he examined it and told his partner to keep everybody back, even other police officers.

Using a sharp knife, Lynch and his partner removed a piece from one side of the suitcase. They could see the dynamite stacked inside. Now they knew they didn't have a valise filled with old clothing and an alarm clock. They also knew lives would be lost in the panic resulting from a bomb blast in that crowded area. They might restrict the immediate area and prevent damage from the direct blast, but they could do little to quiet a frightened crowd.

Slowly, piece by piece, they enlarged the hole in the side of the suitcase, attempting to get at the timing mechanism or the detonating cap itself, but time ran out on them. The damage was terrific. A reconstruction of the bomb, based upon testimony of witnesses who handled it before the police were called, led to the belief that it contained *twenty-four* sticks of dynamite.

Another case involving a delayed action bomb resulted in the deaths of a whole planeload of people. The bomb maker sought to kill only one person, but his bomb was set to go off while the plane was in flight in order to make the murder appear to be a plane crash. The plane disintegrated and all aboard were killed. His plan failed when a study of the scene led to a suspicion that the plane disintegrated while in the air.

The clock mechanism generally utilized in bombs of this type is an ordinary alarm clock with the contact being made by the alarm "clapper" stem in the same manner as fire-setting mechanisms. When the alarm goes off, the stem starts vibrating and will make contact. Both the fire-setter and the person who prepares a bomb of this type will remove the normal alarm bell so that its ringing just before the fire or blast will not serve to identify the mechanism.

Direct action may be the result of an act by a person

receiving or examining the bomb, or by the person placing it. Direct action falls into three general classifications: actuated by the person receiving or examining; set off by the person placing the explosive—either fuse or electrical contact; automobile bombs or "booby traps," manually operated by some person performing a normal act.

"Infernal machines" or "suspected packages" mailed to their victims usually have their contact attached to the string wrapping of an inside box or on the lid of the box itself. The package is usually well wrapped; when the outside wrapper is removed, the package is found to contain another wrapping with a lighter string securing it in place. When that string is cut or removed, contact will be made. If not string-actuated, then the contact is generally a piece of wire fastened to the inside of the box lid. When the cover is raised, the wire makes contact. Such bombs may contain stick or loose dynamite, a few wires, and a small battery.

A mercury switch can be spring-actuated so that it will also make contact when the cover of a box is raised, but it is usually encountered in bombs "planted" in buildings. A switch of this type can be actuated, once set, when the package containing it is tilted in any direction. It can be set to go off when tilted as little as 30 degrees.

A plunger contact may also be encountered on "planted" bombs in buildings. A hole is drilled in the bottom of the package—usually a suitcase—and a plunger set on a spring is placed in the hole. While the bomb is being carried to the scene, the plunger is held in place by a small pin; when it is planted, it is set bottom down and "armed" by taking out the pin holding the plunger in place. The weight of the bomb now keeps the plunger from moving out through the hole in the bottom of the "package," but it is ready to go off whenever the package is lifted. These plungers can be set to make contact when the bomb is lifted a quarter of an inch.

Intimidation bombs placed during racial and religious violence, or involving some labor trouble, are usually set off by the person placing the explosive. Regular blasting equipment has been wired up and used in some cases, but the usual device is an ordinary fuse. The explosives are tied together and placed against the outside of the selected building. A fairly long fuse is ignited in order to provide time for the criminal to leave the scene. This criminal depends upon stealth to avoid discovery.

A recently encountered method is one in which the criminal or criminals depend upon speed to conceal their identity. Operating from a car, they use a short fuse and throw the bomb from the speeding car. As a general rule this group of bomb-throwers will use a few more sticks of dynamite to insure damage even from a poorly thrown missile.

Automobile "starter" bombs seem to be fairly common in the West and Midwest. A quantity of dynamite is lashed under the chassis or the dashboard of a car and wired up with a blasting cap, one wire hooked to a spark plug and the other grounded to the chassis. When the victim pushes the starter, the contact is made and the blast goes off. Another automobile bomb is arranged so that the heat of the manifold ignites a fuse, thus effecting a delay of anywhere from 30 minutes to an hour.

A recent case involved a regulation Army hand grenade of the demolition type. A simple "booby-trap," it was tied to two nails driven into the floor and the ring tied to the door handle. However, this type of grenade affords a few seconds' delay after the pin is pulled, and the woman who opened the door summed it all up in one glance at the ring and the nailed down grenade and "hit the deck" away from the doorway, saving herself from the effects of the blast and fragmentation.

The fact that most of our Service personnel are not only familiar with the use of grenades but have access to them at some time or other during their service points to their possible use in booby traps.

Safety Precautions—A package suspected of containing an explosive and possibly a delayed timing mechanism or one which may go off when the package is lifted or tilted must be handled with great care. The best method is to *leave it alone* and evacuate the building and area for a safe distance until bomb squad personnel from a large city police force or Armed Services unit can arrive at the scene.

The investigator must remember that it has always been an axiom of experienced Army and police personnel that the good bomb experts are all dead. The records of "unexploded bomb" or "bomb disposal" units during World War II are replete with "deceased" notations, and even the Dupont organization lost an expert who was examining and attempting to open a suspicious package in Easton, Pennsylvania. All that can be expected of an arson investigator is what might be expected of any police or fire officer, and that is to safeguard the scene and attempt to minimize the damage if and when the suspected bomb does go off.

CHAPTER SIX

PYROS

PYROMANIA may be described as an overpowering desire to set things afire, literally "fire-madness." It may be used to describe the condition of any individual evincing an unreasonable tendency to set fires regardless of the amount of destruction which may result.

For years officials concerned with public safety, police officers and firemen particularly, termed practically all fire-setters fire-bugs, psychos, or pyros indiscriminately. Today, finer distinctions are made in terminology. When a person is motivated to set a fire by what may be termed a "normal" or rational motive such as profit, or the need to conceal a crime or to facilitate a crime such as extortion, it is improper to term him a victim of pyromania. It is the fire-setters without apparent normal motive who are justly termed pyros.

A pyro has no rational motive for setting fires. He does not burn for profit or to conceal crime, nor does he burn for sabotage or racketeering purposes. Although some may burn for a vague sort of revenge or to satisfy some shapeless resentment, these arsonists cannot be classified as actual hate fire-setters. However, pyros do want fires. That's why they set them. Except for the "psychotic" arsonist, who suffers from a marked defect of reason, all pyros secure some gratification, exaltation, or relief as a result of the sights and sounds attending the fire-setting.

The reasons they give for setting a fire are sometimes fantastic. In May of 1935 a series of New Jersey forest fires resulted in a young male delinquent being confined to an institution. In 1942 this same young man was sentenced to five to six years in a state penitentiary for again setting forest fires. Immediately after his release he moved to New England and in 1947 confessed to setting forest fires in both Maine and New Hampshire, some of them of considerable magnitude. His only "reason" for setting all of these fires was to better the blueberry picking in the burned-out areas. He said he was fond of blueberries and believed that burning off the underbrush in blueberry patches would mean good berry picking a few years later!

Insofar as a layman is concerned, pyros are usually classified in accordance with the extent of their mental derangements or the basic factors leading to their fire-setting. The "psychotics" suffer from such defects of reason as not to know the nature or quality of their acts. Better able to distinguish between right and wrong are the morons, imbeciles, and feeble-minded individuals who are grouped together and classed as mental defectives. In descending order follow the "sex pyros," the "hero," and "would-be fireman," and lastly the juvenile fire-setters with indications of pyromania.

RELEASE FACTORS

All normal persons know that fire-setting is wrong, know that to burn another's house or building may result in extensive damage and possibly loss of life. Normal inhibitions prevent such fire-setting.

Almost all pyros know arson is wrong, that it will damage property or cause loss of life, but they sublimate this knowledge to an apparently more pressing desire to have a fire regardless of possible damage or harm.

While almost any incident or series of occurrences can snap the narrow thread separating apparently "normal" individuals from pyros, it is usually stretched to the breaking point or broken entirely by one of the following: a poor home life, unemployment, a confused sex life, or the excessive use of alcohol. One or more of these four factors may help breed conditions which lead to intolerable pressures which only seem to be released or relieved by acts of firesetting or some equally violent outlet.

Poor Home Life—Emotional disturbances resulting from friction between parent and child or husband and wife sometimes assume tremendous proportions to one of the individuals concerned. Reaction to some break in a normal home life may be immediate or not exhibit itself for years. Such reaction is one of the major factors in juvenile fire-setting.

Lack of satisfactory home life among males living alone has manifested itself time and again as a contributing factor to fire-setting. Furnished room "bums" in urban areas, itinerant laborers or migrant workers in rural areas, the "tramps" of the West and the "homeless men" of the East, have frequently been identified as pyromaniacs. Vagrants, persons without a home, are more likely to desire the destruction of other people's homes and thus, no doubt, are more responsive to the pressures resulting in pyromania than a person with a normal home life.

Unemployment—Personal economic security is always an anchor to windward when a potential pyro is riding out an emotional storm which might lead to arson without a rational motive. Sudden loss of a job may result in a defeatist attitude. The plans of years may be suddenly torn asunder by loss of economic security. Continued unemployment may wreck the normal reasoning ability of many an individual.

Confused Sex Life—A normal heterosexual relationship may be difficult to establish because of extreme shyness, partial impotence, or fear of acquiring a venereal infection. Any of these may lead to homosexual experimentation.

A young man who admitted his involvement in sexual irregularities since he was thirteen years of age was responsible for the burning of the Rochester Club in Rochester, N. Y., one of the most beautiful club buildings between New York and Chicago. An idea of the possible damage can be gleaned from the fact that close to $700,000 had just been spent on modernizing the interior of the club and a total of $1,000,000 insurance was carried!

There's no question that the frustrations engendered by failure to lead a normal sex life serve as fuel to prime the fires of pyromania. Suppression of an aroused, but previously latent, homosexuality may have the same effect.

A study of the case histories set forth in Lewis and Yarnell's *Pathological Firesetting* (Pyromania) reveals numerous instances in which a confused sex life made a major contribution to pyromania. Exhibitionists and exposers, sex deviates, peeping Toms, and passive participants in homosexual play are cited time and again. Indicative of the type of confusion that may be encountered is one in which the fire-setter admitted to an obsessional urge that culminated in fifty-six masturbations in one day.

Normal inhibitions are ineffective with such confused personalities.

Excessive Use of Alcohol—While drinking to excess is frequently fostered by feelings of insecurity resulting from poor home life, unemployment, or sexual maladjustments, it may also have some more obscure cause. However, no matter what the reason, there is little doubt that such use breaks down normal inhibitions and releases previously dormant desires and drives.

Several incendiary fires which occurred in a Connecticut city pin-points a typical alcoholic pyro. In August, 1942, a fire of suspicious origin occurred in a furniture store. During the investigation a former fire chief called attention to a man who had been convicted of arson in 1935.

This man was questioned and admitted that after having several drinks he had started for home but had stopped to rest on the steps of the furniture store. After awhile he decided to set the building on fire, went through an unlocked door in the cellarway, and started a fire in a pile of papers. He watched until the fire got a good start and then left in the same manner by which he had entered. He walked around the block to give the fire time to make headway, returned to the building, and stood talking to a couple of men until one of them remarked that he smelled smoke. To this the fire-setter agreed and all three started to investigate. The arsonist turned in the alarm, offered to assist the fire chief, put a handkerchief over his face, and went into the cellar with the chief and several firemen whom he assisted in extinguishing the fire.

This fire-setter also confessed to setting another fire and to turning in several false alarms, but denied responsibility for other fires which the officials believed were undoubtedly his work. He gave as reasons for setting the fires that he wanted to be a hero, wanted to stir up the neighbors, to assist the firemen, to be a volunteer firemen, but he admitted he only had such ideas "after a few drinks."

Sometimes a few drinks will be sufficient to incite some individuals; sometimes real intoxication must be reached before the urge to set fires is noted. And in a few individuals a desire to see a fire or hear the apparatus was noted during periods of recovery from the aftereffects of an over indulgence in alcohol—the so-called "hang-over" periods.

In any event the effect of alcohol upon some humans has led to the designation, "alcoholic pyro." This is the person who is generally rational insofar as an urge to set fires is concerned, but who becomes a victim of pyromania after taking a few drinks.

THE "IRRESISTIBLE IMPULSE"

The glib explanation of some arsonists that they "couldn't help themselves" cannot be accepted by an arson investigator unless other acts before or after the fire-setting episode tend to show that the fire resulted from some delusion or hallucination.

When the suspected individual hears voices, labors under a persecution complex, or commits some bizarre act such as prancing around the burning building in the nude, then a true irresistible impulse may be present. Otherwise the investigator must view any attempt to blame the fire-setting upon a compulsive drive as a subterfuge to avoid punishment for the act of arson.

It must be remembered that what is sometimes termed "unbearable tension" associated with an inability to deal with the daily problems encountered in our complex social structure does not qualify as a true "irresistible impulse." Nor does the need to set a fire which sometimes results from the pent-up rage attendant upon some social or physical inferiority qualify as such an impulse. In recent years some investigators have set themselves up as amateur psychiatrists and assigned an "irresistible impulse" or "uncontrollable urge" to all pyros encountered in their investigations. Others have sought confessions by suggesting to suspects that such impulses or urges are in the field of excusable acts. Nothing is further from the truth. Actually an arson investigator rarely encounters a person so far gone mentally as to be unable to resist any such impulse or urge.

"PSYCHOTICS"

The arson investigator need not attempt to differentiate between the various psychoses in classifying pyros. He is concerned first with who set the fire, how it was set, and the reason for it. Only when a mental defect apparently precludes any reasoning process may the investigator term a fire-setter "psychotic," probably activated by some inner drive of a delusional character.

When the actions of a fire-setter indicate a need for prompt commitment for psychiatric care, the investigator may suspend efforts to discover why the blaze was set until after an examination of the prisoner by qualified psychiatrists.

It must be remembered, however, that legally a person must stand trial for his acts if he is rational at the time of court appearance and capable at the time of the fire-setting of distinguishing right from wrong and able to understand the nature and quality of his act. This is the gauge of criminal responsibility, and all "irresistible impulses" or "uncontrollable urges" when offered in explanation for setting fires must be measured accordingly.

MENTAL DEFECTIVES

Morons, imbeciles, and feeble-minded individuals who become pyros—oddly enough, considering their mental equipment—generally escape detection and apprehension for some time. Some just want to see a fire, some to watch the apparatus, others to enjoy the excitement and noise of the event; but the activity of an arsonist with inadequate mental equipment invariably is marked by a continuing series of fires showing a definite pattern.

The fires of these mental defectives are highlighted by numerous fatalities. Their limited mental equipment makes it impossible for them to realize the possible loss of life. Lacking the intelligence to fear arrest and the consequences of their acts, these arsonists sometimes remain at the scene, literally fanning the flames until the fire has gained real headway.

A case in point concerns a juvenile mental defective in Baltimore. In May, 1944, when only ten years of age, this boy set fire to some trash in steel drums and he and his parents were warned. On November 17, 1947, as a result of two fires in a school building, he was committed to a state training school for boys, where he was confined until September 4, 1949, at which time he was released, having made a very good record at the institution. Within two weeks in November, 1949, he set ten fires. In the first of these two children were burned to death.

Another factor which contributes to the large number of deaths in such fires is the fact that a good proportion of these mental midgets want to see the flames and hence don't send in an alarm. They become so preoccupied with the fire and their own delight that the thought of fire engines sometimes escapes them. Fortunately, a goodly number are more interested in the engines than the fire and promptly dispatch an alarm.

SEX "PYROS"

One male arsonist told investigators that after he has a few drinks he gets the urge to set fires; he likened it to "getting hot and bothered" with a woman. Sex pyros set fires to achieve sexual stimulation and orgasm. A great many of the other pyros utilize arson as a substitutive sexual act, but these arsonists actually derive a sexual thrill from setting a fire and watching the flames.

Illustrative of how deep-seated this pyro-sexual drive may be is a case in which fire-setting tendencies became apparent at the age of nine when the subject was arrested for setting fire to a school in his home town of Evansville, Indiana. After his release, no record shows until 1935 when he was convicted at the age of 24 of second-degree arson in Evansville for a fire which caused $11,000 damage. It later developed that this fire was only one of a series he set on the same night. Committed to the Indiana Hospital for Insane Criminals, he was released a few years later in 1938.

Shortly after his release a number of incendiary fires of the same pattern occurred in Evansville and the authorities sought this recently released pyro, but he fled his home and was not heard of again until his arrest for a series of costly fires in Nashville, Tenn., one of them causing damage estimated at $150,000. This man was found to be normal in other respects when he was examined and re-examined prior to trial on the Nashville charges. Today, at forty-one years of age, he faces twenty-eight years in prison, yet he soberly tells questioners his only "motive" is sexual gratification, that fires get him "excited."

In reality, a sex pyro is a *fetishist*. Instead of women's undergarments, baby clothes, or like objects, the fetish is a fire.

Sometimes a sex pyro is really mixed up, his sex deviations meandering down several paths at once. A recent case in California well illustrates this type of individual. In all, seven fires of apparently incendiary origin occurred within a few weeks of each other. Investigation narrowed suspicion to a teen-aged youth.

The "break" in the case came when a five-year-old girl told her father of an older boy who gave her a ride on his bicycle, drove her into a nearby garage where he removed all of her clothing and fondled her before dressing her and driving her back home. Her father immediately reported the incident to the police and it was noted that the description of this boy tallied with that of the youth suspected of the fire-setting.

Police picked the boy up, and when identified by the little girl he admitted the attack and the fire-setting. He claimed that just before the fires he'd have a ringing, buzzing sound in his head and that during these periods he would walk and walk until he'd get an urge to enter a house.

Once inside a home he'd search for women's underclothing and after fondling the articles for awhile, he'd scatter them about a room and set it on fire.

VANITY FIRE-SETTERS

Serious fires and even strings of eight to ten fires have been traced to little men who wanted to be big heroes in the eyes of others. Equally serious blazes have been set by would-be-firemen arsonists, frustrated firemen whose top enjoyment consists of the sights and sounds attendant upon fire engines and firemen in action. Some of these would-be-firemen also secure great satisfaction from actually aiding the firemen at the fire scene. And some individuals combine both drives, wanting to be both heroes and fire-fighters.

The classic story of such arsonists concerns a man who set an early morning fire in a tenement house hallway (the fifth in a two-week series in the same neighborhood), raced through the premises banging on doors and screaming, "Fire, get out, fire," at the top of his lungs. Then he met the firemen on their arrival and volunteered to help them with the hose.

When the fire was under control the police officer first on the scene took the fire-setter by the arm and brought him to the fire chief. "Chief," he said, "this is the man who sent the alarm and then came back and awakened all the tenants. He deserves a lot of credit."

The chief's reply was interrupted by a fire lieutenant. "Chief," this officer said, "this is the man who also helped to handle the hoses and assist in extinguishing the fire."

"Yeah," said the chief, "and I'm pretty certain he's the man who set the fire!"

The chief had recognized the fire-setter as the "hero" of two previous suspicious fires. An interrogation soon resulted in a full confession.

Another case involved a volunteer assistant fire chief who

set a fire, but in his eagerness to report it and get to work putting it out failed to check on the success of his "plant." He led firemen to the "fire," but all that they found upon their arrival was a basement room filled with smoke and littered with crumpled newspapers. An unkind fate had snuffed out the ignition blaze with only a slight scorching around the point of origin. The arsonist couldn't explain how he could see the "smoke and flame" coming from the "burning" building from his point of observation at street level just before he turned in the alarm.

Fortunately, from the investigator's standpoint, vanity fire-setters are "repeaters." The thrills attendant on one fire do not satisfy their vanity permanently. They may feel some elation for days, or even weeks, but memories of previous fires whet their appetites for more blazes. Basically they are exhibitionists and their "public" is a necessary adjunct to their exhibitionist tendencies. Many cases show a shortening of the intervals between fires as a series of blazes continues. And as the frequency of the fires increase, so also does the desire for the spotlight of recognition. The pyro rises to new heights as a hero or would-be fireman. At this stage he is satisfied with nothing less than saving life in a large fire, or attempting to supervise and direct the firemen in their fire-fighting efforts.

When the fires increase in frequency, it is very often noted that their size also increases. It's a case of the pyro wanting more and bigger fires than those he set previously.

One case in point occurred in Massachusetts. For about six years, fires were set on weekends and on holidays such as the Fourth of July and Halloween. Until about four years ago the fires were set largely to grass and forests, but in the last few years they included shacks and small sheds. Each year the fire-setters became bolder and set fire to property of more value. Brush fires increased, also large forest fires, one of which burned for over four days. In 1946 twenty-seven calls for brush fires were received in seven hours, and in July, 1947, twenty-two calls were received for brush and shack fires.

When the case was finally broken, it was discovered that one of the persons involved was the brother of a police officer; also involved were a nephew of a former chief of police, a son of a newspaper reporter, a lieutenant in the fire department, and a member of the board of engineers (which elects the fire chief). In all a total of nine men were found guilty.

Though this has always been a difficult case to understand —a manifestation of group pyromania by a number of people who wanted the thrill of fighting fires—it well illustrates the increasing tempo of fire-setting by pyros.

Somewhere along the line, depending upon the alertness and training of police and fire personnel, this type of fire-setter draws suspicion to himself, and once centered, it is usually not difficult to tie a suspect in with previous cases or to place him under surveillance and arrest him when a new attempt at fire is made.

JUVENILES

Children oftentimes set fires at home or in school, but cannot be considered among the pyros until a behavior pattern can be established.

Youngsters under twelve years of age play with matches and serious fires sometimes result, but to classify such children as arsonists is unfair. However, if a study of a youngster's behavior shows a definite indication of any of the previously described manifestations of pyromania then it is reasonable to classify him as a potential pyro and provide adequate treatment and care for him.

A case of this type which literally demanded proper care occurred in Kansas City, Mo. Four fires blazed within a period of one month, all in one single block. Prior to these fires, and in the same vicinity, there had been thirteen unexplained rubbish or grass fires. Responsibility for these fires was finally placed on a boy of *eight*. The youngster admitted setting many fires. Two of them had done serious damage. His school teacher said he was of definitely retarded mentality. She cited an incident which took place when she asked her pupils to draw a picture showing what spring meant to them: this child drew a bright sun and a burning house with many firemen around it.

Many teen-age boys and girls are emotionally ill equipped to shoulder the duties and responsibilities which increasing age places upon them, physically and mentally. While most youths successfully attain emotional and physical maturity without outward signs of internal difficulties a few will react to these pressures and tensions by committing various acts against the community, and sometimes the act is fire-setting.

Two cases which reveal the extent of the activity of fire-setters in this age group occurred in widely separated cities:

In St. Louis a boy of *twelve* set twenty-two fires and was responsible for false alarms on four occasions. He believed that he had set a great many more fires, but could not remember the exact locations. He was apprehended by police officers who saw him running from a burning automobile. As a juvenile delinquent he was sentenced to an indefinite term at the state farm. He has set two fires at the farm since his commitment.

A boy of *fifteen* in Springfield, Massachusetts, started two different fires a week apart in a four-story apartment building. He was a great reader of detective magazines and especially interested in articles concerning arson. He had experienced some difficulty with the authorities, having been charged with breaking, entering, larceny, and indecent assault. In addition to the apartment house fires, he admitted setting three others, two in barns and one in another apartment house. He was found guilty, was committed to a hospi-

tal from which he escaped, was apprehended again and sent
to a reformatory for five years.

During this age period hatred of parental authority may
blossom fully, and hatred of what the psychiatrists term the
"mother figure" or "father image" may lead to setting a
revenge fire—actually a rebellion fire.

Otherwise, "everyday" juvenile fires fall pretty well within the framework of pyromania, and the arson investigator
will experience difficulty in distinguishing between the fires
of juveniles and the fires of adult pyros because of the simi-
larity in pattern or technique.

The pattern of juvenile fire-setting can be readily visual-
ized by the following transcript of a confession secured in a
case involving several youths:

Q. Where do you live?

A. Weston, N. Y.

Q. How long have you lived there?

A. About four years. I was born in Sharon, Conn., June 10,
1936. My family was living at Astoria, N. Y. at the time.

Q. Are you employed at present?

A. No, and I don't go to school. I work weekends for my father,
Richard B......., off and on. He does tree work at Weston.

Q. Do you know Albert L....... of Weston, N. Y.?

A. Yes, we used to hang around together. I only hang around
with him off and on, but try to stay away from him as much
as I can 'cause we have been in trouble together a couple
of times.

Q. Do you know whether Albert L....... is inclined toward
setting fires, or does he get any satisfaction out of seeing
anything burning?

A. Well, he just likes to fight fires mostly.

Q. Have you ever seen Albert L....... start any fires?

A. Just one at A..... & B....... garage.

Q. Will you tell the date this occurred and how he set this fire?

A. I don't recall the date, but think it was before Thanksgiving
time. This night, I was at Johnny W's....... soda fountain,

and it might have been there or some other place I met Albert L........ I think we went down to his girl friend's house. Her name is Frances H......., and she lives in Weston. It was around 7:00 P.M., and we left her house, headed back toward W's....... store, but the store was closed. Bob headed North toward the A....... & B....... garage, and I followed. He said something like: "Let's go up the street. I'm going to burn a building down." I followed him up to this garage, the door was open, so he walked in. He found some kind of greasy or oily rag in the garage and he set a lighted cigarette on the rag. I was against it all the time and I was afraid to try to stop him because he can beat up most of the kids in Weston. I took off and ran down the street, and we went to his house. He called his girl in Dover, Barbara H......., and then about 9:00 P.M. we took a walk up by the garage. We noticed that there was quite a fire going in the north side of the building, where Bob had started the fire. There was a small bench there near the wall, and a lot of paper which I guess helped get the fire going. We both ran down to the W......-N...... Food Store in Weston and Al turned the alarm in by pushing the button which starts the fire siren. The button is located about the middle of the building, towards the street, on the east side. The fire did a lot of damage to the garage. I read in the paper that there was about $2500 damage to the building, besides a delivery truck which was burned pretty bad.

Q. Walter, do you go by any other name?
A. Everybody calls me Teddy. It's just a nickname.
Q. Did you have any part in setting the fire?
A. No, I had no part in it. I was against it all the time. I didn't think Al was going to do it anyway. I thought he was just kidding, but he was serious about setting the fire.

MODUS OPERANDI

The point of origin for any non-profit motivated fire is usually in the public portions of buildings. The majority of pyros further identify their work by setting their fires in hallways and cellars. These are the two favorite locations of these arsonists. However, unlike other fire-setters, their "plants" as a rule are nothing more than some paper, rags, or trash, and a match. Oftentimes their fires burn out without spreading through the building in which set. The vanity fire-setters may make more extensive ignition efforts because they want the fire to assume suitable proportions for their role as hero or fireman's helper.

The individuals who set vanity fires will also break and enter for the purpose of stealing and setting a fire. There appears to be a dual motivation in such cases, with the desire for the fire taking precedence over the intent to steal. Other pyros hardly ever break and enter a building, though they may open unlocked doors and enter.

However, juveniles hesitate to enter strange buildings. In the younger age groups their fires will be found in their homes or the homes of friends and neighbors. Older youths have a slight tendency to place their fires within their own neighborhoods, thus offering the investigator some clue as to their identities.

PATTERN OF PYRO FIRES

The fires of pyros invariably build a pattern for the skilled investigator to trace and thus identify the fire-setter. A profit-motivated or hate fire may have the appearance of the work of a pyro, but it will not fit into a pattern as will a series of fires set by a pyro.

This of course must be qualified by observing that a professional torch or an arson ring hired to set insurance fraud fires during times of financial stress may very well use the same method of touching off each "job," particularly if the first few "contracts" have been burned out satisfactorily and payments have been made promptly by the companies.

Another switch on this pattern of fire-setting for which

the investigators must be on the alert is the possibility of a fraud fire-setter capitalizing upon a series of fires. When a series of fires have occurred in an area and the authorities as well as the public are justly convinced that a pyromaniac is active, a "smart operator" who has been looking for an opportune time to have a profitable fire may very well touch off his own property and loudly bewail his ill luck at becoming another victim of the "fire-bug's" activities.

All pyros develop a uniformity of technique in their fire-setting. It may be in any one of the following areas or a combination of more than one, but the uniformity of technique can be broken down into the following phases: area of operations, type of buildings selected for the blazes, location of point of origin, basic materials composing the "plant," time of night or day, and day of week or month.

Once having set a fire in a certain manner and successfully avoided detection and arrest, a fire-setter seems to become a victim of habit. Habit, or opportunity, also seems to govern the selection of an area of operations or type of building in which fires are set.

The grouping of fires by the basic materials used in the "plant" serves tentatively to identify all such fires as the work of one man. The grouping of related points of origin is a nebulous identification. When such information can be localized as to type of building and area of operations, it is a bit more definite and the identification is more valid.

However, when a pyro's activities become so systematized that the fires can be singled out by the time of day or night, or the day of the week, then a full pattern of activity can be established. In a case which follows on the next few pages the pyro showed a pattern of from 12:30 A.M. to 6:30 A.M. on every day of the week. Upon his arrest he admitted he never set a fire before midnight or "much after daylight came up."

Another case showed a pattern for Thursdays and Fridays.

Twelve fires occurred in less than three months in a small town in West Virginia just outside the city of Charleston. The damage was trifling in most cases, but one destroyed a warehouse and another burned out a yacht and boathouse. The fires were set by an alcoholic pyromaniac who received unemployment compensation on Thursday of each week and wound up by setting fires on that day and on the following day, Friday. He was twenty-eight years of age and on the day of his arrest he had consumed over seventeen bottles of beer and a quart of wine. His apprehension was aided by studying the time element in his pattern of fires and ascertaining if any local firms paid their employees on Thursdays.

Of course, it's true that such leads are slim ones, but in pyro fires there are very few leads of any kind and the study of the pyro's technique does lend some direction to the investigation. At least the *modus operandi* will build itself into a pattern identifiable as the work of one arsonist.

SURVEILLANCE

When such an identification has been made, a "plant" or fixed surveillance can be established which will ring the neighborhood concerned with police or fire officers in civilian clothes during the hours of the pyro's operations. A variation of this technique is mobile surveillance of the crowds at fires. One of the foremost arrests of a pyro in recent years was effected by this technique.

A series of fires in the crowded tenement section of Brooklyn pointed clearly to the work of a pyro. He operated in the early morning hours in what is known as the Bedford-Stuyvesant section, an area of former private dwellings converted into multi-family housing without regard to the provisions of New York's Tenement House Law. Some of these buildings did not have fire-retarding of any kind, many lacked fire-escapes, and some were classified as complete fire-traps.

A detail of detectives was assigned to a centrally located police station in this area and Fire Marshal Martin Scott and his assistants began using the fire station of Engine Company 219 on Dean Street, around the corner from the police station, as a base of operations. Sgt. Frank Weldon, in charge of the police Burglary Squad in Brooklyn, also contributed his manpower.

On June 27, 1952, at 5:15 A.M., an alarm sounded in Engine Co. 219 for a fire in a four-story brick tenement at 9 Gates Avenue, near Fulton Street. An hour or so earlier another fire had occurred at 681 Classon Avenue and Sgt. Weldon of the Burglary Squad "rode" on that one so that he could look over the spectators. When the second alarm came in, he followed the apparatus to the scene.

Firemen told him on his arrival that it was the same story: the fire had started in a baby carriage in a well behind the first floor landing and it seemed to be an incendiary fire. It was this pyro's pattern—to enter the unlocked front door of a tenement and start a fire in one of the baby carriages usually found in the hallway.

Sgt. Weldon looked over the crowd of early morning spectators, most of whom seemed to be men on their way to work. As the firemen went about their task of putting out the fire, the excitement diminished and the crowd dwindled. It was then Sgt. Weldon noticed a neat, slightly built man of about thirty standing on nearby Fulton St. When he noticed Weldon looking at him, he grinned nervously and walked down Fulton St.

On a hunch Weldon went back to his unmarked police car and followed his suspect. He planned to follow the man to see if he would set another fire. For quite a few blocks the suspect seemed relaxed, but then he apparently became suspicious and started to run. Weldon drove up and collared him at Classon and Atlantic Avenues, twelve blocks from the fire scene.

The prisoner was a twenty-seven-year-old porter with no previous criminal record. At the time of his apprehension he had no weapons and he offered no resistance. He gave his name as Irving Green and stated he lived at 141 Herkimer Street, a nearby location.

Questioning of Green brought a quick confession. The papers of June 28 quoted Green as telling Fire Commissioner Jacob Grumet, a former Assistant District Attorney, "I've been setting them (fires) for years. I enjoyed the excitement." He avoided capture, he explained, by always working after midnight and never setting more than two or three fires a night. His fire-setting equipment consisted of two or three kitchen matches.

He also admitted that he always turned in an alarm because he wanted to watch the engines arrive. In fact, it was this latter habit that led to his indictment for a fire on Bedford Avenue in which three adults and four children had lost their lives. Green readily admitted this fatal fire and reenacted the actual fire-setting. Clinching the case was his identification by one of the tenants in the burned building as the stranger he'd encountered in the burning hallway who told him, "Don't worry, I've turned in a fire alarm."

Green's case history showed psychiatric treatment at Kings County Hospital for a mental condition over a period of several years and treatment for nervous disorders from the age of seven when it was alleged he had suffered a head injury. Possibly in the years to come psychiatric tests will alert law enforcement officers to such pyros and lead to their apprehension, but presently the surveillance technique is the only available method and this case not only typifies the feasibility of such technique but also indicates how effectively police and fire units can operate together.

A successful "plant" or fixed surveillance can operate only in a limited area. A case in a Connecticut city was solved by this technique. Since this particular pyro's area of operations encompassed only a four-block area, it was decided to surround the blocks (instead of going directly to the scene when an alarm was sounded) and to hold anyone leaving the area for a few minutes' questioning.

These fires occurred between the hours of 11 P.M. and 1 A.M., and they were all set in cellars. In a couple of instances a man had been seen escaping over a rear fence just before the fire was discovered. On three occasions he had set two fires within three or four minutes. During one of the fires, newspapermen went to what later proved to be the pyro's home to locate a telephone. After listening to the conversations, the man remarked, "I hope they catch the firebug."

Shortly after the establishment of the "plant" one of the detectives stopped a man crossing the street; a few minutes later a fire broke out a block away. Under questioning, the suspect confessed and the entire neighborhood breathed easily again. It was a difficult case because the suspect lived in the area and only the tight surveillance managed to net him.

Surveillance of previously convicted pyros is also standard procedure when a series of pyro fires break out. Local arson investigators should always know the whereabouts of convicted and suspected pyros in their area in order that such persons may be placed under surveillance without delay.

"Plant" or mobile surveillance of bars and grills in the affected area has yielded results that frequently surprise investigators. Arson detectives should always remember the amazing effect of alcohol on some people as a trigger to their fire-setting tendencies.

A check of neighborhood peeping Toms or exhibitionists (exposers) has also been found worthwhile because of the tie-in between a confused sex life and pyromania. One habitual peeping Tom set nineteen fires in Philadelphia and Delaware County, Pennsylvania.

Whatever the surveillance technique employed, it is almost the only certain method of apprehending a pyro. True, he may be caught in the act, but not until he has set fire after fire, and possibly not for years. And he may be "turned in" by a stool or informer, but this too is very unlikely. Surveillance of some kind is the most feasible method of apprehending these fire-setters in the shortest possible time.

THE STINE AND WALZER CASE

The Stine and Walzer case concerns two typical pyros. Frederick Stine was forty-seven at the time of his arrest on November 6, 1939. Robert Walzer, his partner in arson, was only twenty-two. Both were vagrants who worked only now and then.

These two men, in an arson rampage which showed the pyro pattern in the increasing frequency of their fires as well as in the steadily mounting seriousness of their fire-setting activity, set a total of *over one hundred* fires. Twenty-four of these blazes were in the state of Washington, thirty in Oregon, twenty in California, eight in Illinois, and from one to eight in every state west of the Mississippi, except Arizona, New Mexico, Oklahoma, and Louisiana.

It was in 1937 that the fires first became noticeable, covering three states, Washington, Oregon, and California. In 1938 and 1939 they continued to occur with alarming frequency. Most of them were confined to railroad right-of-ways and nearby industrial areas.

It was this area of operation that first led to the belief that the fires may have been set by tramps or vagrants traveling on freight trains. Later, when it was discovered that the same fire-setting technique of using oily waste from freight car journal boxes had been used to start most of the fires, the possibility of all the fires being the work of a pyro was explored. This theory was supported by the fact that in practically all of the cases any semblance of motive on the part of the owners or insureds was lacking.

Police, fire marshals, and special agents of the National Board of Fire Underwriters received their first lead during a week in which four incendiary fires occurred in large industrial plants in Tacoma and Seattle, but failed to exploit it. A battalion chief at the scene of the fourth fire noticed a young man who seemed to be enjoying the fire and pointed him out to police officers. However, nothing worthwhile was secured after some questioning and the young man was released. The next day he was picked up again, this time in the company of an older man he described as his father, and questioned again, but several hours of questioning both men secured no results whatever.

For a six-month period fires of this nature decreased in this area. At the time no connection was made between the decrease in fires and the questioning of the youth and his "father." From October, 1938, to November, 1939, fires of this type again occurred in rapid succession throughout the state of Washington.

A valuable "trace" was located in late 1939. At several fires casts were made of a peculiar footprint, a print of a shoe with an oddly trade-marked sole, but without a suspect this evidence appeared to be of little use in curtailing the fires.

It was a special agent of the National Board who learned that a young man and an older man who claimed to be the youth's father had been observed and questioned at one of the most recent fires. This was the "break" in the case. The agent recalled having heard of the questioning of a year ago in which a young man and his father were interrogated about a suspicious fire. This agent, together with a deputy state fire marshal, immediately proceeded to the area of the most recent fire. After an intensive search the father and son team were apprehended at the local Young Men's Christian Association. Stine was wearing shoes whose soles were identified in pattern with the casts made of the peculiar footprint.

Both were sentenced to long prison terms, but their three years of mobile arson left a record unparalleled in American criminal history and their case will always be a horrible example of the tremendous damage which can be wrought by pyromania. While no attempt was ever made to total the amount of damage involved in all of Stine and Walzer's fires, it is known that twelve of their blazes caused losses totalling $730,000, and it is safe to say that the total losses resulting from their fire-setting amounted to *several million dollars.*

This case certainly spells out "fire-madness"—an unreasonable tendency to set fires regardless of the amount of destruction occasioned.

CHAPTER SEVEN

CRIME AND ARSON

Arson is employed now and then to facilitate the commission of a crime, but it is more frequently used as a device to destroy the evidence of crimes such as murder, burglary, and larceny.

ARSON TO FACILITATE OTHER CRIMES

The modern professional criminal of today weighs the penalties for his crimes against the possible profit therefrom. To commit arson solely to further the successful commission of another crime offers little "percentage" to these criminals. If apprehended, they can be charged with both crimes. Weighing the amount of profit involved in each crime, these criminals prefer to commit two robberies, for instance, rather than one arson and one robbery. It is senseless to commit the major felony of arson in an attempt to facilitate the commission of a lesser crime.

It is only the occasional offender, and usually the youthful one, who believes an act of arson is worthwhile for the purpose of lowering the possible chances of arrest while committing some other crime. One of the few cases of this type in recent years took place in Peekskill, New York. It is also a good example of addle-headed thinking on the part of the youthful criminals involved.

It was in the fall of 1952 that two would-be tough guys

committed a series of burglaries in the above city. One of
their acts was to break into and steal from an orphanage in
which they had been sheltered at one time a few years
earlier. Another, and their last "job," was the burglary of a
pharmacy located on the street-level in a two-story frame
building occupied by several tenants in second-floor apartments. The two burglars gained entry quietly enough apparently by prying open the front door, but experienced a
great deal of difficulty in opening the locked cash register.
They banged it around with tools found on the premises but
couldn't open it. Realizing they were making noise sufficient to alarm the upstairs tenants, the two men abandoned
their efforts and fled through the front door.

Having made good their escape, the two relaxed and discussed their failure. One of them expressed concern regarding possible fingerprints left on the cash register, the tools,
and elsewhere about the premises. No one will ever know
the exact extent of the discussion, both boys telling conflicting stories, but it is a fact that one of them was seized with
the idea of setting fire to the store and thus obliterating any
chance of the police identifying them through fingerprints.

A short distance from the burglarized store the boys found
an excavation marked off with four kerosene flares of the
open "bomb" type. They picked up one of the burning
flares, returned to the pharmacy, and piled paper napkins
and tissues from the counter around the flare. The fire
blazed up, and the boys ran out, no doubt well satisfied
with their bright idea.

The fire did destroy any possible fingerprints. It also destroyed the pharmacy, gutting the store and making it necessary for the firemen to rescue some of the tenants whose lives
had been endangered while they slept. But the fire did not
destroy the marks made on the cash register in attempting to
open it, nor the signs of forced entry upon the front door,

nor the report of the first fireman to enter the store that he found it open, nor the "bomb" used as a fire tool.

Classifying the crime as another burglary in the series which had been occurring in recent weeks, the police concentrated all their effort on solving the burglaries. Determined detective work soon resulted in the arrest of the two former orphanage inmates as the burglars. Further investigation implicated them in almost all of the recent burglaries, and when faced with the facts both boys made damaging admissions.

Neither youth considered the tenants in the upstairs apartments when they set the fire. Panic-stricken thinking can excuse a lot of things, but not the wanton disregard of human life manifested in this case. Later, one was to plead guilty, and while the other refused to plead, he was found guilty upon trial. Instead of being charged solely with burglary, unlawful entry, or a lesser charge, however, the first boy pleaded guilty to second-degree arson and the second youth was convicted of first-degree arson—both major felony convictions spelling out many years in prison.

Arson as a technique to facilitate some other crime has diminished in frequency in the past ten years in a direct ratio with the ability of police to reach the scene of a crime quickly. There is little advantage to draw off the police from the area of the crime when a telephoned alarm by some chance passer-by will result in the transmission of a radio alarm and prompt response by police in radio cars. Mobility of police and rapidity of police communications have made it unprofitable to attempt to outwit local police by such an archaic technique as fire-setting.

Arson to facilitate a crime has only one possible use at the present time and that is to draw off and temporarily occupy a watchman, guard force, or a police unit without automobiles or radio. It may be encountered in rural areas, very small municipalities, or about warehouses or factories employing watchmen or guards.

An unusual use of arson is as a technique of murder. The "Lady in the Bath" case described in Chapter VIII was one in which fire was to be the murder weapon; if successful, the burning gasoline would have cremated the victim. Cases of this type can easily be confused with those in which fire is the weapon of a suicide. In Miami, Florida, a forty-six-year-old housewife soaked her body and clothes in alcohol and committed suicide by touching a lighted match to herself.

FIRES TO DESTROY EVIDENCE

For ages arson has been a classic device to destroy evidence. Murderers think of it, seeking to destroy the corpus delicti; burglars seize upon it to conceal their entry and larceny; and embezzlers see in it the only possible solution for their knotty problems. Other individuals who fear that a survey of their books or personal records may pin-point them in a criminal investigation of some kind also look upon arson as a possible device to destroy records.

MURDER

Killers burn with a three-fold motive. First, they seek to hinder identification, as prompt identification of the deceased usually results in some tentative theories on the killing and starts the police checking on all those who knew the victim. Secondly, they seek to destroy evidence of the attack, hoping that the fire will consume all traces of the "foul play" normally suspected when a dead body is found under suspicious circumstances. Lastly, the killer may hope the fire will consume the body enough to bar identification as human remains, or to so conceal the fact of death as to effectively hide the act of murder.

A truly amazing instance of using arson for this three-fold

purpose occurred during 1943, and was almost successful. Not only was the thrill-seeking murderer in this case seeking sexual satisfaction, but he also sought to perpetrate the "perfect crime."

In September of 1943 a fire of incendiary origin destroyed a summer cottage on a lake in Connecticut. "Tramps or kids" was the supposition, but no likely suspect turned up. Almost a year later, in May of 1944, the owner and his wife visited the property to remove the debris from the cellar in contemplation of rebuilding. The wife was using a rake to pile up the debris for her husband. She struck a shoe which stubbornly remained stuck in the debris no matter how she tugged on the rake. She bent over to pull it out by hand and discovered it to be on a human foot.

Further raking disclosed a skeleton of what appeared to be a woman. The state police officers carefully removed the remains and an autopsy disclosed a bullet hole in the skull, apparently made by a small calibre slug. Determined efforts to identify the remains were successful: the girl had been reported missing by her parents shortly after her disappearance nine months before. The trail soon led to a seventeen-year-old high school boy of New York City. He was arrested and during questioning it developed that he had written a theme in high school entitled "The Perfect Crime." In it he told of a forced entry into a bungalow, rape, murder, and arson—all without detection. He boasted that the individual responsible for these four crimes was free and at no time under suspicion. And since his victim had not been found nor his crime discovered for nine long months it's small wonder this youth boasted.

Confronted with his theme, the boy readily admitted the crime. He had arranged with the girl, a fellow student, for a trip to the country. They were going to "run away" together. At nighttime he broke into the bungalow and forced himself upon the girl. They spent the remainder of the night there; then in the morning, while she was lying on the floor reading a magazine, he shot her in the head with a .22 calibre rifle. He buried the body in the basement, procured kerosene oil from the kitchen, and set fire to the building.

The near success of this murderer does point up the need for a thorough search of debris at all fire scenes so that the possibility of some murderer successfully concealing his crime is materially lessened.

Hampering the Identification of Deceased Persons—Techniques of identifying dead human bodies has made tremendous progress in the last half century. Even a large fire may burn only the fully exposed portion of a body. The underside of a body or any parts in contact with a floor or other flat surface generally remain almost unmarred by fire. And even when partly consumed, a body may be identified from fingerprints, dental work, tattoos, scars, and the like. In cases of almost total destruction, enough bones are generally found to alert police and eventually lead to full identification.

Destroying Evidence of Attack—A murderous attack will leave many easily discernible signs, but all too frequently fire has served to conceal these signs. Arson investigators must realize that in homicide cases the body is usually the best evidence of the cause of death and when fire destroys a large portion of the body, it may be impossible to determine the cause of death. Post-mortem examinations of fire damaged remains present a special problem to any autopsy surgeon. Therefore arson investigators must learn to keep an open mind on the possible causes of death until the autopsy report is received. What may at first appear to be an accidental death resulting from the fire may turn into a murder when an autopsy discloses several skull fractures.

A case of this kind concerned an old-age pensioner, seventy-five years of age. This old man lived alone for twelve years on a ninety-acre farm near a small town in Monroe County, Ohio. He was last seen alive on January 2, 1953, and when he had not been seen for over a week one of his neighbors went to his home on the evening of January 9, 1953. He discovered that a fire had occurred in the front room in which the old man ate, slept, and lived. The fire had burned a large hole in the flooring and had engulfed the bed, but apparently had died out from lack of air in the closed house.

Investigation revealed a leg hanging on a cross beam while other skeletal remains, burned beyond recognition, had fallen through the hole into the basement.

Possibly this fire and the apparently resultant death would have been written off as careless smoking except that one of the neighbors noticed two almost empty gasoline and kerosene containers near the burned area. This was unusual enough to point out to neighbors and warrant a report to authorities. An autopsy of what little remained of the body was made and it revealed traces of gunshot wounds.

Alerted, the sheriff checked on all suspicious persons in the neighborhood and learned that a former resident of the area, who had moved to Columbus, had been seen in the vicinity a week prior to the discovery of the fire. An investigation of this former resident revealed that the man had paid numerous long-standing bills after January 2, the approximate date of the old man's death, and had made a bank deposit the following week. Arrested and questioned on January 16, two weeks after the killing, he signed a statement admitting the murder.

He said he knew the old man kept his life's savings in the house, and he had come back from Columbus to steal the money. He had to kill the old man, he explained, because the occupant recognized him. He shot him in the back, right after locating the $1500 in savings, and returned to his home in Columbus.

All that night he worried that he had been seen in the vicinity and would be identified as the old man's assailant when the crime was discovered. The next morning he returned to the farm with some gasoline. He poured the gasoline over the bed, wrapped the old man in a quilt, spread kerosene over the body, and then ignited the pyre.

It was his final act of closing the front door to aid in making the fire appear to be an accident that led to the fire dying out for lack of air and to the discovery of his crime.

Concealing Murder by Burning—Effective concealment of murder requires almost furnace heat for some length of time, and even then it is almost an impossible task as some portion of the body or some object thereon will not be fully consumed. In one case a large timber fell across a body and effectively prevented complete burning; in another case the burning through of a door ventilated the room and drew the fire upward into a stairway. In both cases prompt extinguishment contributed to the failure to destroy the bodies by fire.

Some years ago, quite a number of husbands and lovers seized on the automobile as a funeral pyre for unwanted wives or sweethearts. Following the murder, they'd toss a few gallons of gasoline on the body and about the interior of the car and then throw in a match. In some dozen cases the fire was discovered by passing motorists, campers, farmers, police, and even by a car-load of volunteer firemen returning from a convention. The fires were usually quickly extinguished and enough of the victim's body recovered to prove a corpus delicti.

Condition of Body—An examination of the body will indicate whether death took place before or during a fire. Murders, or suicides for that matter, are best determined by first establishing the fact that the deceased was dead at the time of the fire. It is possible that a victim could be drugged and then the premises set afire, thus utilizing arson as a weapon of murder, but no known cases have been encountered in many years. If an autopsy discloses the cause of death as heat, toxic gases, fumes, or injuries caused by falling walls or like material, it is generally reported as an accidental death.

A complete autopsy is the only feasible method of examining human remains damaged by fire. While burns of the skin made before death sometimes cause blisters containing fluid to form on the body, it is also a fact that blisters also form after death, and while these do not contain fluid, they may easily be mistaken at the fire scene for those which form before death.

The first thing to determine about any burned remains is whether or not death preceded the fire. It is far better to await the report of a skilled autopsy surgeon than to attempt a rough determination at the scene. The best proof that an individual was alive during a fire is the presence of carbon monoxide in the blood and noticeable damage to the lungs. The most lethal of the toxic gases produced in ordinary fires is carbon monoxide. The blood from the body of a person dying in a fire is certain to show the presence of carbon monoxide, and it is believed that the inhalation of this gas probably causes the lung damage once credited to inhalation of flame or highly heated air. Such proof can only be adduced by the autopsy surgeon during a post-mortem examination of the body of the deceased.

Position of the Body—The position of the remains is frequently indicative of accidental death or murder in arson cases. In most fire deaths the last acts of the deceased are to escape flames and reach open air. Body face down on the floor with the hands reaching toward a window or protecting the face is a classic death position of fire victims. Some are found in bed or a few feet from it, overcome as they slept or awakening too late to fight off the cumulative effect of carbon monoxide poisoning. Bodies found in other positions may be viewed with suspicion until there is proof that death was caused by fire. Bodies found in unusual portions of the house or not in bedrooms during the hours usually spent in sleep are also signals to alert the investigator.

In any event the arson investigator must not move or disturb the body until the arrival of detectives assigned to the homicide unit of the local police department. After they have taken photographs and attended to their other duties in connection with the murder, the arson investigator can go ahead with his tasks in cooperation with the detectives and the medical examiner or coroner.

Personal Effects of Deceased—When other signs are not indicative of a murder, it is possible that the proceeds of the crime preceding the murder and arson may aid in uncovering the fact of murder as well as the murderer.

In the case of the aged farmer just reviewed it was the prompt spending of the money that supported the sheriff's initial suspicion. In a 1949 case it was an attempt to destroy the personal effects of a man who perished in an incendiary fire that led to disclosure of the crime and punishment of the criminal.

The fire took place in a small upstate New York town and broke out in five separate places. There was no doubt of incendiarism; the two-story frame dwelling had been saturated with kerosene. Only the quick work of the fire department and neighbors checked the fire and saved the building. The dwelling had been rented for some time and the body of the male tenant was discovered by the owner, who had been of material aid in fighting the blaze.

Men and women throughout the county wondered who would have a motive to set such a fire? Gossip soon developed the fact that the owner and the tenant had recently been in a vicious argument about payment of a debt owed the landlord.

Possibly the owner heard the same talk and became alarmed. He was found attempting to burn a wallet and several check books belonging to the dead man a few days later. Surprised with such incriminating evidence, the owner confessed and later pleaded guilty, claiming he had killed in the heat of an argument and only set the fire to conceal the crime.

BURGLARY

The presence of evidence of forced entry at the scene of a fire as well as the "topsy-turvy" condition of the contents of a home or office will generally indicate whether a burglary preceded the fire. Questioning of firemen as well as examination of the premises should reveal signs of forcible entry. Tools used by the burglars may be found about the scene and tool marks may also be discovered where entrance was effected or upon the doors of safes or cabinets, or upon desk drawers. The bungling burglars of Peekskill, described previously in this chapter, left all of these tell-tale signs.

Youthful burglars seem to have a marked tendency to set fires after their burglaries. Other acts of vandalism such as turning on the faucets in upstairs bathrooms, slashing upholstered furniture, or chopping up valuable pieces of furniture such as pianos and television sets also have occurred. Therefore, it is questionable whether burglary followed by arson is really an attempt to conceal the basic crime or the manifestation of some destructive urge. Since vandalism and arson for destructive effect are very close, it is reasonable to assume that youthful burglars don't really think they'll hide their burglaries but just burn "for the hell of it," as one of them attempted to explain it.

EMBEZZLEMENT

Trusted employees handling cash frequently steal some of the money in their care. Discovery may be prevented for some time by manipulation of books and records, but ultimately the only "out" is flight or destruction of the books and records by fire.

A twenty-six-year-old woman cashier of a vacuum cleaner store in Colton, California, was faced with the need for such a decision on December 24, 1948. An audit was to be made of her accounts on January 1 when a new manager was due to take over the management of the store. She wasn't short much, just about $1800 which she had taken from time to time to meet household expenses.

On the night of the fire she had returned to the office alone and scattered papers from her desk and files over the floor of the main office and in the manager's office. She then pulled the hose off a natural gas jet which fed a gas heater, turned on the gas, set fire to the papers, and walked home. The nature of the fire hastened the audit, and the young woman's shortage was discovered. She was first queried about the money, then about the fire. She promptly broke down, told the whole story, and later pleaded guilty.

Incidentally, books are one of the most difficult things to destroy by fire. Several embezzlers have even placed wisps of cotton saturated with kerosene between the pages of their books, but little destruction has occurred. In fact, some of the cotton was discovered unburned between the pages of the books.

Any circumstance such as all the books having been left out of a fire-proof safe or cabinet "by accident," the grouping together of books at one desk or in one office when they normally are not kept together, or the discovery of open books spread out upon a desk when normally they'd be kept closed and stacked one upon the other—any one of these is suspicious.

The thinking of these embezzlers is hampered by their great need to destroy the books. In many cases the books have been found "tented" upon a desk with rolled newspapers stuffed into the "tent" formed by the up-ended open books in a desperate effort to accelerate burning.

The fact that incomplete combustion may lead to discovery of the books in such positions apparently never occurs to these thieves. When discovered and questioned on this point, the arsonists are usually ready to talk of their troubles.

PILFERAGE

Theft of merchandise by a trusted employee is closely akin to embezzlement of cash because to conceal the pilferage the employee must juggle stock inventory records. Eventually he too will have to flee or try to destroy the records by arson.

Managers, department heads, foremen, and inventory clerks are in a position to conceal their thievery by arson. Furthermore, when the thief holds a position of some authority, he can use it to write off as a fire loss the amount of merchandise stolen.

Two good examples of this type of case occurred in widely separated parts of the United States.

In California 135 bales of cotton were damaged by fire in a large factory. In addition, 143 other bales had been slashed open and quantities of gasoline spread about where the cuts had been made in each bale. The fire was obviously of incendiary origin.

No motive was immediately apparent, the insurance barely covering the loss at market value, but an audit of the books of this firm revealed a shortage in the inventory of baled cotton amounting to slightly over $40,000. Investigation into office and plant procedure revealed that the shortage could not have occurred without the knowledge of the shipping clerk. He was questioned and this fact pointed out to him. Unable to avoid admissions relating to his failure to report the shortage, he soon made a full confession and implicated another employee. The two had stolen and disposed of a great amount of cotton and had set the fire to cover up the shortage.

An odd development in this case was the discovery of an earlier shortage in baled cotton involving still another employee which probably never would have been discovered if the other two employees had not started on their career of crime.

The locale of the second case was the farm country of Nebraska. A fire in a grain elevator was considered suspicious because in spite of all the precautions usually taken against fire in such establishments, the blaze had spread rapidly.

Again no motive was immediately apparent, but before a check could be made of the books of this firm, an employee came forward and claimed he had received a shock about a week prior to the fire when he turned off an electric switch in the driveway of the elevator.

A check was made by an electrician, and all the wiring was found to be in good order. While it was not impossible for this employee to have received a shock, no evidence of any short was found, and it was therefore considered highly unlikely that he was telling the truth.

Since this employee was in charge of the grain accounts, an audit was made and a large shortage uncovered. He admitted forging names of payees on checks given in payment of grain which was never purchased, but for a considerable time he denied setting the fire. He finally confessed, admitted using kerosene to accelerate the flames. He later pleaded guilty to forgery and arson.

DESTRUCTION OF RECORDS

Many normally honest persons see in the destruction of their personal or business records a fine opportunity to avoid questioning at a civil or criminal trial, or during an investigation, hearing, or examination before some legislative body or grand jury. And, of course, dishonest individuals seize upon fire to avoid payment of taxes or to defraud creditors in bankruptcy proceedings. Sometimes the fire will be only "window dressing," a subterfuge to claim destruction of records while in fact such records were removed and destroyed or hidden away at some other location prior to the fire.

Not long ago an extremely wealthy man was accused before a state crime commission of destroying his personal records by fire. Respected and holding a position of prominence in the business world, he was nevertheless questioned as to whether he had instructed two of his employees to set a fire in premises used for the storage of his records. Many of his friends were heartened by his prompt denials, but lost heart when he failed to produce the employees in question and fight the accusation.

Arson to destroy records may be encountered in any business or profession and at any level of government. The merchant, doctor, or public official may all seek the lapses of memory permitted by a destruction of records.

ASSOCIATED CRIMES

The arsonist may commit many crimes which have a direct relation to the basic act of burning. It's a case of first the arson and then the associated crime.

Assault at the scene of a fire occurs when some person is unlucky enough to chance upon the incendiary in the act of preparing his plant or setting the fire. It may sometimes take place as the arsonist flees the scene. Not only may the eye-witness be assaulted, but such assault may also result in death. An excited arsonist is likely to use any convenient weapon or to strike with great force.

Conspiracy is inherent when two or more plan the crime of arson and act jointly in its commission. While arson itself encompasses the same field as conspiracy to some extent, it may be possible to add a count to an indictment in some jurisdictions which would spell out conspiracy as separate and distinct from the arson. It may also be possible to so charge a group of persons when no actual burning took place. As a general rule, conspiracy is present when two or more individuals join together for arson, but it is usually merged in the greater crime.

Fraudulent claims spell out violations of the laws of most states, and if paid off prior to discovery may be the basis of larceny charges. The temptation to profit from a chance fire by greatly exaggerating the actual losses is always present.

Intimidation of witnesses is always a possibility in any case involving a major felony. Assault and even the murder of eye-witnesses is not unknown. If there is any fear that the prisoner's friends or accomplices may seek to deter a witness from testifying, then process to hold such person as a material witness should be secured.

Perjury, subornation of perjury, and even bribery of jurors must not be overlooked as possibilities. Material witnesses who change their stories without reasonable cause or justification have oftentimes been won over by the defense. Relatives and friends of the defendant may substantiate an unjust claim of alibi. All contribute to defeat justice, and certainly some attempt should be made to bring them to justice for perjury.

Extortion seems to be an unlikely crime to associate with arson. It is a fact, however, that many a business man who considered himself fortunate enough to have a "successful" fire found that he was unfortunate in his selection of a torch. Such criminals don't consider themselves blackmailers; it's just a case of being down on their luck and needing a few dollars. What could be simpler than asking a former "friend" for a little money?

An unusual case of this type occurred in a large city in

Michigan. The basic fire took place during the month of October, 1938. It was an extensive fire, involving insurance totalling more than $36,000. Investigators were lucky enough to find an eye-witness who observed the torch running from the building. A speedy trial sent this professional arsonist away for five years.

However, certain that this was a conspiracy case in which the occupant of the premises was involved, the torch was visited in prison and questioned as to his associates in the arson. He resisted all efforts to secure the full story of the fire and was released in four and a half years.

Only a few weeks after his release, the insured in the case, the occupant of the fired premises, reported the torch to the police, charging attempted extortion. It seems that the torch had visited him and requested financial aid.

The torch promptly told a detailed story of the arrangements preceding the fire. He had been employed to arrange the fire. He named a prominent business man of the city as intermediary and a notorious criminal as one of his accomplices in the actual fire-setting.

The story confirmed the suspicions of the local fire and police authorities as well as agents of the National Board of Fire Underwriters. After some investigation documentary evidence was secured supporting the torch's story as to payments of money at the time of the fire.

Satisfied that the true story was now unfolding, an attempt was made to locate the torch's accomplice in the setting of the fire. After considerable difficult work, an agent of the National Board located this criminal in a Western city and secured admissions concerning his part in the fire. Heartened by his success, this agent now contacted the intermediary and confronted him with some of the facts in his possession. Again, damaging admissions were made.

A visit to the now cooperative torch to iron out a few inconsistencies in the overall picture led to his release on the attempted extortion charge and the arrest of the three others in the conspiracy. Two of the conspirators confessed, but the insured still denied his guilt. He was tried, convicted, and sentenced to a maximum of twenty years in prison.

Briefly, crime and arson bear a close relationship. Fire is a device that aids other crime, conceals the evidence of crime, or breeds it.

CHAPTER EIGHT

BASIC LINES OF INQUIRY

FIRES occur daily all over the world, most of them resulting from other than criminal causes. However, when a fire is set by an incendiary there is generally a determined effort to make it appear to be a non-criminal fire.

In only a minority of arson cases is the fire so ignited that firemen and investigators can promptly report that a fire-setter was responsible. As previously stated, arsonists scheme and plan to make a fire appear to be of accidental origin. That is why the detection of arson involves a great deal of investigative work.

Some crimes, by their nature or manner of commission, require little or no detection. Any person can detect a felonious assault. The victim of the attack promptly tells police of the assault. So too with crimes such as burglary and robbery, the victim promptly reporting to the police. Once the commission of a crime is known to the police, its investigative phase gets underway. This is concerned with the recording of the circumstances surrounding the crime and the identification, arrest, and prosecution of the person or persons responsible for it.

Although some fires or murders will stand out as definite criminal acts because of the manner of their commission, arson is among the small group of crimes, such as murder and larceny by fraud, which are not easily detected.

In any criminal investigation there are basic lines of inquiry which must be explored in order that the investigator will not only complete a comprehensive investigation but, what is more important, will be capable of detecting crime—discovering that a crime has been committed. In murder, for instance, the basic lines of inquiry concern the dead body and the cause of death. In fact, the only way to detect murder is to find a dead body and then pin-point the cause of death as resulting from some criminal agency.

The basic lines of inquiry to be followed in arson cases have been mentioned in previous chapters as they concerned the type of fire-setter or fire under discussion. These four lines of inquiry are: origin of fire, establishing motive and opportunity, developing prime suspects, and identification of the fire-setter and accomplices, if any.

To be fairly certain that the crime of arson has been committed requires more than merely determining the fire to be of other than accidental origin or that a "good" motive existed. The *who* is very important in arson cases. *Who* had the opportunity to set the fire? *Who* among those that had the opportunity are likely suspects? And to be really certain that arson has been committed it is sometimes necessary to almost conclude the investigation by determining *who* set the fire before marking the fire's origin as "incendiary."

For instance, only this past summer in a large New York city a partially constructed dwelling, insured for $32,500, was severely damaged by a fire which had obviously been started by spreading gasoline around the premises and touching it off with a match. There was little doubt that this fire was deliberately ignited, but when the fire-setters turned up in the persons of two boys, aged four and six, the arson case went out the window. The *who* in this case was learned a few minutes after the fire was extinguished; otherwise the authorities would have started a full-fledged investigation.

Investigators must remember that sometimes one of these

basic lines of inquiry may be followed to advantage in a sequence other than listed here. Evidence of motive and opportunity, if secured first, very conceivably might call for speedy and full development in preference to exclusive concentration on the origin of the fire. The same may even be true of identification of the fire-setter. A case may present itself which literally screams: "If this is arson, then the policyholder is the arsonist." In certain instances, a case of this type might warrant an immediate background check of an individual even before a full determination of the origin of the blaze or the opportunities for fire-setting.

Regardless of the sequence in which information is sought along these basic lines of inquiry, it is a certainty that adherence to this inquiry pattern will prove most successful in leading to the solution of the case under investigation.

Of course, as is true in any other line of endeavor, teamwork is usually the key to success. With the proper coordination of the interested agencies there is no reason why several phases of an investigation cannot progress simultaneously. While the fire scene is being searched, other officers can be locating persons to be questioned. At the time a lab analysis is being performed by technicians, investigators can also be checking out alibis. And while a suspect is being interrogated, other investigators can be looking into his credit rating, previous fire record, criminal record, personal background, and business activity.

In other words, an investigation is not necessarily a one-step-at-a-time procedure. Many parts of the puzzle may be worked on at the same time and frequently the completed picture develops rapidly.

ORIGIN OF FIRE

The first line of inquiry in any arson case concerns the origin of the fire. Evidence must be obtained to establish the fact that the fire was of incendiary origin. As has been noted previously, it is a rule of law in regard to arson that every fire is presumed to be of accidental origin. This presumption has to be overcome before the state can make an arson case. Therefore, a prime fact to be established, and proved by competent witnesses, is that the burning was by criminal design and by a person criminally responsible. In other words, the state must prove the *corpus delicti,* or body of the crime.

In connection with the *corpus delicti,* it should always be borne in mind that before the crime of arson can be charged it is imperative that proof be introduced showing that a fire actually occurred at a specific time and at a specific place within the jurisdiction of the court wherein the case is to be tried. This emphasizes the importance of the testimony of the firemen and the necessity of fire department records and reports in any arson case.

In the preceding chapters the detection of fire-setting has been grouped loosely into the elimination of accidental causes and the recognition of arson. This insures the familiarity with accidental causes of fire necessary before an attempt can be made to recognize arson. It also was planned to give the reader some knowledge of the modus operandi of all known types of fire-setters. Fundamentally the detection of arson can be summed up as establishing the fact that the origin of the fire resulted from a criminal agency by:

1. The elimination of accidental causes.
2. Deduction as to probable ignition method.
3. Establishing the criminal responsibility of the fire-setter.

Reducing this to the simplest terms, the three steps are:

1. Was the fire deliberately set?
2. How was it set?
3. Who set it?

ESTABLISHING MOTIVE AND OPPORTUNITY

The apparent origin of the fire, as determined by fire department officers and investigators, frequently does not furnish sufficient information as to the type of fire-setter even to permit a conclusion that arson has been committed. It is often necessary in arson cases for the investigator to develop some theories as to motive and opportunity before he can proceed to classify the fire tentatively.

Hence, in addition to his first basic line of inquiry as to the fire's origin, the arson investigator must now find the answers to these two questions:

1. Who would want the fire?
2. Who had the opportunity to set it?

Was the fire one of motive, or in the group previously described as lacking in what is termed rational motivation? In the first group a blaze may result from a desire for profit, or to conceal another crime, etc.; while the fires in the second group result from the mental wanderings of pyromaniacs.

The investigation of fires with rational motivation requires a great deal of probing as to who would benefit by a fire. When such individuals have been located, a number can be eliminated for one reason or another, and then the inquiry can be pointed toward the determination of which of the remaining persons had the opportunity to set the fire.

DEVELOPMENT OF PRIME SUSPECTS

The third basic line of inquiry is pointed toward the identification of the criminal and his accomplices, if any. To accomplish this identification, however, it is first necessary to develop what are known as "prime" suspects among the individuals having motivation and opportunity to set the fire, or to pin-point a prime suspect in pyro fires by studying the fire pattern. The investigative techniques used to develop a prime suspect naturally depend on the type of fire concerned.

Suspected fire-setters with rational motivation are usually developed by a check of their activities, questioning, and background study. Friends, eye-witnesses, and others who may possess information about the fire are interviewed. The owner of the building, the occupants of premises affected by the fire, and anyone who might profit from the blaze in some manner are queried. Background studies of possible suspects, highlighted by some information secured during questioning sessions or by the facts surrounding the fire, may show a "need" for the blaze, or fully develop a suspected motivation.

In fires without normal motivation set by pyros there is some questioning, particularly of eye-witnesses and persons living or doing business in the area of operations of the arsonist, but surveillances of the area or of known pyros is the time-proven method of effecting apprehensions in these cases.

In any event the investigative techniques utilized by arson investigators to develop prime suspects are:

1. Search of the fire scene for physical evidence.
2. Background studies of policy-holder, occupant of premises, owner of building, or other person having a major "interest" in the fire.
3. Interviews and interrogations of the person who discovered fire, the person who turned in the alarm, firemen, eye-witnesses, owner of building, occupant of premises, policy-holder, and all others who may possess information as to the fire or fire-setter.
4. Surveillances.

The integration of all facts secured as a result of interviews, interrogations, surveillances, background studies, and the evaluation of physical evidence will narrow the field of possible suspects to a very limited number, oftentimes to only one bona fide suspect.

IDENTIFICATION OF FIRE-SETTER

The final basic line of inquiry to be pursued by an arson investigator concerns which one of the prime suspects is the fire-setter and who were his accomplices, if any?

This identification of the incendiary results from the full development of leads, clues, and traces. The testimony of persons, particularly eye-witnesses, and the development of expert testimony by the application of laboratory techniques to physical evidence is of top value in this identification of the fire-setter, as well as in court upon later trial.

It should always be kept in mind that when the "fire-setter" is mentioned, the term applies to the man behind the scenes as well as the actual fire-setter. The term includes all conspirators.

THE WOOD CASE

The following well-known case is a good example of the manner in which each of the basic lines of inquiry, when properly explored, will result in full identification of a fire-setter.

On January 2, 1943, a Saturday, at 11:45 P.M., a fire occurred in a one-story frame dwelling of six rooms and bath in Sanger, California. It was the home of Mr. and Mrs. John T. Wood, a middle-aged couple.

Two persons were known to have been in the house at the time of the fire, Mrs. Laura Wood and her brother, James Brown, who lived with his sister and her husband. Mr. Brown was asleep in his room when awakened by screams. He rushed out of his room and smelled smoke at the same time he identified the screams as coming from the bathroom down the hall. When he reached the bathroom door, he noted smoke coming from a smoldering pile of what later proved to be clothing at the base of the door. He found the door locked from the inside, but it was presently unlatched by his sister, Mrs. Wood. He noted his sister was naked, hysterical, and badly burned. He also noted that the shower curtain and window curtains were burning. Mr. Brown assisted his sister from the burning room, called for firemen, and attempted to put out the still smoldering fire.

Among the first firemen to arrive at the scene was Harry Martin, a veteran fire-fighter. He noticed that Mr. Brown had extinguished most of the fire in the pile of clothing outside the bathroom door, but that the shower curtain was still smoldering. He also noted that Mrs. Wood seemed to be in great agony and that she was severely burned about the arms and feet.

Fireman Martin learned from Mrs. Wood, as he secured an auto to take her to the hospital, that while she was taking a shower someone had thrown a cold fluid which she now realized smelled like gasoline through the bathroom window into the room. A moment after it splashed on her, the whole bathroom caught fire. She had her back to the window and saw no one. She had heard a noise in the house a few minutes earlier and, thinking it was her husband, had called out, but no one answered.

Investigation by Fire Chief Bridges and Fireman Martin disclosed that an electric wall heater was turned on at the time the gasoline was thrown into the bathroom and accounted for its ignition. The white-hot coils of the heater were perfect for the purpose of the arsonist.

The Chief and Fireman Martin extended their search into the back yard of the house and found a one-gallon glass jug a few feet from one of the bathroom windows. A few feet from the jug they also picked up a small white-enameled pan. The jug containing about a pint of whitish fluid and the pan a minute quantity; both smelled of gasoline.

The two men also noted that the partly burned pile of clothing found in front of the bathroom door consisted of a woman's dress and undergarments. They also noted that a window screen had been removed from one of the bathroom windows and that this window was open, with the screen on the ground below it.

It can be readily seen that Fireman Martin and Chief Bridges had now established the incendiary origin of the fire.

Chief Bridges took possession of all the physical evidence —the gallon jug, the white-enameled pan, the window screen, and the partly burned clothing found at the bathroom door. He informed the sheriff's office of his findings and with the undersheriff assigned to the case turned this evidence over to a nearby laboratory in Fresno.

As is normal in such cases a wave of public indignation greeted this attempted cremation of Mrs. Wood, and all public safety agencies concerned, from the fire department through the sheriff's office to the district attorney, soon possessed considerable circumstantial evidence that Wood was desirous of getting rid of his wife, that he had in fact asked her for a divorce, but that she had refused to grant him one.

Now a motive had been established.

Two days later a sixteen-year-old boy who lived across the street from the Wood home reported that he was returning home from a party the night of the fire and as he approached his home on the side of the street away from the Wood house he noticed Mr. Wood on the other sidewalk walking rapidly away from his house. As Wood came directly opposite him, this boy looked at the older man. Wood noticed him, turned up his coat collar, and increased his gait. The boy thought nothing of it until the fire, but hesitated to come forward because he didn't want to become "involved." This youth also stated that Mr. Wood appeared at the fire scene about five or six minutes after the arrival of firemen.

This information as to opportunity backing up a probable motive made Wood a prime suspect.

In rapid order the following events lead to Wood's identification as the fire-setter and attempted murderer:

1. Mrs. Wood, when questioned by the district attorney at the hospital, stated that on the night of the fire she had undressed in the kitchen of her home and put on her slippers, pajamas, and bath robe, leaving her clothing on a kitchen chair. She identified the partly burned clothing found burning outside the bathroom door as the clothing she had removed the evening of the fire and left on one of the kitchen chairs.

2. The laboratory in Fresno reported that an analysis of the gasoline in the jug and gasoline extracted from the clothing mentioned above showed this gasoline to be identical with gasoline found in a storage tank at Wood's place of business, a plumbing establishment.

3. On the Monday evening following the fire Mr. Wood telephoned Sanger police and told them someone was prowling around his house. When the police arrived, they found Mr. Wood in his backyard armed with a shotgun. He told them repeatedly that he'd shoot anyone who came prowling around trying to burn his house down, and pointed out to them a small pool of gasoline on the concrete steps leading to his back door. The officers notified the fire department of an attempt to burn.

Chief Bridges promptly arrived, noted the gasoline and also a wooden match lying in the middle of it. However, since no gasoline had been ignited, it seemed likely that the match had been burned out before being placed in the gasoline. He sent samples of this gasoline to the laboratory in Fresno with a request for a rush analysis comparison, against the standard of the gasoline known to come from the storage tank at the Wood plumbing establishment.

4. The "woman in the case" was located. A resident of

nearby Fresno, she admitted to the district attorney that Wood had been a regular visitor to her home for the past few years.

5. The district attorney questioned neighbors of this woman and storekeepers in the vicinity of her home and elicited the information that Wood was seen there almost every day, particularly toward evening, and that groceries that he purchased at a neighborhood grocery store were often delivered to the residence of this woman.

6. The laboratory in Fresno reported that the gasoline sample secured by Chief Bridges from the back steps of the Wood home in what Wood described as an attempt by some prowler to set his home afire was the same gasoline as in the storage tank at the Wood plumbing shop.

This rapid identification of the fire-setter was accomplished in exactly five days, Wood being arrested on charges of arson and attempted murder on January 7, 1943. He was sentenced on June 12, 1943, to from two to twenty years on the arson charge and from one to fourteen years on the charge of attempted murder. His trial was brief.

CHAPTER NINE

THE FIRE SCENE

THE fire scene holds the key to the origin of any fire. A careful, methodical, and thorough search of the scene of a suspicious fire is a basic part of the initial investigation. First, the scene must be protected so that evidence is not destroyed or removed either by careless persons or the guilty individual. Secondly, every person assigned to a search should know what he is looking for. And lastly, the preservation of physical evidence from the time of discovery to the time of presentation in court is an extremely important factor.

Evidence can be destroyed or removed if the scene is not guarded; it can be overlooked by inexperienced personnel assigned to the search; and its evidentiary value can be ruined by improper handling.

PROTECTING THE SCENE

In order to properly protect the fire scene it is imperative that the cooperation of local firemen and officers be secured. Experienced arson investigators request that fire personnel exercise care in overhauling (See Glossary) around the place of origin in all fires which in their opinion seem to be suspicious. Of course, a solid hose stream applied directly to the point of origin will do a lot of damage to material in that area. In this respect it would be advantageous if fog nozzles or similar hose tips, as well as a minimum of water, could be utilized when a fire immediately appears suspicious to the firemen, but such precautions are well nigh impossible on most occasions. If such precautions can be exercised, evidence of an ignition device, "plant," or "trailer" can be preserved rather than broken up and pushed away or flooded out of doorways.

Most experienced firemen will use great care in overhauling so that evidence will not be damaged or destroyed. Likewise, salvage work is generally postponed until after the scene is searched.

The assignment of a fireman to guard the fire scene is of the utmost importance in order to properly protect evidence. If the fire has caused extensive damage, it may be necessary to assign more than one guard. In any event, they should be instructed to prevent any unauthorized person from entering or leaving the premises and to remain on the post until properly relieved. Guards should be relieved at four-hour intervals so that they will be fully alert. The guarding of the scene must be continued until the arrival of the arson investigator and usually until the completion of the search. It is imperative that a chain of security be stretched from the time of the fire to the time of the discovery of evidence so that defense attorneys cannot lessen the value of the evidence by claiming tampering or fraud of some kind. Quite often the occupant of the premises may complain about being denied access to his premises and oftentimes may threaten civil suit. This situation is encountered frequently both in fraud fire cases and in legitimate fire losses.

Each case must be handled on its merits and any arbitrary and capricious barring of occupants from their premises without justification is to be avoided, but when some foundation is established for labeling a fire as suspicious, then the establishment of a guard is more than justified. However, unless the circumstances are highly suspicious and a prolonged delay in the search is unavoidable, it is doubtful whether an occupant can justifiably be denied access to his premises.

POINT OF ORIGIN OF FIRE

The importance of locating the point of origin has been discussed in the chapters concerning suspicious fires and touch-offs. Each of the tell-tale signs indicating the point of origin has also been fully explored. However, since the scene search is directed primarily to materials in and about the point of origin, it is again necessary to stress the great importance of locating this site of the original fire. The entire investigation sometimes hinges upon its location and the evidence found at that spot.

Searchers will find the ignition device or trailers or materials used in the plant somewhere around the point of origin, but it must be borne in mind that the region of most intense burning, sometimes known as the seat of the fire, or the spot where the fire was first observed, may not be the point where the ignition originated. As has been pointed out earlier, on many occasions trailers are laid from one room to another, or down a long hallway, or even on staircases leading from one floor to another. However, from the investigative standpoint it is essential that the heart of the fire be located and the reason for the concentration of fire at that point be determined. When this spot has been isolated, then it is advisable to try to work back along the path and look for any signs that might indicate the use of trailers, inflammable liquids, or any such devices or accelerants.

The point of origin in which the investigator is initially interested is the spot where the fire first actually broke out and started to feed on combustible material and spread throughout the building. From this point the search can go both backward and forward.

A fundamental step in helping to locate the point of

origin is the interviewing of persons who may have information concerning the location of the blaze when it was first noticed, its direction of travel, or the materials lying about the area before the fire.

When fires occur in commercial establishments, employees and the occupant of the premises can supply information as to the exact nature and quantity of combustible material about the premises. In residence fires, members of the family can supply this information. The investigator must ascertain what material was supposed to have been located at the point of origin prior to the fire in order that he may recognize the unusual when he comes upon it.

Firemen are invaluable in locating the point of origin. Their trained eyes note the site of the fire upon arrival, and often they can estimate quite accurately the point of origin from this initial observation and their experience with fire travel in similar buildings. By all means listen to them, make note of their observations and opinions, and integrate the information secured from them with the stories of eye-witnesses.

The person who sent in the alarm and other eye-witnesses to the start of the fire or its initial progress are good witnesses. They can tell what they observed. They should be questioned as to the exact location and the size of the fire at the moment they first discovered it. They should also be questioned on the intensity of the fire and the direction of fire travel from the time of sending the alarm to the arrival of the firemen and apparatus.

MECHANICS OF SEARCH

A methodical search requires planning. Look over the scene, make appropriate plans, and either get promptly to work or secure the necessary help without delay. The scene of an extensive fire may require a labor force to aid the investigator in locating evidence. A blaze extinguished after scorching a hallway is one thing, but a fire in which several floors have collapsed presents an entirely different problem.

The actual sifting of the debris which constitutes the major portion of most fire scene searches is a problem solely for the assigned investigators. Naturally, the closer the search moves to the suspected point of origin, the greater the care to be exercised in handling ashes and other debris. It is far better to use a fine mesh hand screen than to carelessly shovel through debris.

If protection cannot be secured from the weather, or there is some reason why the clearing of debris must be accelerated, it may be necessary to cart the debris from the suspected point of origin and remove it to some building offering not only protection from the weather but also a large floor area for examination purposes. Such a location must be guarded or securely locked when the investigator is not actually present.

In important cases many investigators prefer to work under lights rather than to establish a night guard and postpone continuation of the search until the next day. This is a highly desirable procedure as it accelerates the entire investigation.

IGNITION DEVICE

It becomes almost second nature for an investigator to mentally picture the possible ignition devices which may have been employed and to be on the alert for the unearthing of such devices. The wax or wick from a candle, wires from an electrical "set," an alarm clock, or some other mechanical contrivance are all items of physical evidence which aid in proving the incendiary origin of the fire. The more elaborate the timing device, or "set" as it is sometimes termed, the greater the chance of finding physical evidence which can be identified as some form of device for delayed ignition of a fire. Chemical "sets" offer little residue for the searcher, but lack of evidence pointing to some timing device, plus the apparent absence of direct ignition, may indicate that chemicals were used to start the fire. If such seems to be the case, it is always advisable and usually helpful to consult a chemist or a lab technician at the time of the search.

PLANT AND TRAILER MATERIAL

Many arsonists avoid delayed ignition techniques because they realize that most of their timing devices are not fully consumed by fire and can be uncovered during a careful search of the scene. These incendiaries may simply light a match. If discovered, they deny being at the scene and offer an alibi to prove it. But the materials in their plant usually give them away. The arsonist wants a fire, a big one, one that is not readily extinguished. He can't just apply a match to a few pieces of paper. He must get together some material that will burn, and he may use inflammable fluids to accelerate the fire. The same is true of trailers used to spread the fire. And regardless of whether the material was used in a plant, a trailer, or both, some evidence can generally be found. It may be the unusual, a chair or a bag of rubbish not in its normal place; it may be that some of the material itself will be found unburned; or it may be tell-tale residues—but all of it is evidence.

THE UNUSUAL

In any fire scene search, it may be established as a general rule that the investigator seeks the unusual. The normal or usual is of little help in determining arson. The investigator does not know too much about the evidence for which he is searching—he seeks something out of order, some material or thing foreign to the premises, or something normally present but out of place or in other than a normal condition.

It may be partially burned threads of cotton waste found in a garment factory fire after questioning had revealed that no such material was on the premises. It may be paint cans and remnants of paint-smeared rags in a hall closet of a private dwelling which indicates the point of origin. Nothing unusual in itself, but out of place. A cellar or garage is the normal place for the storage of hazardous material of this type.

A fire in the living room of a small home seemed concentrated about a large sofa. Nothing unusual until a search revealed one of the partially burned pillows had been slashed with a knife—a typical fire-setting technique.

Some unusual condition is generally created to accelerate fires. Briefly, the search is concerned with what material was burned during the initial stage of the fire, where did it come from, was it normally in or about the point of origin, and what was the source of ignition?

OBJECT OF SEARCH

The object of a fire scene search is to locate the place of origin and find enough of the materials used in an ignition device, plant, or trailer to permit the investigator to picture the modus operandi of the fire-setter and reconstruct the actual fire-setting. Then, through the evaluation of such evidence by experts, to develop expert testimony for use at a later trial which will be of sufficient evidentiary value to exclude the presumption of accidental origin and prove the fire resulted from the acts of an arsonist.

Two other objectives of a fire scene search are to secure physical evidence which may point to a rational motive for the fire, if one exists, and to tie in the suspect with the scene of the fire or materials used in its ignition.

For instance, if the search reveals two separate and distinct places of burning, it is usually fairly clear that the fires were set, but this condition does not always point to a motive. However, if in a large retail store one point of burning is in the midst of a quantity of highly flammable stock and the second burning is concentrated in a small rear office wherein the books and records were strewn loosely on desks and cabinets, it becomes quite apparent that someone wanted to damage the merchandise and at the same time destroy the business records. This circumstance would most certainly narrow down the field of suspects and thus facilitate the investigator's task.

When the suspect can be placed at the scene as a result of some item of physical evidence found during the search, the investigator is well on his way toward establishing opportunity, and the identification of material used in the fire-setting with a suspect serves as good evidence in most cases, or at least aids in limiting the field of possible arsonists.

PHOTOGRAPHS

Photography in fire scene searches is a vital phase of the investigation; its importance should never be minimized. Every arson investigator should have a working knowledge of photography. Not only should he know how to take pictures, but he should also know the technique of developing and printing.

Taking pictures at a fire cannot be started too soon; the best time is while it is still actually burning. Pictures of a fire at its height aid in determining the validity of the testimony of witnesses to the fire's inception as to location of blaze, direction of wind, flames, smoke, etc.

The rule at fire scenes is to take too many rather than too few pictures. As the search progresses, pictures are made in an orderly sequence, details of each being carefully entered in a notebook. When the point of origin is pin-pointed, photographs will thoroughly record its appearance. When evidence is discovered, a photo will be taken of its position at the time of discovery, when half uncovered, and when fully uncovered. Additional photos to identify salient features of the piece of evidence will be taken as required for full identification.

When a case involves two or more separate burnings, photos will be taken of each burning from several angles and a sketch to scale should be drawn to show that neither of the fires could have spread from the other. In the case cited at the end of this chapter photographs of two separate burnings were taken and supported by an aerial photograph to show their distance and the impossibility of the fire spreading one from the other.

Investigators must remember that many courts have refused to permit an arson investigator to testify as an "expert." In such an instance he can only tell what he observed during his search of the scene. Photographs—and possibly sketches—will aid the investigator in revealing to the judge and jury just what he observed at the fire scene. Aided by the photographs, the investigator can demonstrate that the fire was of incendiary origin without voicing his opinion.

The investigator must also remember that courts and juries are not trained to see evidence as he has been taught to see it and that this makes his task of presenting his evidence one of primary importance. Photographs must show the evidence the investigator desires to show, clearly and without distortion.

Care must be taken not to inject anything into the picture which was not there at the time the fire occurred. Courts frequently have declared inadmissible as evidence photos showing laborers, firemen, or investigators at a fire scene pointing to some item of evidence, photos containing signs and rulers, and pictures which place emphasis on specific spots by the use of circles of chalk. The best evidence is a picture of the scene as it appeared at the time the investigator first viewed it or of an item when it was first uncovered.

Another important point in presenting photographs in

court is their identification. For this purpose the back of each photograph is rubber stamped along the following lines:

Case No._____

Date_____

AM
Time_____PM_____

Subject_____

_____

Conditions_____

Photographed by_____

Processed by_____

Such data permits ready identification and is a marked improvement over clipping or pasting photographs to separate pieces of paper carrying such information; obviously the paper and photograph may become separated and positive identification is then impossible. When the pertinent data is stamped on the reverse side of the picture, it becomes an integral part of the photograph. To date, this manner of identifying pictures has never been seriously objected to by defense counsel.

Persons testifying as to the taking of pictures or the processing of film must know their business. Quentin Dean of the Michigan State Police explored this point in a paper presented at the fifth annual arson seminar at Purdue University in 1949 when he said:

Occasionally we come up against a defense attorney who knows something about photography, and if the prosecutor does not object, the cross-examination of the photographer can become pretty rugged. I have had them take me through every step in the process from the time the picture was taken until I brought it into court. What kind of camera did I use? What size flash bulbs? What shutter speed? What lens opening or "F" stop? What kind of film? How was the film developed? How long was it developed? Is the picture an enlargement or a contact print? If an enlargement, how many diameters was it enlarged from the original negative? What kind of paper was it printed on? What type of developer was the paper developed in? What type of fixing bath was used? And a multitude of other questions that have no bearing at all on the case at hand, but if not properly answered may have a bearing on the credibility of the witness.

Therefore investigators who qualify as "amateur" photographers with little or no knowledge of the more technical aspects of photography should not take pictures at the scene of a fire. After all, why ruin a case when in this day and age the services of a competent photographer can be readily procured. Practically all police departments, sheriff's offices, and fire marshal's staffs have the necessary camera equipment and dark room facilities, and the personnel to operate them.

A number of city fire departments have camera equipment and firemen assigned to handle the necessary photographic work at each fire, suspicious or otherwise. In fact, we know of several progressive volunteer departments that have maintained excellent photographic records of all their fire-fighting jobs over the past few years. Very recently this practice paid off handsomely when the driver-photographer was on hand to snap a picture of a burning candle set-up in a cardboard carton surrounded by newspaper, kindling wood, and a plastic curtain. Three fires were already in progress in three separate buildings in a bungalow colony and this fourth one was just ready to "go" when it was discovered, photographed, extinguished, and preserved for evidence.

In the event that a law enforcement agency is not equipped to handle its own photography, the services of a commercial photographer can be utilized, but always under the direction of the investigator. It is the responsibility of the investigator to point out the areas to be photographed, to decide on the direction and angle of each picture, to select the desirable distances from which the pictures are to be made, and to handle personally each such essential detail.

However, since photographs are of top importance and because of the possibility that an expert photographer may not be available it is desirable that all arson investigator's should seek some qualification in this field. Technical training by an experienced photographer or in a school of photography is desirable, but if not possible then a reading of some of the numerous books on the subject will give the investigator a working knowledge.

Some cameras are not suitable for arson work. For instance, the reflex type camera is not too practical because many pictures at fire scenes have to be taken from directly above or directly below the subject, and viewing with this type of camera is extremely difficult. The press type of camera with an eye-level view finder has the advantage over other cameras in this respect and it is also desirable because of its versatility. Synchronized flash equipment is a necessity, as most buildings damaged by fire do not have any electricity and other types of lighting are not available.

Any picture, even one taken by an amateur, is better than no picture at all.

SKETCHING THE SCENE

A possible advantage of sketching over photography as a means of graphically illustrating a fire scene is that a sketch contains only the essentials while a photograph may be over-crowded.

A detail sketch is concerned with the immediate scene, possibly only the point of origin, while an area sketch gives some information as to the area surrounding the immediate scene. Any larger sketch borders on map making and it would be better for the investigator to secure a map of the area from the county surveyor or other official and make notations on it rather than to attempt to draw a large map-like sketch.

The scale of a detail sketch varies from 1/2 inch-one foot for small rooms to 1/4 inch-one foot for large rooms, while the scale of an area sketch may be from 1/8 inch-one foot to 1/2 inch-ten feet, depending upon the size of the area sketched.

In addition to the scale each sketch must have marked thereon the compass direction. This is usually shown by an arrow pointing to magnetic north with the letter "N" at the arrow's tip. The investigator can secure this direction by the use of a compass or by orienting his sketch in accordance to directions shown on an official map of the area. It is also general procedure to prepare the sketch so that the top of the paper is toward the north.

Measurements should be shown on the sketch with as much accuracy as possible; estimate nothing—measure everything. One of the "must" items for an arson investigator is a good quality steel tape.

At least two measurements must be given from some one point of reference in order that objects of evidence or a major feature of the fire scene can be definitely located. The reference point itself must be an easily identified focal point, such as a chimney or wall corner. The idea is to have one easily located point from which all measurements originate in order that every feature of the sketch can be accurately located with ease and certainty.

Each item of evidence shall be plainly marked—"five gal-

lon gasoline can," "two-inch candle stub," etc. Arrows leading to the item permit this lettering on the borders of the
sketch. Large articles of furniture can be marked directly,
"chair," "couch," counter," etc.

In the lower right-hand corner will be shown the location
concerned in some detail, the date, and the signature of the
person making the sketch. The scale is generally shown immediately above this information.

A plane sketch can assume a three-dimensional appearance by using the cross-projection method of representation.
The center of such sketch is the floor area and then spread
out on each side of the sketch are a representation of each of
the four walls. A series of four photographs made from the
center of the room aid in graphically illustrating this sketch.

MODELS

A cross-projection sketch lends itself quite readily to the
construction of an actual scale model representing an interior
fire scene. The sketch is copied accurately upon heavy draw-
ing board (cardboard) and cut out. The cardboard is then
lightly cut along the lines joining the walls and floor, then
bent upward and held in place with scotch tape. A ceiling
can also be represented and placed on the top of the completed model so that it is easily removed to obtain a view of
the interior.

More elaborate models can be prepared at surprising low
cost by this cross-projection and cardboard method which
will give honest representation to a large floor area. Of
course, this type of sketchwork requires a certain amount
of innate ability and it is no secret that many competent investigators are pretty poor at a sketching board. If a person
cannot reproduce on paper a fairly accurate representation
of the layout of the room, building, or area in question, he
would be better off not trying to use this medium.

SPECIAL PROBLEMS IN SEARCHING THE SCENE
OF AUTOMOBILE FIRES

Ignition devices, or a great deal of plant or trailer material, are generally not used in automobile fires. Gasoline is usually placed in the interior of the car or around the motor area. But the body of the car is oftentimes so badly damaged that little evidence is left. Sometimes a search for the point of origin is academic. However, when too much gasoline is used it will sometimes run through openings in the car floor and burn under the car, causing soot to form on the underbody of the automobile. This is one of the few indications of the use of flammable liquids in a thoroughly burned auto.

Another indication may be secured by filling the radiator with water. If the radiator core is heavily damaged in the corner (usually lower right) close to the fuel pump, it could indicate that the fuel line was disconnected and the starter used to pump gasoline through the line. This is one of the techniques used to secure the necessary gas to fire a car. Sometimes the drain plug in a gas tank is removed and plier marks may be found on it if it is replaced after a quantity of gasoline is secured. However, when gasoline is siphoned out of the tank, there are no tell-tale signs on the tank.

The best evidence at auto fire scenes is generally a circumstance or condition that points to a possible motive. Were the tires changed before the fire? Were the accessories removed? Does the car have some serious, costly-to-repair, mechanical defect? If the answer to any of these or to other like questions is in the affirmative, there is a strong hint of incendiarism.

Another good field for search in auto fire cases is the flight area. When an auto is burned, the arsonist must do his work in a lonely and secluded spot. The means of transportation back to his business or home sometimes leaves marks. Tire tracks other than those of the burned auto may be a valuable lead in the investigation of these cases. The auto burner usually needs an accomplice to assist him in fleeing the scene of the fire hurriedly and without detection. When more than one person is involved in a fire-setting scheme, the chances for a break in the case are strengthened immeasurably.

In general, the scene of a suspicious automobile fire should be treated in the same manner as that of any other suspected arson site.

IMPORTANCE OF THE FIRE SCENE

In the fall of 1951 a very interesting fire investigation developed in a resort area not far from New York City. Information secured in this case is set forth below in order to highlight the importance of the fire scene to later prosecution of an arson case.

Two large frame buildings, the main units of a forty-acre hotel property, were severely damaged by fires of unknown origin. The two buildings involved were 350 feet apart and so located that neither building could be seen from the other. The larger of the two buildings, which was practically gutted by the fire, was three stories high, while the second building had only two stories. Both buildings had large basements.

The volunteer fire department responded to the alarm and found the main building, located on a knoll several hundred feet from the highway, heavily involved in fire which was raging in the cellar, and almost immediately discovered a fire of similarly serious proportions burning in a second building. They promptly summoned assistance from neighboring communities and went to work.

The fire in the second building was brought under control before the entire structure was destroyed, but the flames had spread from the basement up the rear stairwell and mushroomed throughout the entire unfinished second floor and destroyed the roof.

The assistant fire chief of the local department happens to be a full-time paid police sergeant in the town. He was on the scene very early and helped direct the fire fighting operations. Together with other fire department officials, he pointed out to the investigating agent the point of origin of this fire at the foot of the open stairwell in the basement of the building. The burning at this point clearly indicated that the flames had spread from this area upward into the first and second floors.

Since neither the local police or fire department had a photographer available, the investigator secured the services of a local commercial photographer and a picture series was started under the close supervision of the investigator. The water was first allowed to drain out of the basement of the second building. Then before anything was disturbed, pictures were taken of the burning and the debris at the point of origin—the spot where the stairway had formerly terminated.

After the photographs were taken, the debris was sifted for any possible evidence of incendiarism. The sifting was under the supervision of the investigator and the police sergeant-assistant fire chief, and in the presence of the owner of the property.

When the debris, several feet deep, was finally cleared away, it was found that at a point under the stairwell a section of the concrete floor had been broken, exposing an uneven patch of soil in the otherwise solid floor of the basement. The mass of debris had apparently acted as a seal, for when it was finally shoveled away, a strong odor of kerosene was noticed by all those present, including the owner—who promptly asserted that no kerosene had ever been stored in the building.

Further visual examination revealed distinct traces of kerosene in the sandy, stony soil of the broken floor area. The soil was promptly loosened and two large glass jars were filled and sealed. After marking the jars, the police sergeant-assistant fire chief took them to the State Police Scientific Laboratory at Albany for analysis. The laboratory report confirmed the suspicions of the fire officials and the investigator. It read: "Contents of both jars have a strong odor of kerosene. Kerosene was recovered from the sand contents."

During the search of the basement of the main building, the investigator noticed an electric clock in the kitchen wall, the hands of which were stopped at 7:29. This was also included in the picture series as possibly pointing to the time of the burning.

Another very significant condition noted by the firemen while they were fighting the fire in the main building was that a number of windows on the first floor of the building were open from the bottom, leaving no protection against intruders except the screens. Further, a door at the end of a long hallway on the second floor giving access from the hallway to an open porch on the roof of the dining room had been left open; only a screen door guarded this entrance against burglars or vandals. Of course, these open windows and door provided excellent drafts for spreading a fire.

The fires were reported to the local police headquarters at 8:25 P.M. by a local resident who was driving by on the highway. At the time the fires were discovered, no one is known to have been on the premises. The owner and his only current employee had left for New York City by automobile approximately two hours before; the owner's wife had departed for an out-of-state destination two days earlier in response to a telegram message; the owner's mother had been taken by her son to New York City four days prior to the fires, and there were no guests at the resort that week.

The employee, when interviewed, advised it was the first time in his nine months of service that the premises had been left alone and unprotected. Further, this employee's day-off fell on the preceding day, but despite this fact the owner had suggested that he accompany him to New York City on the evening of the fire.

When on the morning after the fire the owner was asked to account for the absence of his wife, his mother, and himself, and the fact that he had invited his employee to accompany him to New York City on the evening of the fire, he gave glib answers.

When asked why the windows and the second-floor door were left open when everyone was absent from the premises overnight, the owner explained that the building was apt to develop a musty, damp odor when closed up. At the conclusion of the questioning the investigator asked him what he attributed the fire to. His answer was a shrug and, "You tell me."

That day the investigator concluded his report with: "With two separate and distinct fires breaking out simultaneously in two large, widely separated buildings at a time when these buildings were vacant and only a few hours after the owner had departed from the premises, plus the discovery of kerosene at a point where one of the fires appears to have originated, there is every reason to look upon these fires as having been deliberately set."

When further investigation revealed that the resort had not been operating profitably and that the owner was in financial straits, it was decided that the case should be presented to the district attorney. However, he decided that there was insufficient evidence to present the case to a grand jury, and since the district attorney's decision is final is such matters, it appeared that there would be no prosecution for what was pretty obviously an act of arson.

However, the investigator—in co-operation with the adjuster—put the case to the insurance companies involved. Even though a criminal case was not developed out of this suspicious fire loss, there was sufficient evidence to resist payment and at least prevent the insured from making a "profit" on this fire-setting. Since the insurance on the two buildings exceeded $125,000, there was a sizeable profit involved.

Attorneys were retained by the companies involved and the owner was examined under oath. On the basis of facts previously developed during the investigation and the results of this examination under oath, the insurance companies refused to pay the owner under the policies involved. The latter instituted civil action to collect under his insurance contracts, but lost his suit when the defense proved to the jury's satisfaction that the insured was responsible for "willful burning of the premises," and "false swearing" during his examination under oath. In support was all the testimony of the fire officials, the photographs, and other court evidence such as the laboratory analysis of the kerosene soaked soil. The jury's finding indicated that a criminal case of some merit could have been presented to the grand jury.

The final photograph in this case, incidentally, was an aerial photograph of the property. This was made in order to impress the jury with the remoteness of each of the burned buildings from the other, thus discounting any possibility that the fires had communicated from building to building.

The important point in this case, however, is the fire scene search. While the evidence as to the time of the fire showed opportunity, and proof of the poor season experienced by the hotel as well as the financial conditions of the insured pointed to motive, it was the testimony (supported by photographs) of witnesses examining the scene which established the place of origin in each building and consequently the proof that the burning had been deliberately planned.

CHAPTER TEN

INTERVIEWS AND INTERROGATIONS

THE arson investigator must interview a number of individuals during the initial stage of his investigation. Interviewing witnesses or other persons who possibly possess information of value is one of the major techniques of securing information. Information secured in this manner also leads to the testimony of witnesses in the event of a trial. (*See* page 200.)

WITNESSES

Since physical evidence must be supported by evidence other than the testimony of experts, it is essential that the investigator develop additional testimony so that the jury trying the case will have the opportunity of hearing ordinary or lay witnesses.

The psychology of a jury is a strange thing. Regardless of the value of the physical evidence in the case, or the worth of expert testimony, juries like to hear ordinary people testify. Perhaps it's because they are on more familiar ground listening to the stories of ordinary witnesses rather than the difficult-to-understand terminology of experts.

Cooperative Witnesses—The investigator should use a physician's bedside manner when interviewing any person concerned with an arson case. There is absolutely no excuse for making a witness angry. A good working knowledge of the technique and psychology of interviewing is summed up in the advice of an experienced fire marshal. "Be nice to people," he tells new men in his office. "People will talk if you treat them as equals."

An investigator, however, must remember that one or more of the individuals interviewed may become prime suspects later in the investigation. He should be careful during any interview not to reveal any pertinent fact about the fire to the person being interviewed. The interview should be a pleasant one, but the investigator certainly should not permit the person being interviewed to turn it into an interrogation of the investigator.

An interviewer is limited to asking questions. If the person being interviewed wishes to cooperate, the questions will be answered. If the answers are not responsive, or sufficiently precise, then the interviewer rephrases the question, clarifies it, or phrases a new question which will secure the desired information.

Uncooperative Witnesses—On some occasions a witness will be reluctant to answer the investigator's questions or unwilling to admit that he was a witness. Usually these individuals have some reason for their failure to cooperate. They may fear bodily injury from the fire-setter, his friends, or his relatives. They may fear becoming "involved"—possible loss of pay while waiting in court to testify, the inconvenience of appearing in court time after time because of numerous adjournments, or dread of the usual badgering encountered during cross-examination by the defense counsel.

Other witnesses may fear the appellation of "stool pigeon," or "informer." Many inhabitants of rural areas are inclined to be close-mouthed when questioned. Oftentimes a wife is reluctant to answer questions when her husband is absent. Other witnesses may refuse their cooperation because they are related to the suspect or the person *they suspect* of setting the fire.

When a witness is uncooperative and there appears to be no readily understood reason, then the investigator must consider the witness as a possible suspect. Guilt sometimes closes the mouth of an apparently innocent witness and investigation may reveal him to be the fire-setter or an accomplice.

Uncooperative witnesses may be persuaded to talk only after the reason for their silence has been ascertained. Logical arguments along general lines can be used to persuade them to testify. The investigator can appeal to their sense of civic duty, of social responsibility, or of decency, but all such arguments are vague and impersonal, therefore weak and unconvincing. It's far better to find out why they are silent and then argue against the specific reason for silence.

A little suggestion that this is the behavior only of individuals who are "yellow," lacking in "guts," works with certain types of fearful witnesses. Another approach may be a guarantee of police protection or, better yet, a logical presentation of the really remote possibility of their being attacked: "Why should the fire-setter want to get into more trouble? . . . Do you think he wants another 'rap' for assault against him? . . . Why, if he beat you up or hurt you in any way, it would be an admission of guilt! . . . What would it gain whoever set the fire to hurt you? When you've made your statement, it's too late to change it, so there would be no 'percentage' in his hurting you."

If "involvement" is feared, then every effort must be made to convince the witness of the importance of his testimony and the little inconvenience he's likely to experience. Some experienced investigators use a two-fold argument in such instances. First, they strive to bring home the personal danger factor. For instance, a next door neighbor might be reminded: "It could have been your house too, if the fire had spread." A business associate might be reminded: "And of course anyone even remotely associated with a crime of this nature possibly could become involved." While an employee might be told that the fire-setter was hiding behind his employee's misplaced loyalty. Secondly, it could be explained to the witness that this is virtually a "wrap-up" case, that with his help it is almost a certainty the defendant will plead guilty. With this development, very little time, if any, would be lost upon trial.

When the reluctance to give information is due to national origin or regional habits it can generally be overcome with the aid of a person of the same origin or a local police or fire officer. In the first instance, someone who understands the native tongue is of great help, while a local officer aids in creating the impression that the investigator is not an "outsider," but is actually cooperating with the local authorities.

The questioning of a wife who is hesitant because of her husband's absence may very easily be postponed until her husband can be present. However, she must be encouraged to tell her own story and not lean on him for assistance.

Relatives of a suspect, on the other hand, should not be questioned at all when they appear to be uncooperative. The same is true of a witness who may become a suspect. Both should be treated as hostile witnesses.

Hostile Witnesses—A hostile witness is one who cannot be persuaded to cooperate. Such a person should be interrogated rather than interviewed. In cooperation with an active prosecutor the lips of a hostile witness may be unsealed before a grand jury. Contumacious refusal to answer is contempt, unless fear of self-incrimination exists, while a false answer may result in a charge of perjury.

In most jurisdictions the provisions of law relating to material witnesses can also be utilized in securing information from a hostile witness whose testimony will be vital to the proper adjudication of the case.

Missing Witnesses—In arson cases it may happen that a witness will flee his normal haunts while the major suspect remains smugly at home. When a witness flees the jurisdiction of the court, the investigator should promptly notify the local prosecutor with a view to having the witness returned in accordance with the local laws relating to the return of fugitive witnesses. Sometimes, however, it may pay the investigator to search out the witness and try to persuade him to come home and cooperate.

TIME AND PLACE OF QUESTIONING

At-the-fire questioning is ideal. It is first-hand, fresh, and it saves a great deal of time. Witnesses are present at the scene and can be questioned in a half hour, while at a later time it may take hours or days to contact one individual witness and many days to interview all of them. Otherwise the home or office of a witness is suitable for an interview. He will be in familiar quarters and considerably more relaxed than when being questioned in a police building or a fire marshal's office.

Except in the case of suspects the questioning must be very prompt. Learn to get the facts before they become hazy in the minds of witnesses or before the fire-setter "reaches" them and tells them what to say.

In some instances the investigator can do a great deal of preliminary work by telephone, thus not only cutting down the time spent in locating witnesses, but also permitting a brief inquiry as to the nature and character of the information available from each witness.

Some so-called witnesses may not be worth a visit. However, never fall into the lazy investigator's habit of supposing a witness knows nothing or will testify along lines better covered by previously questioned witnesses. The best rule is to contact all of them, determine the nature and extent of their possible contribution to the case, and then act accordingly.

The questioning of an insured or a suspect can be more

formal and may be held in the office of the investigator. Follow-up quiz sessions are usually scheduled for the investigator's office, too, because they are most likely to result in admissions or confessions, and the investigator will require the facilities provided in his office.

INTERVIEWS

While the circumstances of any case will undoubtedly dictate the order in which information will be secured through interviewing, it is suggested that fire personnel be interviewed first, followed by other witnesses or persons with information concerning the case, then the insured, and lastly the suspects.

Fire Personnel—On-the-spot questions along the following lines should be asked the fire officer in charge and the other firemen. These questions are not exclusive, nor need they be posed with any exactness. They are suggested merely to guide the interviewer as he listens to the fire officer or other fire personnel talk about the fire. They should be of great help in obtaining a fairly comprehensive picture of the fire rather than merely securing facts which impressed the fire personnel.

1. Who turned in the alarm? From where? At what time was the alarm received?
2. At what time did the apparatus arrive at the fire scene?
3. Where was the fire's location, and were premises occupied at the time? If so, who was the occupant; the owner of the building—other tenants?
4. Who was observed about the premises?
5. What were the nature and characteristics of the burning:
   a. Specific location, comparative size, and general extent of the fire at time of arrival.

b. Intensity and direction of travel. Weather conditions, particularly if windy.

c. Separate fires, location and relation to other fires.

d. Color of smoke and flames; any noticeable odors?

e. Any apparent attempt to hinder entry or fire-fighting by strategic placing of obstacles or any unusual difficulty encountered in extinguishing fire.

f. Type of heating in building; coal furnace, oil burner, gas heat, etc. Was heating unit in operation? Was electricity on or off? Was gas turned on? Building sprinklered? Did sprinkler heads operate?

g. Any physical evidence of fire-setting discovered?

6. How was entry secured; were doors or windows open? Any sign of forced entry?

7. Why was fire classified as incendiary, suspicious, cause unknown, or origin undetermined?

This final question summarizes the information relating to incendiarism in the possession of fire personnel and may be helpful in that some fact not covered by the above questions may be revealed.

Information secured from fire personnel is generally authentic, firsthand information, but sometimes an investigator encounters conflicting details about the fire as he questions firemen. This is normal and the investigator must be patient, for no two men recall their observations exactly alike. They may both see the same thing, but usually they'll describe what they believe they observed with slight variations. When any marked discrepancies on important features of the fire are encountered, the investigator should record both versions and trust that later questioning or other evidence will indicate the correct one.

Some experienced investigators interview fire personnel

at their quarters shortly after a fire in what might be termed the usual post-mortem discussion of the fire. Others like to roll with the alarm and catch fire personnel at the fire scene before the post-mortem session unconsciously channels the recollections of each individual into a group pattern.

Discoverer of the Fire—The person who discovered the fire is very often an important witness as to the nature and origin of the fire. His testimony of what he observed during the first few moments of the fire may be of vital significance upon trial.

This witness should be questioned along the following lines:

1. When did you first observe the fire? (What fixed this time in the mind of the witness, i.e., looking at watch, on way to 7:55 A.M. train, on way to 6:00 P.M. date, T.V. program just ended, etc.)
2. Where (exactly) was the fire when you first became aware of it? Where were you at this time? (Also with some exactness.)
3. Who else was at the scene, leaving it, or in neighborhood? (Descriptions of person or car to be as distinctive as possible.) Would you recognize him, it, or them again if given the opportunity?
4. What was the nature of the fire when first observed? What was the color of the flames and smoke? Was there any distinctive odor, such as gasoline, turpentine, celluloid, etc.? Was it an unusually "intense" fire in your opinion or experience?
5. How did you happen to notice the fire? What attracted your attention to it?
6. What do you suppose caused the fire? (Sometimes a fire discoverer is full of ideas about a fire's origin. If these ideas are associated with persons he saw about the scene, they may be of value. Possibly someone flee-

ing the scene or loitering about, perhaps a failure on the part of the occupant of the premises or the building owner to manifest interest in the fire, even some unusual conduct among the first spectators to arrive at the fire may have registered with a degree of sharpness in the mind of the witness.)

Investigators should keep in mind the possibility that the person who discovered the fire can be utilized as a "first assistant" in the investigation. An ideal arson case would be one in which the investigator was at the scene and discovered the fire, but since that is not possible, the investigator should utilize to the fullest extent the best available witness to the first few moments of the fire and, generally, that witness is the person who discovered it.

Neighbors and Other Residents of Community—A neighbor or some chance passer-by may be equally as valuable a witness as the person who discovered the fire. Such persons should be questioned along the same lines as the discoverer. The testimony elicited from these individuals can be used later to corroborate the testimony of the fire discoverer if necessary. And in many instances these witnesses may observe something not seen by the discoverer of the fire.

In the previously discussed "Lady in the Bath" case it was the brother of the victim who heard her screams and discovered the fire, but it was the son of a neighbor who saw the defendant hurriedly walking away from the fire scene, thus definitely placing him at the scene and proving he had the opportunity to set the fire.

Frequently valuable information relative to possible motives may be secured from neighbors, local merchants, and other residents of the community who might know something of purely local interest, which may be of value in pointing to a motive for the fire. Don't overlook these sources of information; more than one case has been broken on a local tip.

The Insurance Agent or Broker—Data concerning the insured and his insurance can easily be secured from the agent or broker handling it. The important features of this interview are concerned with the following:

1. Any recently acquired insurance or increase in coverage?
2. Is insurance adequate, too little, or are premises over-insured?
3. Coverage of any other premises?
4. Who is the insured? What is his reputation in the community, his business background?
5. Who brought in the insured's business originally?
6. What is the history of previous fires?

Of course, the agent or broker may not be able to properly answer all of these questions, but much information can be secured from him and with little expenditure in time or leg-work.

The Adjuster—The investigator cooperates with the adjuster for the company carrying the insurance on the burned building or property, or both, and the adjuster is always more than happy to reciprocate.

Adjusters as a rule are shrewd, intelligent individuals. In their daily work they are constantly confronted with matters of a controversial nature and, while they must satisfy honest claims, they are also required to protect the insurance companies they represent from either unjust or dishonest claims. Handling business of this nature would sharpen the wits of any person and make him particularly alert to fraudulent claims. Some veteran adjusters state that they can "smell" a fraudulent claim, and experience has proved them right on a number of occasions.

An adjuster must deal with the insured or his legal representative and determine among other things the amount of loss or damage sustained, whether the loss occurred during the life of the policy, whether the property lost or damaged is that described in the insurance contract, and whether the ownership of the property coincides with the person named in the policy. An adjuster must also ascertain all other facts pertinent to his task of either bringing about a proper adjustment or proving that no liability exists. Of particular interest to the arson investigator are any facts uncovered which indicate that an insured has concealed or misrepresented any material fact or circumstance concerning the insurance, or is guilty of fraud or false swearing in connection with the loss.

It may also be highly informative to ascertain what public adjuster, if any, has been retained by the insured. Today, most of these operatives are able and trustworthy and at times cooperate with the investigator. However, this field of activity is open to corruption and has been freely exploited by unscrupulous individuals in the past.

The Insured—This may be either the occupant or the owner (or both) of the premises in which the fire occurred, or the registered owner when an automobile is burned. In other cases, goods on consignment may be covered by a third party, or a customer's belongings may be covered under "floater" policies.

In fires apparently for profit or whose origin is undetermined, but possibly motivated by profit, the insured must be handled as a suspect. Unless the circumstances clearly point to another motive for incendiarism it is a good rule to handle all insureds as possible suspects. And it is because of this classification as possible suspects that insureds are usually questioned after other witnesses.

Naturally, when an insured is questioned for the first time, the questioning will be along the line of an interview rather than an interrrogation. Later, if suspicions are deepened, a real interrogation will be undertaken. The insured should be handled easily, he should be encouraged to talk, and questions should be asked only to fill in gaps in the insured's story. Pointed questions directed toward possible areas of incrimination should not be asked. Incriminating information is more likely to be "spilled" when a seemingly pointless question is asked—when the phrasing does not alert the person being interviewed.

The interviewer should ask the insured to review his activities during the few hours, or possibly a day or two, before the fire and for several hours following the blaze. Starting the insured on his recitation of events well ahead of the possible time of the actual fire-setting is of top importance; this strategy cannot be slighted. The insured should be required to relate not only his whereabouts and his activity at various times, but also the identity of his companions at such times, and what persons he met or saw as he traveled about. Time is an element to pin down with great exactness, as are the routes and manner of travel from place to place.

Of equal importance is the story of the insured if he admits being present at the scene of the fire. In this case he should be asked to describe exactly where he was, what he was doing and what he did when he saw the fire. What he actually observed may be of great importance, as well as what it was that attracted his attention to the fire.

In such cases, the insured is in the same class as the discoverer of the fire; therefore the *outline* of questions as suggested for the person who discovered the fire is also pertinent in these instances.

A major point which must be determined is just who had access to the premises—who had keys. Unless the fire occurred in a portion of the building accessible to the public this question of access is extremely important in determining who had the opportunity to set the fire.

Also of importance is accurate information from the occupant of the burned premises as to just what material was located at the place of origin prior to the fire—if strange material is identified at the spot of burning, can the occupant explain its presence?

INTERROGATION OF SUSPECTS

On first contact with a suspect it is important that the investigator not relay his suspicions. The suspect is to be treated in the same manner as any other witness. He is asked a few preliminary questions as to his name and address, relationship with others in the case, if any, his occupation, etc. This affords the investigator a chance to size up the suspect's general demeanor and apparent intelligence and educational background. Of course, it is highly desirable to have some knowledge of the suspect prior to the questioning, but this is not always possible.

However, it is a hard and fast rule that the interrogator be thoroughly familiar with the case before interrogating any suspect. He must have visited the fire scene, questioned other witnesses, reviewed all the physical evidence in the case, and obtained as much background information on the suspect as possible. In pyro cases he must know something of the suspect's previous history, whether he has ever been arrested, the charges, and any history of mental or emotional disorders.

In automobile fire cases the interrogator should be armed with any facts pointing to dissatisfaction with the car (usually mechanical trouble); to domestic problems (husband or wife uses car for illicit romance, or drinks to excess and then drives); or to financial involvement (unable to meet payments, or in need of ready cash).

In fraud fires the financial status of the individual, as well as the status of the business concerned in a commercial fire, is of top importance. So too the record of previous fires of the suspect, members of his family, or concerns with which he was formerly associated.

The investigator must remember that if the suspect is guilty, he knows a great deal about the fire. If a guilty suspect finds out his interrogator knows very little about the blaze, then he'll relax, confident in his own knowledge that he can successfully "ride out" the questioning. For this reason experienced interrogators avoid questions which reveal their lack of knowledge concerning the circumstances surrounding the fire. Naturally, they also avoid pointed questions which reveal evidence in their possession.

Guilty suspects are somewhat like wild animals at bay during interrogations. They are fighting for their freedom, they have a lot at stake, and as a result they are alert and on guard. The investigator, of course, doesn't have such an overpowering interest in the outcome of the questioning and at times must overcome a tendency to "coast"; otherwise a suspect may gain more information from the quiz session than does the interrogator.

Do not bluff, threaten, or belabor a point with the intent of continually keeping a suspect on the defensive; such actions not only breed negative answers but very frequently reveal lack of knowledge of the fire. Let the suspect talk. Get him started by asking what occurred (if he was a witness to the fire) or what he was doing and where at the time of the fire (if he was not present at the fire scene). Listen; let the suspect believe you are accepting his story; plan your counter-attack and be patient.

WRITTEN STATEMENTS

At this point in an interrogation of a suspect, or at the close of an initial interview of an insured, or at the conclusion of an interview with a witness whose testimony may be material, the investigator should reduce the statement to writing.

This may amount only to the investigator making a few notes in his own handwriting; summarizing the witness's story in the language of the witness and then asking him to sign it; or asking the witness to write a brief statement himself. On the other hand, it may be a lengthy recital by a major suspect, taken down in shorthand and then transcribed.

In the case of a suspect, this should be a detailed account of his whereabouts for a reasonable period preceding the fire; who was in his company; why he visited the persons or places mentioned; routes used; persons observed by, or who might have observed, the suspect; when he was last at the fire scene and why.

The statement of an insured should follow similar lines but may also extend to whether or not anything was removed from the premises, the condition of his business, the type of materials stored, etc.

The statements of witnesses are intended only to "hold" them, not as a means of developing an interrogation. As a rule they are taken only when the investigator believes there is the slightest chance of the witness modifying his statement at a later date by "changing his mind" about pertinent facts. Sometimes a witness is persuaded to change his story and "dump the case" by refusing to testify to the truth as related orally at the outset of the investigation. A signed written statement helps to hold a witness to his original story.

Such a statement should also be taken when the witness is in ill health or it is feared he may flee the jurisdiction of the court. In the latter case, as mentioned previously, court process should be secured to guarantee the appearance of a material witness.

The statement of a witness need only encompass the relevant and material elements of his possible testimony. Anything about which he may be expected to testify in court should be in the statement of a material witness. The key facts should be clearly and concisely stated and, if warranted, the witness should be encouraged to draw a sketch or floor plan and note thereon key points of his story.

Statements can be in either narrative or question-and-answer form. For various reasons, based on local experience, different law enforcement agencies have adopted different policies as to the form of statement desired. Many successful prosecutions have been based on each type, so that it cannot be held that one form is superior to the other. It is important only that the statement contain all the pertinent details to which the witness can testify and that these be set forth in the language of the witness.

For purposes of clarity, it is usually preferable to have the pertinent facts set out in chronological order, but conceivably there are occasions when a different outline might be more effective. The statement should open with a notation of the time of day, the place in which it is being taken, the persons present; and it should very specifically identify the person making the statement.

A completed statement should be read to the person making it, or, even better, such person can be asked to read it aloud. A witness other than the investigator should be present during this reading so he can attest to this fact. Later repudiation in court is often based on the claim that the witness did not read or understand the statement.

The statement should be signed by all present: the person making it, the witness, and the investigator. However, if the suspect balks at signing, a note can be made of this fact together with the reason given, if any, and then the witness and investigator can sign as usual. This preserves the value of the statement.

DEVELOPING AN INTERROGATION

After an initial statement of facts is secured from a suspect, the interrogator asks that the story be repeated. He can plead a poor memory or confusion over some details. Another maneuver is to bring in a fellow investigator, introduce the suspect, and then ask that the story be retold to the new arrival. Care must be exercised, however, that this later technique doesn't take on the aspects of the undesirable "team" interrogation—questioning by relays of interrogators.

When a suspect does not claim an alibi but admits his presence at the fire scene, a reenactment of his movements in accordance with his statement is sometimes helpful in revealing inconsistencies. Either in the re-telling of his story or during the reenactment, the interrogator may encounter discrepancies in the suspect's story. His manner of exploiting such inconsistencies is a true measure of an investigator's ability.

In conjunction with such questioning, or in place of it when no discrepancies are apparent in the suspect's story, the investigator should attempt to develop possibly incriminating evidence of which the suspect is fully aware. If the facts warrant, the suspect will be questioned sharply and directly as to why he was carrying the insurance policy in his pocket, why an inventory was found in his valise, why he carried an almost empty five-gallon can of gasoline in his car, and like questions.

If these lines of questioning are not productive, the interrogator may proceed to some point in the suspect's story he knows to be untrue and attempt to break down the suspect by showing the palpable falsity of his story. If the interrogator is not possessed of such information then he must schedule a session of further questioning for a time after he has had the opportunity to check on the facts in the suspect's story. When he finds portions of the suspect's story to be false, he can again question the suspect and hope he "panics."

As a general rule investigators in arson cases are questioning inexperienced law-breakers rather than individuals who make crime a profession. The majority of arsonists, other than pyros, are "one-shot" criminals. These amateurs almost always "panic" at some point in an interrogation. Sometimes the reaction is not too readily recognized, but it occurs when they realize suddenly that the investigator has found out something pointing to their guilt. This shakes their carefully nurtured belief that the interrogator knows nothing about their involvement in the crime. ("You got nothing on me, go ahead, lock me up, go ahead, you think I did it, go ahead, prove it!")

Regardless of their vocal gymnastics, suspects worry at this point. And the skilled investigator hammers away at a suspect, carefully cultivating the suspect's sense of panic in an attempt to break him down and secure some slight and apparently harmless admission. From this first step other admissions may follow and, if the panic is complete, a full confession will result.

However, "pro" criminals don't panic. A professional torch, for instance, fully realizes how little he has to gain in admitting anything. He merely shrugs when the enormity of the discrepancies in his story is pointed out, while a normally honest amateur offender will suffer agony at being caught in a lie.

A conference with the prosecutor in such cases may result in an offer to the "pro" to become a witness for the state against others in the conspiracy. A "pro" usually talks only when he believes it is to his advantage to talk. It is up to the investigator to weigh the evidence in the case and then confer with the prosecutor; possibly the evidence against all concerned is sufficient to warrant going to trial without "bargaining" with the torch. This is the best procedure because if the case is won it insures full punishment for the torch as well as the other conspirators, but as a matter of fact most prosecutors hesitate to go to trial in arson ring cases without a state's witness, if one can be made available through "bargaining."

The professional torch is the most desirable witness because of the scope of his testimony. Usually he's been cheated a little bit by his "customers" and can give testimony not only in the immediate case, but in cases going back for several years.

Prosecutors and arson investigators must bargain for nothing less than the full story of a torch's activities. These criminals may seek to escape punishment by relating the facts only in the case under investigation, but the proper persuasion and a good bargaining lawyer will frequently result in a full story encompassing all their activities from the beginning of their criminal careers or since their last prison terms.

This technique of bargaining with torches, if upheld in the courts, would probably assist greatly in lessening the number of fires involving professional arsonists. After all, who is likely to employ a man to set a fire if, when caught, he'll turn against them and assist in sending them to prison?

In any case involving two or more persons it is always possible to "work" one against the other and gain an advantage by such talk as: "He's sacrificing you. . . . He tells us it was all your idea in the first place," . . . and such lines of questioning. As a last resort it is possible that the prosecutor will agree to some attempt at mitigation of punishment in return for cooperation and testimony against accomplices, even in the case of an occasional offender.

The history of fraud fire prosecution is replete with cases in which one accomplice has testified against his fellows in crime. "I saved myself," he'll explain. "I didn't want to go away." Every person involved in a fraud fire case is worried—worried that one of his associates has "given him up." This mental attitude aids in developing a state's witness and in some cases it's really a race to see who will save himself and "give up" his co-conspirators.

ADMISSIONS AND CONFESSIONS

When a suspect admits some fact which is at variance with his plea of innocence, while still denying the setting of the fire, it is an admission. Such admissions are of good evidentiary value as they are against the interest of the defendant, but they are of even greater value for use as leads in developing more salient features of the investigation. Admissions are really of value when used as levers to pry the case apart and develop independent evidence.

A confession made to an arson investigator is termed an "extrajudicial" one—"judicial" confessions are made in court under fixed circumstances—and should extend to every material element of the crime. It should show the burning, the criminal intent, and expose the person making the confession as a principal in the fire-setting. It should also show when the fire was set; where the blaze was started; where the fire-setter procured the materials for his "fire-trap," if any, and other details of the *modus operandi;* who aided, counseled, or advised him in his act; and why the fire was set, the motive. Other points may be of importance depending upon the individual case. For instance, flight after the fire-setting is a good point to have in a confession because it helps serve as its own corroboration.

A confession is a first-person recital of facts very similar to the initial statement of a suspect or insured, except that it is a little more formal, or it may be in question and answer form. The date, place, persons present, and the person confessing are identified in the first paragraph. Then the confessor tells his story, again *in his own words.*

A beautiful example of a confession taken down in the words of a suspect was secured in a 1952 arson case in

White Plains, New York. In order that this point may be fully understood this confession is set forth below:

I, Charlotte D......., age 35, living at 138 So. Main St., Portchester, N. Y., wish to make the following true statement of my own free will, without the use of force, fear or favor, and knowing that what I say may be used for or against me in a Court of Law.

I wish to state that on August 15, 1952, I was working in Scarsdale, N. Y., and I quit at 5:00 P.M. I took the New York Central train to White Plains. I arrived in White Plains at about 6:00 P.M. After I arrived in White Plains I went to the Sugar Hill Bar, which is located on the corner of Brookfield St. and Martine Ave. I went inside and had one glass of beer. After I had this beer I went outside on the corner where I saw three girl friends of mine. We talked for a short while, and then the four of us decided to go to the liquor store on Spring St. and there I bought a pint of Paradise Port Wine. The four of us girls then walked down Hamilton Ave. to the Parkway where we went into the park. We drank the pint of wine which I had bought. The four of us girls then went to the liquor store on the corner of Main St. and Central Ave. where we purchased one quart and five pints of wine. We then went back into the park and drank all of the wine that we had bought. At about 9:00 P.M. we left the park and went to Ferris Ave. where we visited a friend by the name of Alice M........ While at Alice M.......'s I had more wine and some beer. At about 11:30 P.M. myself and another girl left Alice M.......'s, and we went to the Sugar Hill Bar. While there I drank beer and whiskey. Sometime after midnight I left the bar by myself and I went to Edward H.......'s apartment which is at #12 Winchester St. Edward let me into his apartment. There was a girl there by the name of Sally M........ After I was in Edward's apartment I sat on the bed and counted what money I had. Edward asked me to get off the bed and sit in a chair, which I did. Edward then told me not to come into his house anymore as he didn't want me there. I got up then and started out. Edward then got up and started to push me out. When I got outside, Edward came running out and accused me of throwing something at the house and he knocked me to the ground and he went back into the house. I was mad at Edward for knocking me down and I wanted to get even with him. When I got to the chicken market at Martine Ave., I saw a whiskey bottle lying on the sidewalk. I picked it up and I went back to the gas station on the corner of Winchester Street and Martine Ave., where I drained about two tablespoons of gas from a pump hose into the bottle. I then walked to #12 Winchester Street. I walked to the corner of the building by the alley and poured the gas from the bottle onto the building. I then took a book of matches and tried to ignite the shingles. I then heard a woman yell at me and I ran away and went to the Sugar Hill Bar.

In court, upon her trial for attempted arson, this alcoholic, revenge fire-setter spoke in the phraseology of her confession. It would have been a difficult confession to successfully repudiate.

Each page is numbered and initialed or even signed by the confessor. Corrections are permitted and aid in disproving later claims that the confession was not "understood." These corrections may be numbered consecutively and initialed. A few intentional typographical errors in the preparation of the final draft assure some corrections so as to guard against later repudiation.

In the closing paragraph the confession usually contains some or all of the following comments: the number of pages, the number of corrections, the fact of initialing them, a note of it being read aloud or read by the person signing, and a line to the effect that it's a true statement, voluntarily made. Finally, it is signed by the person making it, witnesses, and the investigator. Frequently witnesses sign below a brief note to the effect that they heard it read and by whom, or observed the reenactment, or witnessed the signing of the confession—whatever the case may be.

A question and answer type statement taken by Chief Assistant District Attorney, Frederick E. Weeks, Jr., of Westchester County, New York, is reproduced here for the purpose of pointing up the importance of inquiring into every essential element of the case. Mr. Weeks fully explored the time, place, the fact of a burning, who did it, manner of the fire, and its motivation. His procedure may well serve as a model.

The statement opened with a standard identification of the confessor, the time, place, the names of all persons present, and then continued:

Q. Peter W......., I understand you want to give us a complete story about the fires at 12 Lake Street, is that right?
A. That is right.
Q. And we talked earlier today?
A. Yes.
Q. And you understand I am the Chief Assistant District Attorney of the County?
A. Yes, sir.
Q. And you are willing to tell us the complete story now?
A. Yes, sir.
Q. What is your full name, please?
A. Peter W.......
Q. How old are you?
A. Fifty-three.
Q. You have been living at 12 Lake Street, White Plains?
A. That is right.
Q. For how long?
A. Approximately six years.
Q. During the past six years there have been apparently six fires in that building there or the house next door or the barn or garage at No. 12. Now, will you tell us, please, just what you know about those fires? According to the fire records,

the first one was December 27th, 1945, at 3:30 A.M. Now, do
you recall that fire? That is the one in the closet and consisted of Christmas decorations, blankets, pillows, lamp
shades, second floor hall closet. Do you recall that fire?

A. Yes, I opened the door and dropped a match in there.

Q. That was around 3:30 in the morning?

A. I imagine so.

Q. And why did you do that?

A. Well, I can't explain the reason for doing these things. I may
have had a grudge, I don't know, I imagine so.

Q. Just some urge?

A. That is right.

Q. Is that it, a grudge?

A. Yes.

Q. And if so, who would the grudge be against?

A. No one in particular.

Q. Had you been drinking at the time?

A. Yes, sir.

Q. Now, the next fire listed is April 5th, 1948, 11:28 P.M., the
first floor, curtain, shades, window casings scorched. What
do you know about that fire?

A. I was sitting in the hall down there and I was drinking and
I dropped a match alongside the window.

Q. By "dropped a match" do you mean you just dropped it or—

A. Threw it.

Q. With the idea of it catching on to something and blazing?

A. Yes, sir.

Q. Had you been drinking at that time?

A. Yes, sir. That is why I was sitting downstairs in the hall.

Q. Before midnight?

A. That is right.

Q. Now, the next fire listed that we have here is 14 Lake Street,
that is next door, Mrs. ....'s home. Mrs. .... was
your landlady before you moved to Lake Street?

A. That is true.

Q. When you lived in her home on Central Avenue?

A. That is true.

Q. 4:22 A.M., September 22nd, 1948, first floor closet there. Now did you start that fire?

A. Yes, sir; I did.

Q. And how did you start that one?

A. Just put a match to the closet.

Q. And what was in there that would catch on, any papers?

A. Clothes, I imagine.

Q. And why did you do that?

A. No particular reason. I can't answer that. I never had any grudge or ill feeling towards Mrs. ....

Q. Did you have to open the door to the closet?

A. The door was ajar.

Q. But you had to open it a bit, did you?

A. That is right.

Q. Now, the next fire that we have a record of is at the barn there in the rear of 12 Lake Street, on October 24th, 1949, around 11:23 P.M. What do you know about that fire?

A. I went upstairs in the attic of the garage and set fire to some material by the door.

Q. What sort of material?

A. A lot of things up in the attic.

Q. Well, I mean, was it furniture?

A. It was furniture up there.

Q. And why did you do that?

A. Just had the urge.

Q. Had you been drinking at the time?

A. Yes, sir.

Q. Had you tried to secure that barn to use as an upholstery shop?

A. Yes, sir; well, I mentioned the fact; yes.

Q. That was before you started the fire, though?

A. Oh, yes.

Q. Now, on October 26th, '49, that is two days later, a fire in the stairway at 12 Lake Street, 1:37 in the afternoon. What do you know about that fire?

A. I don't recall that one, Mr. Weeks.

Q. You don't recall that one?

A. No.

Q. In other words, there was no fire two days after you set fire to the barn?

A. No, sir.

Q. Now, do you know anything about a fire in an old abandoned barn across the street?

A. No, sir; I know nothing about that.

Q. You don't know anything about that . . . between Stewart Place and Lake Street there?

A. No, sir.

Q. Now, coming down to October 26th of this year, 1950, did you set a fire that day?

A. I did.

Q. In No. 12 Lake Street?

A. Yes, sir.

Q. And how did you set it?

A. I threw a match down the hall.

Q. What hall was that? Supposing you tell us just what you did.

A. I went downstairs the back way and I threw a match down the stairs there.

Q. At what time of day did you do it?

A. I imagine around 12:30.

Q. In the afternoon?

A. Yes, sir.

Q. And why did you do that?

A. Well, I just wanted to give them a little trouble, I guess, so I could take the building over.

Q. What do you mean by taking the building over?

A. Superintendent.

Q. You had had trouble with the superintendent there?

A. The caretaker.

Q. You had had trouble with him, had you?

A. Oh, yes.

Q. Did you want that job to be caretaker there?

A. Not then I didn't; no. At one time I did. That was right after Mr. O . . . . . died and the estate took over; and Mr. O . . . . . wanted me to take the job as caretaker before he died. He didn't want to have anything to do with it, he was just going to live there.

Q. Had you been drinking when you did that on the 26th of October, this year?

A. Yes, sir.

By Chief MacIntyre:

Q. If you had been drinking that morning, you hadn't been drinking too much. Right? I am talking now about the last fire up there, the 26th of October. You told us in the other room that you had been drinking the night before.

A. That is true.

Q. That you had a hangover.

A. That is right; and there may have been some left that morning in the bottle.

Q. You weren't drinking to any great extent that morning but you had been drinking the night before and had a hangover and probably were in an ugly mood or something?

A. That could be; yes.

Q. That is up to you to tell us.

A. Well, I mean, I had been drinking.

Q. And you had been drinking in addition that morning to the night before?

A. That is true. I know there was a bottle there. I am pretty sure I had been drinking.

By Mr. Weeks:

Q. Now, as a result of that fire on October 26th, 1950, you were injured, were you?

A. Yes, sir.

Q. And how were you injured and what part of your body?

A. My arms and a couple of marks on my hand; one arm.

Q. What type of injury was it?

A. A burn.

Q. How were you burned?

A. From trying to put the fire out. It got the best of me. I think that is why I got the smoke, too, Mr. Weeks.

Q. And why did you want to put the fire out after you had started it?

A. Well, I started to realize the seriousness of the thing, if it ever got too far going.

Q. Didn't you realize the seriousness of the other fires you started there?

A. No, sir.

Q. Well, the other times were you more drunk than you were on the last time, the last occasion?

A. Just about the same.

Q. Now, who did you tell that you had been burned?

A. Only my wife, I think. I don't know of anybody else.

Q. And were you treated for those burns?

A. I was treated down at the Veteran's Hospital.

Q. You weren't treated here in White Plains?

A. No, sir.

Q. Why didn't you go to a physician or hospital here in White Plains?

A. I didn't realize it was that serious, truthfully. It didn't bother me so much then.

Q. And when was it that you went to the hospital?

A. Around the 29th.

Q. A couple of days later?

A. Yes, sir; on a Sunday. I am pretty sure it was the 29th. A Sunday afternoon.

Q. You said, I believe, the reason you started the fire on October 26th was because of your grudge?

A. That is right.

Q. Against the owners of the property and the caretaker there?

A. Not against the owners of the property.

Q. Just the caretaker?

A. Yes.

Q. And you had wanted the job as caretaker at one time, is that it?

A. Yes, because I had done a lot of work in that building.

Q. Earlier today you were questioned over there in my office.

A. Yes, sir.

Q. At that time you denied setting the fires and finally said you might have but you didn't recollect doing it?

A. That is true.

Q. Now, what has led you to now come and tell us the truth?
You are telling us the truth now, are you?

A. Well, because I feel I need some kind of treatment to get
off this drinking business; and I don't get any ideas like that
when I am sober.

Q. And the story you told us this morning was not the truth,
you are telling us the truth now, is that it?

A. I am, sir.

Q. Now, did you ever try and set any other fires there?

A. No, sir; not that I recall now.

Q. Do you recall a fire on the porch there in some porch furniture a year or so ago?

A. I do; vaguely, though. I do recall there was a fire on the
porch.

Q. Did you start that?

A. I believe I did.

Q. Do you remember fanning that fire after it got going in the
furniture, in the cushions?

A. No sir; I do not.

Q. But it is probable that you did if you were seen there at the
time?

A. It is probably so; yes.

Q. Have you set any other fires in the neighborhood there?

A. No, sir.

Q. Do you know the W.... home around the corner on North
Broadway?

A. Yes.

Q. Did you ever set a fire there on the porch?

A. No, sir.

Q. Did I ask you how old you are?

A. Yes, sir; fifty-three.

Q. Have you ever been in a mental hospital?

A. No, I haven't.

Q. Outside of this setting fires, have you ever thought anything
might be wrong with your actions?

A. Oh, people tell me that. My wife told me more than once,
"I think you need a little treatment or something." When I
was down to the Veteran's Administration I was talking to

the doctor, Dr. Paul, she is a vocational guide, and she mentioned something, too: "Now, don't blow your top here but I am here to help you out; I think you need mental treatment, too." I went down to finish my upholstery course, and I had to take up slip covers and drapes to complete the course. That is at the Veteran's Administration.

Q. Now, since you were brought into my office this morning by Detective Collins and the other officials, you have been treated all right, have you?

A. I sure have.

Q. You haven't been abused or threatened or anything like that?

A. No, sir.

Q. You have been a pretty heavy drinker?

A. I have, Mr. Weeks. Yes, I admit that. If I take the first drink I will go until I can't drink any more. I have done it quite a number of years, practically half my life, I imagine, and I go on periodicals like that, maybe three or four or five days, maybe a week or ten days.

By Chief MacIntyre:

Q. You haven't been gainfully employed in a long time, is that right?

A. I have been going to school for some time. Up until I started school. I started school in '47 and then I went to the hospital again and that was interrupted. I went back in September of '47 . . . September of '48, and I started school in March, '48, and then I took sick and I left there in May, interrupted my training, then went back in September and completed my course in March, 1950. Then I did a little work there for that boys' school in Hawthorne, and then I left there.

Q. Why did you leave the boys' school?

A. Well, to be truthful, I was requested to leave.

Q. For what reason?

A. Drinking.

A confession may appear to be the end of the case to an inexperienced investigator. It is, in fact, little more than a beginning. All phases of the confession must be checked from start to finish so that the investigator is certain that events occurred as stated, or circumstances were favorable enough for them to have occurred as stated.

A good procedure is to have the person confessing write his statement in his own handwriting and then reenact the crime. When the interrogator is satisfied that the true facts have been disclosed, he can return to his office, call in a stenographer, and have the subject dictate his confession in full detail. This is the best guard against attempts to repudiate the confession.

Too many inexperienced investigators relax after securing a confession, lulled into inactivity by the mistaken belief that the accused will plead guilty upon appearance for trial. True, at the time of the confession the fire-setter may have been willing to pay the penalty for the crime, but during the period of awaiting trial his feelings of self-guilt may evaporate. Normal procedure is to plead not guilty and attempt to repudiate the confession. Hence a confession should be the basis for developing independent evidence sufficient, if possible, to prove guilt beyond a reasonable doubt *without the confession*. When this is not possible, then sufficient evidence to corroborate the confession is *prima facie* evidence that the confessor is speaking the truth.

ADMISSIBILITY OF CONFESSIONS

The admissibility of an extra-judicial confession is to be determined by the court upon trial. Inquiry is naturally made as to whether the defendant spoke through fear or in expectation of immunity when he made the confession and, if defendant was under arrest at the time, the court will explore the possibility of a compulsion existing for any reason.

A preliminary examination by counsel for the defense

is generally permitted to test the competency of a confession, but once received in evidence, its voluntary nature will become a question of fact for the jury to determine. The jury is usually charged to disregard it wholly unless they find it was voluntarily made without threats or menace by acts, words, or situation; without compulsion, real or apprehended; and without the promise, expressed or implied, of immunity or mitigation of punishment.

In a New York case (Peo. v. Weiner (1929) 248 N. Y. 118, 122, 161 N.E. 441) it was held that if the evidence shows without dispute that the confession was extorted by force or fear, or if a verdict that it was freely made would be clearly against the weight of evidence, the judge should reject it. Only where a fair question of fact is presented should the jury be permitted to determine whether the confession is voluntary.

Certain techniques of interrogation have been held to make a confession an involuntary one. The previously mentioned "team interrogation" is a form of duress. When one interrogator becomes tired, another takes his place, and the first interrogator rests. When the second questioner becomes tired, then he too is relieved. But during all this questioning by relays of interrogators the suspect is not permitted any rest and naturally tires.

Lengthy questioning is also frowned upon by the courts as it also tires a suspect and is a form of duress when prolonged beyond reasonable limits. Other techniques such as bright lights, denial of water, cigarettes, and like comforts are also forms of duress. Naturally, actual physical force, beatings or the like, or the threats of such force, destroy the value of any confession.

Some investigators argue that an involuntary confession, even if it is later successfully repudiated in court, permits the development of the investigation and the securing of other evidence which may be admissible. But fortunately such reasoning is not generally encountered. After all, the interrogator is searching for the truth and if he avails himself of any method to *force* a confession, he may not be ascertaining the truth. A tired person may confess to almost anything to have a little rest, and in many instances an innocent person will confess the most heinous crime to avoid a beating or the continuation of one.

And since the promise of immunity is not usually binding unless made by a prosecutor or district attorney or their assistants, most competent investigators who cannot "produce" on such promises won't utilize them as a technique to secure a confession.

A New York court has held: "Lawless methods of law enforcement should not be countenanced by our courts even though they may seem expedient to the authorities in order to apprehend the guilty. Whether a guilty man goes free or not is a small matter compared with the maintenance of principles which still safeguard a person accused of a crime." Every investigator worthy of the name must subscribe to such belief.

"LIE DETECTORS"

There is no such machine as a "lie detector." However, there are machines or instruments which aid a skilled operator in making a diagnosis of apprehension or fear on the part of a person being questioned. These machines do not flash lights or ring bells when the person being tested tells a lie, but they do indicate by means of a graph his emotional responses. From the study of one or more of these graphs an expert can usually detect deception.

Whether the machine is termed a psychogalvanometer or a polygraph, it is basically a machine for measuring emotion and differs only in its circuit and the type and number of physiological changes recorded. Of course, a machine that records blood pressure, pulse, respiration, and electrodermal response appears to be more reliable than a machine that measures only changes in blood pressure. However, the training and experience of the operator is a more important factor. Skilled operators can make a diagnosis with any modern machine, but the best machine is of little use when the operator is lacking in skill, training, or experience.

Professional standards for both examiners and machines have been established in this field in order that the public will not be victimized by a poorly designed or carelessly manufactured machine or an unskilled examiner. The International Society for the Detection of Deception has succeeded in their campaign to assure law enforcement agencies of machines and examiners that measure up to the highest standards.

Standard technique starts with the examiner or operator being given the full details of the case. From these facts an interrogatory is prepared. This consists of three types of questions:

1. Critical—concerning the crime.
2. Non-critical—concerning matters not related to the crime.
3. Emotional standard—to prepare a base for measuring responses to other questions.

After the examiner has completed his analysis of the graphs made by the machine during the examination, an evaluation is made of the subject's response to critical and non-critical questions by averaging the responses of several tests. The accuracy of the diagnosis is increased by this method of evaluation.

Modern operators are not satisfied with one test but may make from three to five tests before making a diagnosis as to whether or not the subject tested was telling the truth. Experience has shown that unfamiliarity with the machine and testing methods usually produces emotional tenseness during the first test. Even innocent persons will tighten up in fear that the machine may unjustly brand them guilty. Such fears are usually dispelled at the end of the first test. The operator may then take from two to five more tests before concluding that the true emotional reactions of the subject to certain specific questions have been measured.

In one research experiment it was found that the diagnosis was correct in 60 per cent of the examinations based upon only one record, 68 to 70 per cent correct when two records were averaged, and 77 to 80 per cent correct when three to five records were averaged.

Even though the record of an examination cannot usually be introduced in court as evidence upon an arson trial, the initial value of this type of examination is in the direction it gives an investigation. When a skilled and trusted examiner reports that he believes the subject has given truthful answers to the questions and apparently has no knowledge of the fire-setting, the investigator can direct his inquiry toward other suspects, saving a great deal of time and effort.

Dr. Fabian Rouke, associated with both Fordham and New York Universities and one of the top men in this field, delights in exonerating the innocent by his examinations. In one recent case he examined a man for the New York Police and reported his belief that the man had nothing to do with the crime, yet all the evidence secured up to that time pointed to this individual's guilt. Needless to say, there was some extensive grumbling among the local police and the press, but Dr. Rouke's diagnosis prevented the arrest of an innocent man. The guilty person was arrested two weeks later during the commission of another crime and made a full confession.

Colonel Ralph W. Pierce, formerly Director, Criminal Investigation Division, U. S. Army, during a lecture at a

1953 Police Institute meeting at New York University, cited another advantage when he recalled several cases of voluntary confessions secured during or at the termination of a lie detector examination. His technique was to casually acquaint the subject with the indications of his guilt as shown on the graphs and suggest that a full confession would save a lot of time.

But the really terrific advantage which this method of detecting deception has over all others is its psychological impact upon a "shaky" suspect who is stubbornly denying his guilt. Investigators must always remember that most arsonists are not hardened criminals but occasional offenders not toughened to the mental rigors attendant upon concealing guilty knowledge from a skilled questioner.

Almost every suspect realizes that refusal to submit to a "lie detector" test considerably weakens his plea of innocence, but the guilty suspect cannot afford to risk such a test. This fact gives the trained interrogator an advantage which he can sometimes successfully exploit: "Well, that's your story. We've been thinking of checking it on the lie detector. If you're telling the truth, you certainly won't object to undergoing a lie detector test. It will definitely clear you. It will satisfy us; we're not satisfied your story is the truth. And it will save us all a lot of time. How about it?"

Refusal to take the test permits questioning along the lines of: "If you're innocent, you must want to clear yourself. I thought you'd jump at the chance of taking a test on the lie detector. You must be scared of something. You must be hiding something . . ." And since this line of questioning is logical thinking, it is not unusual for the suspect to give up at this point.

When these instruments for detecting deception are used early in the course of an investigation, they not only give direction to the initial investigation but place the full weight of their psychological impact upon a guilty suspect before he is hardened and toughened by continuous questioning. Possibly the greatest fault in recent years among law enforcement agents has been the tendency to use these instruments only when other methods of interrogation have failed. In spite of this, many arson cases have been broken by the use of these instruments. There's little question that in a few years these machines will be standard equipment in arson investigation interrogations.

Note:

In 1965, the United States Supreme Court decision in the Miranda case held that a suspect's confession was invalid because he had not been advised he had a right to consult with an attorney. As a result, many police units now use a standardized form advising suspects in criminal cases of their constitutional rights. Written statements are now prefaced by an acknowledgment to these rights and a notation summarizing this understanding is presented to the suspect for his signature. An effective preface is as follows: "I have been advised of my rights to remain silent, and that anything I say may be used against me in court. I know that I have the right to have a lawyer with me during any questioning. I understand this, and wish to make the following statement."

(See pages 283 to 285 for forms which are currently in use in a number of police departments throughout the United States in connection with law enforcement officers respecting the rights of a suspect and the suspect acknowledging his understanding of these rights.)

CHAPTER ELEVEN

EVIDENCE

EVIDENCE is that which tends to prove or disprove any matter in question or to influence the belief respecting it. It is all the means by which an alleged matter of fact, the truth of which is submitted to investigation, is established or disproved.

It is vital that arson investigators be familiar with the technical aspects of evidence in general and the handling and analysis of physical evidence in particular. Otherwise, valuable evidence may be overlooked or ruined by improper handling during an investigation.

DIRECT EVIDENCE

Direct evidence is that evidence directly proving any matter as opposed to circumstantial evidence. It is evidence of a fact in dispute, sworn by those who have actual knowledge of it by means of their senses. Direct evidence has been held to exist when the thing to be proved is directly attested to by those who speak from their own actual and personal knowledge of its existence.

In an arson case direct evidence of the burning by the defendant would be the testimony of a witness who saw the defendant bend down, strike a match, and apply it to the building for whose burning the defendant is on trial. However, direct evidence is the exception rather than the rule in an arson case. The person who commits arson is an out and out sneak. Very few people ever see someone set a fire.

CIRCUMSTANTIAL (INDIRECT) EVIDENCE

In no other crime does circumstantial evidence play such an important part as it does in arson. In fact, most cases are predicated on circumstantial rather than direct evidence.

Circumstantial or indirect evidence consists of facts which usually attend other facts sought to be proved. Richardson in his *Law of Evidence* defines it as evidence that relates to facts, other than those in issue, which by human experience have been found to be so associated with the fact in issue that the latter may be reasonably inferred therefrom.

This type of evidence must *establish* collateral facts from which the facts in issue will follow as a logical inference. Circumstantial evidence can be said to exist when the thing to be proved is to be inferred from other facts *satisfactorily proved* (Peo. v. Palmer (1887), N. Y. St. Rep. 817, 820). Circumstantial evidence consists of reasoning from facts which are known (proved) to establish a point in issue. The process would be fatally vicious if the basic point from which the inference is to be made had not been satisfactorily established. Certainly, one inference cannot be the basis for another inference.

A good case in point is the Stine-Walzer case set out in a preceding chapter. The peculiar footprint found at the scene of several of the fires and the casts made of it, together with the testimony of the expert who made the casts, constituted circumstantial evidence of the presence at the fire scenes of some individual wearing shoes of the type making the footprints. When Stine was apprehended and found to be wearing shoes identical with those making the footprints found at the fires, it was also circumstantial evidence, but in this instance it could be reasonably inferred that it was Stine who had made the footprints.

However, if Stine had been wearing shoes which only corresponded in size to those making the footprints at the fire scenes, it could *not* be reasonably inferred that Stine had made the prints found at the fires. When both the casts made by the police and the shoes which Stine had been wearing at the time of his apprehension were produced in court, it's fairly reasonable to assume that most of the jury inferred Stine's presence at the scene.

When circumstantial evidence is relied upon for a conviction, the proved, collateral facts, when taken together, must be of a conclusive nature and tendency, leading as a whole to a reasonable inference that the accused, and no one else, committed the offense charged.

A good case, also previously discussed, illustrative of this point is the "Lady in the Bath" case—the unfortunate Mrs. Wood, the woman whose husband threw gasoline through the bathroom window when she was taking a shower.

No one saw Mr. Wood actually set the fire; therefore his conviction had to be secured on circumstantial evidence. In this case the "picture" created by the evidence might be said to be a six-piece one:

1. Testimony of the wife, her brother, and fireman as to fire, odor of gasoline, and the fact that the electric heater served as an ignition unit within the bathroom.
2. Testimony of the fireman relative to finding the gallon jug containing a small amount of gasoline plus the testimony of the investigator who seized a sample of gasoline from the drum kept at the defendant's plumbing shop.
3. Testimony of the chemist who made a comparison analysis of the two gasoline samples and found them identical.

4. Testimony of the youth who saw Mr. Wood leaving his home shortly before the fire was discovered (opportunity).

5. Evidence which showed Wood removed his wife's clothes from the kitchen chair, placed them outside the bathroom door, and ignited them—*apparently for the sole purpose of keeping his wife in the bathroom so he could attempt her cremation.*

6. Testimony relative to repeated requests for a divorce and concerning the "woman in the case" (motive).

Taken all together they certainly pointed to the husband's guilt, but he could have controverted them quite easily by proving that he was somewhere else at the time of the fire (alibi), or that the comparison analysis of the gasoline was faulty, thus controverting the testimony of the youth and the chemist.

No piece was missing from the picture painted by the prosecution in this case except an eye-witness account of Mr. Wood throwing the gasoline through the bathroom window, but this could be safely inferred from the evidence produced by the prosecutor.

In a legal sense circumstantial evidence is not regarded as inferior to direct evidence and in many instances it is more reliable than direct evidence, especially since proof by circumstantial evidence usually requires the use of a large number of witnesses, each testifying to some small portion of the overall picture, so that a number of perjured witnesses would be necessary to produce an unjust conviction, whereas one perjured witness giving direct testimony might accomplish such a wrongful act. Justice Walworth, in delivering a charge to a jury in New York, after setting forth the above reasons, said: "For this reason, although from the imperfection and uncertainty which must ever exist in all human tribunals, I have no doubt that there have been cases in which innocent persons have been convicted on circumstantial proofs, yet from my knowledge of criminal jurisprudence, both from reading and observation, I have no hesitation in expressing the opinion that where there has been one unjust conviction upon circumstantial evidence alone, there have been three innocent persons condemned upon the positive testimony of perjured witnesses."

In the last few years there does seem to be some relaxation in the ordinary person's opinion of circumstantial evidence. The great strides in the application of scientific techniques to police problems as well as the wide publicity given to cases in which guilt has been proved by the scientific analysis of physical evidence have in truth educated the ordinary citizen. Today, jurors give full weight to circumstantial evidence which appears to prove the defendant was at the scene of a fire or in some contact with an ignition device or accelerant used in the blaze, when it is supported by some proof that the defendant was the person whose hand set into motion the criminal agency resulting in the arson.

However, investigators of arson must remember that many individuals who may sit on juries still have a marked prejudice against convicting any person solely on circumstantial evidence and a determined effort should always be made to secure direct evidence. When direct evidence cannot be secured, be satisfied with nothing less than a clearcut picture of the defendant's guilt established by *proving* the various items of evidence essential to piece together such a picture.

"BEST EVIDENCE" RULE

Evidence is classified as either primary or secondary when it concerns some document, writing, or other material object. Primary evidence is the "best evidence." It is that kind of evidence which, under every possible circumstance, affords the greatest certainty of the fact in question. Secondary evidence is inferior to primary evidence and can only be introduced when the primary evidence cannot be produced for some good and acceptable reason.

This rule of evidence frequently handicaps the prosecution in cases involving the burning of property to defraud the insurer, because evidence of the insurance is relevant and necessary as bearing upon the motive of the defendant. Primary evidence of the contents of an insurance policy is the document itself and secondary evidence thereof may be excluded. Curtis in his fine book *The Law of Arson* points out that the problem of the district attorney arises from the privilege which constitutionally protects the accused from self-incrimination. If the policy is in the possession of the prisoner, he cannot be compelled to produce it. In many states, however, this circumstance leads to the conclusion that the primary evidence is unavailable to the prosecuting attorney and justifies the introduction of secondary evidence of its contents. In other jurisdictions, secondary evidence is admissible if the accused has been given a reasonable notice to produce the policy and has failed to do so.

SELF-INCRIMINATION

The investigator should remember that a suspect cannot be forced to testify against himself, but any evidence found in the possession of the suspect should be seized at the time of the arrest.

An ordinary business card of a firm of public adjusters seized at the close of an interrogation by Fire Marshal Brophy of New York City was a major piece of evidence in the trial of members of the Brooklyn Arson Ring. In the Boston Post Road Case articles of sentimental value from the burned premises as well as the insurance policy covering the loss were seized from the lessee of the burned premises.

Anything in the possession of the fire-setter may develop into valuable evidence.

The suspect himself may be of some value as evidence. The conviction of a torch in a New Jersey fire was made a little more certain because he was found to be severely burned about the face and chest at the time of his arrest, and could offer no reasonable explanation for his injuries.

While the constitutional guarantee against self-incrimination seems to *mitigate against* successful investigation, the many decisions of courts throughout the country have served to aid the police in overcoming the attempts of guilty persons to utilize this privilege to handicap the basic investigation. For instance, the United States Supreme Court has held it permissible for police authorities to compel a person accused of murder to put on a shirt found at the scene of the crime "for size"—to see whether it fitted or not. It has also been held permissible to seize the shoes of a prisoner shortly after his arrest for the purpose of comparing them with footprints at or near the scene of the crime and later to submit such shoes as evidence.

The common police practice of requiring an accused person to reenact the crime of which he is suspected for the purpose of identification has also been held not to violate a person's constitutional rights against self-incrimination.

The taking of fingerprints has also been held not violative of such constitutional rights, as the prints are taken for the purpose of identification rather than incrimination. The same general line of reasoning also has been applied to taking photographs of a prisoner. Objection of a prisoner to police taking his photograph, one court held, would be similar to a defendant wearing a mask in court to avoid identification upon trial.

A prisoner may be asked to exhibit his body in court for possible identification by means of certain marks, such as scars and wounds, or to stand up and exhibit himself for the purpose of identification. The constitutional guarantee is a prohibition relating to extorting communications from the witness and not an exclusion of his body as evidence.

OPINION EVIDENCE

Evidence of what the witness thinks, believes, or infers in regard to the facts in dispute as distinguished from his personal knowledge of the facts themselves is termed opinion evidence because the witness is, in fact, expressing an opinion.

Ordinary witnesses generally cannot express an opinion; it is usually inadmissible. They may, however, testify to things within the ordinary scope of their knowledge. For instance, whether, in the opinion of the witness, the defendant appeared intoxicated, looked excited, acted peculiarly, angrily, or irrationally. Such witnesses may also testify to matters of color, weight, size, quantity, light conditions, and inferences as to race, accent or language, visibility, sounds, and the like. The subjects on which an ordinary witness may express an opinion are those which do not require special skill or knowledge.

Ordinary witnesses are also restricted as to what they may infer. A lay witness cannot give as his opinion that a certain occurrence took place as a direct result of what some individual did or did not do. In attempting to prove the origin of a fire is incendiary, it has been held to be prejudicial error to permit witnesses to state conclusions they may have reached from things they have seen and facts they have related.

Witnesses may relate facts only, and the jury must be left to draw its own conclusions. As for example, a member of the fire department will not be permitted to testify that he noticed a black smoke at the fire and *drew the conclusion that the building had been saturated with oil.* Nor can he testify that a building burned exceedingly fast

courtesy of Bob Wilder—Times Union, Albany, N. Y.

Lie detector test being given by William Kirwan, Director, Scientific Laboratory, New York State Police.

Two modern devices for the detection of arson in the New York State Police Laboratory.

courtesy of New York State Police Laboratory

Solvent extraction apparatus for the recovery of combustible liquids from cloth, wood, paper, and like materials. Distillation unit for fractional separation of hydrocarbon liquids—gasoline, kerosene, mineral oils, etc.

*and from his experience as a fireman he is of the opinion
that some volatile oil had been used in the fire.*

He can, however, testify that he noticed a dense black
smoke exactly similar to the smoke from burning oil that
he had observed in other fires. He can testify that he noticed a peculiar odor, identical with the odor observed in
a garage fire. He can testify that the building burned much
more rapidly than similar buildings ordinarily burn.

Illustrative of this point is the following opinion: "Common ob-
servers having special opportunity for observation may testify
to their opinion as to conclusions of fact, although they are not
experts if the subject matter to which the testimony relates cannot be reproduced or described to the jury as it appeared to the
witness at the time, and their opinions are such as men in general are capable of forming with reasonable correctness on the
facts observed." (Keccis vs. State, N.J. L-44—State vs. Laster,
N.J. L-586.)

Expert testimony is that given by experts in relation to
some scientific, technical, or professional matter. An expert witness must be qualified by the court prior to his testifying. Qualification is usually a matter of reviewing the
education, training, and experience of a witness in his
particular field. Once qualified, a witness may testify on
matters within his field—generally fingerprinting, ballistics,
chemistry, physics, medicine, psychiatry, the examination of
questioned documents, and the like.

However, of particular interest to arson investigators is
the close relationship of the arson expert to cases of fire-
setting. In other words, if a chemist can give expert testimony relating to chemical examinations, and an expert on
handwriting is permitted to testify as an expert concerning
questioned documents, why isn't an experienced fire official
or qualified arson investigator permitted to give expert
testimony as to the incendiary origin of a fire?

The practice as to the admissibility of expert opinion relative to the origin of a fire varies in different states. The leading case in New York is that of the People vs. Grutz (212 New York 72), in which the court was divided in their opinion as evidenced by the four to three decision.

In this case a deputy fire marshal was asked his opinion of the origin of the fire and in answer enumerated a number of facts which it was quite proper for him to state. These facts, he said, led him to believe that the fire was set. The court held that the nature of the fire marshal's answer did away with much of the harmful effect of the question. The court stated, however, that the case was not one for expert opinion. the physical facts which were the subject of the investigation were so simple that they could be readily understood, when properly described, and it was then up to the jury to draw the appropriate conclusions.

While this decision has been accepted in many quarters as prohibiting expert testimony as to the origin of fires, other jurists believe that the principles are the same in arson cases as in any other criminal cases: namely that if the facts in any given case are complicated or of a nature not readily understandable by laymen, expert testimony would be admissible.

This belief is supported by the opinion rendered by the Supreme Court of Kansas on Nov. 9, 1940, in the case of Kansas vs. Gore (152 Kans. 551; 106 Pac. (2nd) 704) and reading in part as follows:

> It is well to bear in mind at the outset that the admission of opinion evidence in prosecution for arson is governed by the same rules as are applicable in prosecution for other crimes. The general rule is, if a witness has acquired peculiar knowledge or skill, by experience, observation or practice on a subject with which the mass of mankind is not supposed to be acquainted, he may give his opinion on it. It is true there is authority for the view that generally, subject, however, to ex-

ceptions, the opinion of a witness that the fire was of incendiary origin is not admissible. Appellant cites numerous decisions supporting that view.

The substance of the appellee's position and contention was not only that the fire had been set but that it had been set shortly before it was discovered. It seems to us these contentions cannot well be separated entirely, in the instant case, in determining the question of the admissibility of the expert's opinion. The evidence disclosed appellant had gone to the shop at approximately eleven P.M., on the evening of April 28th. He was away from his lady companion between an hour and a quarter or an hour and a half. The alarm concerning this particular fire was given in response to a call at 12:58 A.M., April 29th. Appellant was seen in a cafe just across the street from his shop ten or fifteen minutes prior to the alarm concerning this fire. He returned to his car ten or fifteen minutes after the alarm.

It was the contention of appellee there was no outward evidence of fire in the shop at 12:34 A.M., that the fire had been in progress only a short time when the alarm was given, and that it was of incendiary origin.

When an expert witness, Holder, arrived, the pile in the middle of the floor had already settled, to some extent, by reason of the fact the fabrics at the bottom of the pile had been burned. He stated the fire burned from the bottom up. There was no objection to that opinion. The record discloses the witness examined the burned fabrics, their location in the pile, the unique and unusual arrangement of fast-burning and slow-burning fabrics, and other materials. He named and described the fabrics which consisted of fast-burning and those which consisted of slow-burning contents. He examined the light weight dresses on the hangers which, in his opinion, were scorched from above by the heat as it descended from the top of the balcony. He also named the clothing which was in part, slow-burning, and in part, fast-burning. The ability to analyze the texture of fabrics and to state the quick or slow effect of heat upon them was definitely a matter of professional knowledge. The unique manner in which these various fabrics were arranged in the pile, in all probability, suggested far more to this experienced fireman, whose business it was to search out the cause of fires, than it did to the ordinary layman. Was his knowledge, his inference or opinion, based upon facts in evidence, and his reasons for his opinion as to the cause of the fire, to be withheld from the seekers of the truth, the triers of the fact? Could the reasons for his opinion, in addition to the mere explanation of what he found, afford assistance to the jury in determining the issue before them, and if so were they competent?

Appellant urges the facts were so simple that the opinion or inference of an expert was unnecessary and that the jury should have been permitted to draw its own conclusion on the question of incendiary origin. It was permitted to reach its own conclusions. The jury was not obliged to accept the opinion of the witness. It was instructed it had to reach its own conclusion. Was the jury prejudiced by the opinion of the witness? If it is true, that from a mere statement or description of the conditions found by the expert, it was clear that the fire had been set then it is a bit difficult to see just how the opinion of the witness, if incompetent, resulted in prejudicing the substantial rights of the appellant.

PHYSICAL EVIDENCE

Physical evidence is any clue, trace, impression, or thing so connected with the case as to throw some light upon it. Usually such evidence is mute, requiring the facilities of a scientific laboratory, the techniques used by laboratory technicians, and the testimony of such experts before it is of much value.

Arson investigators should secure qualified aid in any case in which expert testimony may be developed as a result of the analysis of physical evidence. Evidence of top value has been ruined by amateur technicians, by men who could not qualify as experts to testify as to their findings upon trial because of insufficient training or experience in the field concerned.

Today, skilled aid is readily available. Large city and state police units have well-equipped laboratories and are happy to cooperate. On a national basis the fine laboratory of the F.B.I. is always willing to aid qualified law enforcement agencies in cases such as arson.

All that is expected of the investigator is a knowledge of what the technicians in a properly equipped laboratory can do, and the proper manner of handling and forwarding evidence so that its value is not lessened or destroyed entirely before arrival at the laboratory.

If the investigator is not thoroughly trained in the techniques of removing latent fingerprints, making casts and molds, or the recovery of burned paper fragments, he should merely preserve the scene intact until the arrival of the local "i.d." officer or other qualified personnel.

Evidence should be handled and packaged so that it will reach the laboratory *in its original state*. Any contamination by contact with foreign material, breakage, or spoilage must be avoided. Clean wrapping paper and boxes should be used for the transmittal of evidence. Wooden boxes are excellent because articles of evidence can be cleated in place.

Where volatile substances are suspected, however, paper or boxes are not suited to the preservation of the evidence. Articles suspected of containing volatile materials must be placed in large metal or glass air-tight containers capable of being sealed. Such containers must be clean. When fluids are found in containers at a fire scene, or an apparently empty container is found, the container must be promptly sealed.

In this connection many investigators have found it practicable to carry in the rear trunk of their car a "nest" of metal containers—each so graduated in size that the smaller one fits snugly into the next larger one—so that he has on hand at all times, ready for use, at least six such containers which take up no more space than an ordinary oil can.

It is also well for police investigators and fire marshals to have readily available a supply of evidence forms—such as labels, tags, cards, or stickers—which can be easily and securely affixed to each item of physical evidence that is to be retained. Such forms should be captioned and contain spaces for the insertion of all pertinent details relating to the evidence, such as date, time, location, name and number of case, department concerned, who found evidence, where found, names of witnesses or commanding officer, signature of person who packaged evidence, etc.

The forwarding of articles of evidence should be by the shortest, safest, and quickest route. The person finding the evidence should be the one to mark and package it. The same individual should deliver it or ship the package, pick it up when the analysis is completed, and store it in a safe place until necessary to produce it in court.

Physical evidence, in order to be admitted, must be accounted for from the time of finding until presented in court. It must be under the control of the witness during this period. It may be placed in a police property clerk's custody or sent to a laboratory, but the fact that such units preserve the control over the evidence prevents any break in the chain of possession. For this purpose a record of all physical evidence should be kept in the investigator's notebook as to when it was out of his direct control and places to which shipped or where stored.

The witness must be able to testify: "This is the evidence I found; this is the evidence I sent to the laboratory; this is the evidence returned by them; and this is the evidence I've safeguarded until now."

A letter of transmittal is enclosed with the evidence forwarded to a laboratory. In such missive the investigator should note that arson is suspected and give a brief outline of the case. The name of the occupant of the premises should be listed as well as the suspect, if any, or the prisoner if an arrest has been made. The evidence is then described, the place found noted, and a brief statement made as to what is being sought through the examination of this evidence. A note should also be made of the type of examination desired, but this is not exclusive because the nature of the evidence may permit other tests.

Time is of the essence when volatile substances are concerned. Whether or not the lab technicians can extract volatiles from the articles of evidence forwarded to them depends upon the time that has elapsed between the fire and the recovery *and sealing* of the evidence. A portable ultraviolet light is useful in searching for evidence of volatile inflammable substances at a fire scene, because these substances fluoresce when irradiated by such light.

When distillation processing to extract suspected volatiles from fire debris is sought, the investigator should be certain to send as much of the evidence as possible. It is far better to send a whole rug rather than a small piece, a half a door rather than a small panel from it, and thus give the lab technician sufficient material for his tests.

In a Coronado, California, fire the remnants of a rug smelling strongly of gasoline were recovered two days after the fire, immediately sealed in an air-tight container, and forwarded to a laboratory. Twelve cubic centimeters of volatile liquids were extracted and identified as gasoline.

This distillation process to recover volatiles will "squeeze out" over 90 per cent of volatile material in the range of gasoline and benzene and close to 70 per cent of the higher boiling substances in the range of kerosene and fuel oil. Comparison tests will frequently identify the substances recovered as being similar to samples submitted for comparison.

Lloyd M. Shupe, Police Chemist of the Columbus, Ohio,

Police Department covered this point in a lecture presented at the Purdue Arson Seminar in 1949 when he related this incident:

> In a recent arson case the squad brought me some rags and some wood which they said they thought were soaked in kerosene together with five samples of kerosene from different stations in the neighborhood. They asked me if there was kerosene in the wood and if so, if I could tell them which one of the stations it came from.
>
> I was able to extract some oil from the wood and examination of the specific gravity and refractive index showed it to be the same as the sample of kerosene submitted from a Shell Service Station in the neighborhood. One of the attendants at the station remembered selling the suspect a five-gallon can of kerosene a few days before and when confronted with this evidence the suspect confessed his guilt.

Tool marks are sometimes encountered in an arson case and can be identified when sufficient identifying characteristics are present in the impression, and a suspect tool has been located. Even without a suspect tool the lab technician can usually inform the investigator as to the exact tool making the mark. Knives, planes, hammers, screwdrivers, wrenches, bolt-cutters, pliers, and like tools all leave their marks and when found within the control of a suspect at least call for an explanation.

Soil from the scene of a fire when compared with soil lumps found in the insteps of a suspect's shoes placed him at the scene of a fire. . . . A small shapeless fragment of pipe recovered from an explosion scene and subjected to a metallurgical examination was found to be identical with samples of one-inch pipe taken from a large piece of such pipe in the basement of a suspect's home. . . . The restoration of writing obliterated when a fraud fire suspect "doctored" his books led to the discovery of a motive for the

fire and eventually to the conviction of the fire-setter. . . .
Tire impressions and footprints, and like clues and traces,
all aid in placing the suspect at the scene.

In a criminal prosecution for arson the "people" must
prove their case beyond a reasonable doubt. Therefore the
investigator must always be alert for physical evidence and
be diligent in developing the expert testimony which must
accompany it in court so that it will have the necessary
effect upon the court and jury.

CHAPTER TWELVE

PREPARATION OF THE CASE

MANY investigators think that a case is to be prepared only after an arrest and shortly before trial. While it is true that some final preparation may be necessary just before trial, it is equally true that the preparation of a case starts when the investigator receives the assignment initially.

The preparation of a case for trial is similar to building a brick wall. The poured concrete base or "footing" for the wall can be likened to the exclusion of accidental causes and the determination of a fire's incendiary origin. Thus the "footing" or base for the entire case is established as the first step in its preparation. The search of the scene and the development of the case along the basic lines of motive and opportunity can be likened to the bricklayer setting the corners of his wall in order that he may stretch a cord or line from corner to corner to align each brick properly.

Once the fire scene search has revealed physical evidence, or motive and opportunity have been fully determined, or both, then the investigator can line up the remainder of his case. Just as the brick-layer's line guides his work, the development of the basic lines of inquiry guides an arson investigator.

When an investigation follows an orderly plan, a case is prepared as the investigation progresses. In this manner, any gaps that appear toward the final stages are readily visible and can be easily "bricked-up."

ORDER AND CONTINUITY

When an investigation has order it has continuity, and conversely, if the pattern of the investigation moves smoothly along, it has continuity and, necessarily, good order. In the field of criminal investigation, of which arson investigation is a part, order and continuity are secured by what is known as the six classic queries of the investigator: when, where, who, what, how, and why?

An idea of the importance of these queries can be gleaned from the fact that they are also the basic queries of reporters. Each day hundreds of reporters use this series of questions as a guide when gathering facts for their newspapers. In the chapter concerning interviews and interrogations it will be noted that these six queries serve to guide the investigator when questioning fire personnel, the insured, and others concerned with the fire.

A glance at the above listing will show progression in orderly sequence from "when" to "why." This sequence, of course, cannot be maintained in the gathering of evidence, but it can be followed in recording the facts that have been secured. Whether these facts have been obtained through questioning, surveillances, or the analysis of physical evidence isn't of vital importance; what really matters is that such facts are marshalled with a degree of order. The tested method over the years has been to collate facts under six headings in this order:

1. *When* did it happen?
2. *Where* did it occur?
3. *Who* was concerned in it?
4. *What* happened?

5. *How* did it happen?
6. *Why* did it occur?

REPORTS

The same queries in identical order are used to guide the investigator in the preparation of his reports concerning a case. This practice not only makes the report as full and complete as the material on hand permits, but also aids in confining the report to facts. A narrative report without order often contains conclusions of the investigator. The reader of any report should be permitted to draw his own conclusions from the fact; therefore, he is entitled to a factual report—no more or no less.

Most law enforcement agencies have adopted fairly standardized report forms which they consider most desirable and their agents have been instructed in the preparation of these uniform reports. Through this system facts can be easily obtained without unnecessary reading and everyone concerned knows what can be expected in the report and where it can be found, regardless of the individual who prepared it.

The National Board of Fire Underwriters instructs its agents to head their reports with a caption containing the name of the assured, whether owner or tenant, and the place, date, and time of the fire. The instructions then call for a complete description of the building concerned in the first section of the report. This covers the "when," "where," and "who" of the six queries, and the "what," "how," and "why" follow in the remaining sections of the report.

The New York City Police Department follows standard news-gathering procedures in requiring its members to briefly state the facts in the first paragraph of a report in accordance with the six classic queries in proper sequence. The remainder of the report then elaborates on these points in whatever detail the investigation has disclosed up to the time of the report.

In the preparation of an arson report it is important that clarity and simplicity keynote its writing. The six classic queries will give a report order, but simplicity and clarity can be obtained only by correct paragraphing, short sentences, and the use of words with which the investigator is familiar.

A paragraph is a thought unit, the thought being expressed in the topic sentence of the paragraph. The other sentences of a paragraph are used to explore the thought.

A rather common fault is to write sentences of great length. Some good paragraphs are frequently squeezed into a sentence. Short sentences make a report easier to read and easier to "check" for pertinent facts.

Words sometimes play strange tricks on people, particularly unfamiliar words. Of course, there is an attraction in "fancy" words for many individuals, but the importance of being understood decidedly outweighs any need to play with words. Communication of thought and meaning is a vital factor in a report. The investigator not only has to secure the facts, but, just as importantly, he must report on his work in a manner which will inform others of these facts.

All reports should be typewritten. Today, there's no excuse for difficult-to-read longhand reports. As many copies as may be necessary should be prepared, one clear carbon copy to be kept for the case file. All reports should be single spaced with two spaces between paragraphs. A margin of at least one inch should be left on each side of the report for the marginal notes of readers.

Whenever a person's name is mentioned, regardless of his relation to a case, great care must be taken to note the complete name and to spell it correctly. Some explanation is required when a name is listed on public records or in-

surance policies with a variation in the spelling, and both
spellings should be listed.

Preliminary Reports—Most law enforcement agencies concerned with arson investigation require that a report be submitted within a reasonable time of the fire. Hence if the
fire scene search or the initial questioning of witnesses is
not completed within seventy-two hours, it is advisable to
forward a brief preliminary report briefing the facts of the
case to date and explaining the cause of the delay in the
initial investigation.

Progress Reports—At stated intervals during an investigation a report is usually required until the case is considered
"cleared" by an arrest or otherwise. Cases can certainly
gather dust unless reviewed from time to time. These
progress reports should not repeat any matter set out in
previous reports, but should contain only recently developed
matters of interest or assure the investigator's superiors that
the investigation is still active. Such reports also permit
another investigator to enter the investigation without any
lost motion.

Final Report—As mentioned earlier, most law enforcement agencies follow a fairly standardized form in reporting on the investigation of criminal cases. For instance, the
report on a suspicious fire is generally headed with the date
and the place at which the report is written, both close
to the upper right margin. Immediately below and starting at the left margin the following is typed:

From: (The investigator's name and title, if any.)
To: (Full name, unit, etc.)
Subject: Report of fire occurring at (correct time and
          date), at (correct location), occupied (or owned)
          by (full name).

The body of the report then opens about two spaces below the last line of the "Subject." This main text can be

broken up into five major sections containing as many paragraphs as may be necessary in each section. These sections
are for the guidance of the investigator in outlining his
material and are not noted in the report.

The first section should contain a brief but detailed
description of the building, the number of stories, the class
of material in its construction, type of occupancy, number
of rooms, general dimensions, and year in which built or
age expressed in years. For instance: "The fire occurred in
a one-family (or 2-family) three (3) story brick veneer
frame dwelling of six (6) rooms and bath, approximately
36 feet by 42 feet overall, and built in 1912."

The second part is the story of the fire itself. The following outline, which may serve as a "check list" when preparing reports, insures that major facts will be reported
upon:

a. Exact date and time of fire.
b. Who discovered it and the circumstances.
c. Fire units responding.
d. Details of the fire itself, point of origin, color of smoke
   and flame, intensity and direction of travel, and whether
   any separate fires.

The third part concerns evidence. First, the physical
evidence found at the fire scene, then the stories of witnesses, and finally the stressing of any evidence which may
be of use upon trial. Noted in this section would be physical evidence such as:

a. Presence of gasoline or other inflammables.
b. "Fire-traps" of any kind—candles, mechanical or electrical devices, containers for inflammables, etc.
c. Any indication that obstacles have been placed so as to
   impede the work of the firemen.

   d. Any indication that doors or windows have been left open so as to create favorable drafts.

   e. Other physical evidence of incendiary origin.

In relation to physical evidence it is important that the name of the person who discovered it be listed, together with the exact purpose it is expected to serve upon trial, and in whose custody it has been placed for safe keeping.

Information secured as the result of an interview should be summed up as follows:

   a. Time and place of interview.

   b. Name, address, telephone number, occupation, and physical description of witness.

   c. What the witness can testify to in regard to the fire or the fire-setter.

   d. Whether a written statement was taken and, if so, whether it is attached to report.

Miscellaneous evidence obtained in connection with fraud fires cannot, of course, be expected to take the same form in all cases. However, the following conditions are frequently encountered and should be reported with all necessary detail.

   a. Indication that stocks of merchandise, furnishings and fixtures or articles of sentimental value were removed from the premises prior to the fire.

   b. Observations that the closets and dresser drawers in a dwelling house contain far less clothing and personal belongings than normally could be expected in an occupancy of the type involved.

   c. Receipt of information that the officers in the corporation that has suffered instant loss were, in the past, officers of other corporations at other locations that also suffered losses from fires of undetermined or questionable origin.

The fourth section concerns the insured and what insurance if any is involved. Some agencies tend to omit this phase of a report when the loss is not substantial, but it should be included because although many fraud fires burn out without causing any substantial damage, they nevertheless constitute arson with insurance fraud as the motive.

This section should include full data on the insured's identity and pedigree, a listing of all policies, and the names and addresses of agent or broker and adjuster concerned.

Important to this section is information on the condition of the business affected and the financial status of the insured. Debts and other obligations—particularly outstanding mortgages—pending lawsuits or judgments, previous history of bankruptcy or business failure; suitability of location and adequacy of building and facilities are all important in determining motive; and whether any new or additional insurance was purchased shortly before the fire.

Of particular importance would be any significant discussion such as an inquiry as to whether insurance was "paid up" or premiums due, mention of a possible fire ("You know a fire is always possible, Heaven forbid.") or any other act or remark hinting at knowledge of a fire prior to its occurrence.

The fifth section should contain any fact not covered in previous portions of the report. Data on all suspects are noted in this section. Possibly the investigation may be nonproductive and be closed without results, but information on a suspect may be of value in some other case at a later date. When the suspect or person arrested is other than the occupant of the premises, or the insured concerned, it will be necessary to list identifying data as well as pedigree.

Copies of any statements and a confession, if secured, will be attached to the report.

In essence, a final report is a resumé of the case for the information and guidance of the prosecutor. The supervisors of all law enforcement agencies guide subordinates in their preparation of a case and check the completeness of a final report. However, it is the prosecutor who must use the investigator's report as a working outline for the preparation of his court case. The report must inform the prosecutor of the facts in the case, evidence available for court use, and the names of all witnesses together with the substance of what each may be expected to testify to upon trial.

CONFERENCES WITH PROSECUTOR

After receiving a final report a prosecutor will usually confer with the investigator concerning one or more phases of the case. Further investigation, usually resulting in a follow-up report and another conference, is standard operating procedure. The follow-up report is concerned with the leads covered in accordance with decisions reached at the first conference. Later meetings may call for still more investigative work.

Through his own inquiries and analysis of the investigator's report a prosecutor evaluates the admissibility and value of available evidence. He cannot have a lop-sided case, one in which a multitude of evidence points only to one or two of the essential elements of the crime charged, but must have adequate evidence to prove each and every essential element of the crime.

Within the framework of his law enforcement duties the investigator strives to prepare a complete and satisfactory case for the prosecutor, who in turn evaluates the investigator's work. If his evaluation shows more work is necessary, he then confers with the investigator as to the possibility of securing further evidence or other facts. In this atmosphere of cooperation between law enforcement agencies the case is prepared for presentation in court.

REQUESTS FOR INFORMATION

Investigators must develop their private directory of persons concerned with various agencies possessing information which may be useful in their work. Whenever a request for information is answered, the investigator should make an entry in his address book of the name of the person signing the report containing the desired information. Later requests to the same agency can be directed to such individuals rather than the vague "Dear Sir" or, on telephonic contact, the particular individual can be asked for.

Requests for information must be specific. Ask for exactly what is desired, describing it in some detail. All the available descriptive data as to identity and pedigree should be listed. If the request is to an insurance company for "loss" information on previous fires, the investigator must be certain to list the full names and addresses of all close relatives and business associates of the suspect, as well as the person himself.

A prompt thank-you note not only acknowledges receipt of the information, but also lays the groundwork for future cooperation. Telephone calls and personal visits are frequently made to expedite this securing of information and contacts made over the telephone or upon a visit can be further developed by a brief note thanking the individual concerned for his courtesy and cooperation. This may sound time-consuming and appear to be a lot of unnecessary work —and even a bit "corny"—but people like to be thanked, even for the performance of routine tasks. Next time the desired information may be forwarded a bit faster, or a more thorough search made of the records.

Investigators of crimes other than arson can frequently use "stools" and informers to break a case. The nature of arson, unless a torch is employed or several persons are concerned in a conspiracy, is such that no one is in a position to "give up" a fire-setter. Therefore the usual sources of information are commercial or governmental sources. Since the old adage "an investigator is only as good as his sources of information" has great merit, it is wise to cultivate all possible sources.

THE INVESTIGATOR AS A WITNESS

Most investigators make poor witnesses. Knowing too much about the case, they frequently inject extraneous matter into their testimony. A marked impatience is sometimes evident, an attitude never known for its tendency to make friends. The investigator is certain of the defendant's guilt and cannot see why the trial is being dragged out, why he is being asked so many apparently trivial questions.

It's well to review some of the principles of courtroom demeanor for any investigator. No witness has any right to courteous treatment unless he is respectful in his treatment of others. The presiding justice is addressed as "Your Honor," defense counsel termed the "attorney for the defense," and the prisoner referred to as the "defendant."

Friendly relations are frequently strained by the defense counsel. He may bait the investigator for the purpose of making him angry, getting him rattled in order to cloud his ability to think clearly. The actions of some attorneys wouldn't be tolerated in a third-rate bar. The person to whom they addressed their remarks would either take a punch at them or the owner would eject them for making too much noise. Insinuations or even direct accusations of poor eyesight, poor memory, or a malicious intent to "frame" their client ("an innocent man") are not uncommon. The only reaction permitted a witness is an appeal to the court. Under no circumstances should the investigator become angry or even give the appearance of anger.

Regardless of the tactics of defense counsel, the witness should take his time before answering any question, thinking out his answer before he opens his mouth. This doesn't mean that an answer can be delayed for any lengthy period, but it does mean that no court requires a witness to snap out his answers. If the prosecutor raises an objection, the answer is held in abeyance until the court rules on the question or the line of questioning being developed.

Possibly the most important point for the investigator to remember is that a question cannot be answered unless it is thoroughly understood. Do not attempt to answer any question if it is not clear to you. Witnesses have the right to request that the question be repeated or rephrased until they understand it.

The demand for "Yes" or "No" answers confuses many investigators. Of course, the ideal answer to a question is a direct affirmative or a direct negative, but many questions require some qualification in their responses. Defense counsel may shout his demand for an unqualified "Yes" or "No" answer, but if the truth of the matter requires qualification then the answer should be qualified.

Another weapon in the defense attorney's arsenal is the "possible" question. It may be along the lines of a possibility existing as to the accidental origin of the fire. "Isn't it *possible* that this fire could have been of accidental origin?" The answer, naturally, is negative, "No, it isn't possible."

After all, the exclusion of accidental origin plus the evidence of incendiarism is the basis of the arson case. Yet many attorneys secure a hesitant admission from some investigators that "anything is possible, but . . ." And then the big "but" is whether the prosecutor can repair the damaging effect of such an admission. What the investigator must remember in such instances is that guilt must be proved beyond a reasonable doubt, and if there is any "possibility" conceded the defense by an important witness, such as an investigator, then a reasonable doubt may have been created.

Questions should be answered in a firm tone, with some volume. Too low a voice or too much volume annoys all concerned in the trial. Be certain that answers are not directed solely to the questioner or the judge, but answered in such a fashion that all will hear.

It may seem basic to remind any investigator of his appearance—to be neat and clean, not to slouch in the witness chair, or chew gum, or exhibit any other nervous mannerisms. A witness's appearance very frequently carries as much weight as his testimony.

Lastly, and possibly the one thing that can do more to ruin the value of an investigator's testimony, is an apparent desire to "hang" the defendant. This is usually most evident in the giving of unsolicited testimony, but it may also be revealed in the manner of answering questions. The attitude most juries rightfully expect from an investigator can be summed up in the words of one experienced police officer: "I bring them in here and I bring in the evidence I've found; whether it is sufficient for a conviction is up to the court. I've no concern in it."

ANALYSIS AFTER TRIAL

As soon as possible after the trial an investigator should prepare a report for his file exploring the court's determination of the case. Just what evidence seemed to have the most weight in determining the guilt or innocence of the defendant.

This critique, as it might be termed, is all-important to any investigator, for it is a searching analysis of his investigative techniques. Did he or did he not secure a conviction? If not, then what evidence was lacking? What essential element of the case was affected? This form of self-criticism has a high educational value for the individual. It also is of value in the event any research is conducted by the agency employing the investigator.

The good investigator who aims for success in the arson field will not cheat in this analysis. The investigation of arson is a difficult task and failures will be met, but even a failure can be of real value if something is learned from it.

THE CASE FOLDER

A file folder is immediately prepared when an assignment is received. All correspondence is filed therein, together with the carbons of reports, interviews, laboratory reports, etc. Memos of telephone calls or interviews become part of this file. This is a permanent file and such material should be attached to the folder with one of the patented type fasteners unless the folder is of the envelope type.

Wire or tape recordings or movie film will be stored in a suitable cabinet or vault, but notation of its existence, summary of contents, and its whereabouts will be prepared and placed in the case file.

Any data relating to the sentencing of the defendant or his appeals in the case will also be written up and placed in the file. Notification of release from prison, re-arrest, or death should also be entered either in this file or in a file concerned with offenders.

Cross-references to any other case files should be marked plainly upon the outside of the case file folder as well as in the card-index file.

Most agencies close out a case when final disposition of it has been made by the courts or negative results have been obtained after a thorough investigation. Case files are then marked "Closed" and transferred from what might be termed the "Active" file.

"ARSON SUSPECT" FILE

A permanent record on every person who has been investigated as an arson suspect should be maintained in a card index file, regardless of the disposition of the case. This "arson suspect" file should be utilized on every possible occasion. Many of the large investigative agencies which cover wide areas have found it highly advantageous to establish a geographical location card file. This file is cross-indexed and divided into states, counties, cities, etc., and it is also co-ordinated with the regular investigative files and the arson suspect files. It is particularly valuable in pin-pointing a series of fires, such as those set by a pyromaniac or those which indicate the concentrated activities of an arson ring.

CHAPTER THIRTEEN

ARSON RINGS

A GROUP of persons engaged in burglary and robbery is classed as a "mob" or a "gang." They are a closely knit group who plan their crimes and then go out and commit them with greater or lesser frequency, depending upon the needs of the individual members of the mob or the dictates of the boss.

When two or more people band together to commit arson with some frequency, such groups are termed arson "rings" rather than "mobs" or "gangs," because they lack the cohesiveness of a mob of burglars or a gang of robbers. Another factor setting arson rings apart from other groups of criminals is the fact that to profit from arson they must first secure "customers"—individuals who have insurance and want fires—while other criminals can rob or steal whenever they please.

Arson rings are directly concerned with dishonest business men, persons who want a fire as a tool to defraud an insurance company. They were not discussed at length in the chapter on fraud fires because the continuing activity of arson rings permit the use of investigative techniques not usually productive of any results when used in cases involving individual arsonists.

Arson rings have their "boom" years during periods of

depression. "Business" fires increase during this period and the services of a torch are eagerly sought.

THE TORCH

The torch is not the person primarily responsible for the activity of an arson ring. His position in the ring is very much akin to that of a trigger-man in a murder-for-pay mob such as Brooklyn's notorious Murder, Inc. The torch and the trigger-man are the executioners, not the strategists or the planners. The torch is the individual who actually sets the fire, who decides what time and what technique are best suited to the premises.

Each arson ring must necessarily have a torch, but the torch himself may have little or no contact with his customers, the dishonest business men. In well-organized arson rings the torch has only a secondary position; contacts with customers are invariably handled by other members of the ring.

Only in poorly organized arson rings does the business revolve around the torch himself. In such cases a number of people know of a torch, know his prices, and are also aware that he'll pay them a commission on all "business" which they secure for him. These individuals act as "salesmen" for the torch, and in so doing establish a loosely organized arson ring with the torch as the top man.

Because he is actually at the scene of the fires the torch runs the greatest risk of being apprehended by firemen, fire marshals, or police officers. And when it is known that a ring is operating because of a developing pattern of business fires, it is the torch who is usually "given up" by a "stool," or whose identity is discovered by an "undercover" man.

The torch is fully aware of the risk. He realizes that of all the arson ring he is in the most vulnerable position and may be apprehended at any time. However, a torch is always prepared for apprehension. He'll bargain for a lesser sentence by cold-bloodedly giving up his associates in crime.

All members of an arson ring realize the likelihood of their torch turning state's witness. An employee of one of the top men convicted in the Brooklyn Arson Ring case because of the testimony of Sammy the Torch reminded his employer of this fact long before Sammy's arrest; "You know he (the torch) is a dangerous man to have around—some day he will get you fellows into trouble."

"I don't have to worry about that. I have got him out of plenty of trouble before," his employer responded. "You don't have to worry about him, he's 100 per cent. If he ever gets caught he will never squeal on anybody."

To understand why a torch is willing to promptly identify his former associates in arson and testify against them in return for some mitigation of his punishment it is necessary to understand the inherent callousness of a torch—to understand that he is a potential murderer whose mental equipment still flashes a "Go" signal despite the thought of sleeping men, women, and children burning to death as the result of his fire-setting; and to understand that he does not face the thought of the possible death of some unfortunates just once, but that this possibility is faced time and time again, week in and week out.

Two fairly recent cases illustrate the torch's utter lack of normal feelings of horror and pity over the victims —particularly children—of fires. The first case involved several small children. It was only the intervention of Providence and good luck on the part of the firemen that saved their lives. A hard-hitting investigation soon turned up the fire-setters as two professional torches who had participated in the setting of many fires. The initial interrogation developed the fact that both men *knew that several small children lived in the building they planned to set on fire.* When questioned as to why they would jeopardize the lives of these children, the torches shrugged and scoffed at the possibility of the children being hurt. "What have they fathers and mothers for?" one asked, while the other seemed satisfied to mumble defensively, "They could take care of themselves."

In the second case the torch of the Brooklyn Arson Ring was being questioned at the trial of one of his former accomplices and inadvertently revealed the callous, cold-blooded manner in which he approached his fire-setting assignments. The great number of his fires didn't seem to matter, nor did the fact that many of them were set in the nighttime seem to bother this man.

It was during cross-examination by the defense counsel that this testimony was developed:

Q. How many times have you pleaded guilty?
A. Twice.
Q. For what crimes?
A. One in 13th Ave.
Q. A fire?
A. Yes, sir.
Q. What was the crime, arson one or two?
A. Arson one. (Note: Arson one—first degree—involves a dwelling in which there is at the time of the fire a human being; or any building wherein, *to the knowledge of the offender at the time of the fire-setting*, there is a human being.)
Q. How many fires did you set in New York County?
A. About forty-five.
Q. How many fires did you set in Queens County?
A. About three or four.
Q. How many in Brooklyn?
A. I set about forty-five, I meant Brooklyn and New York.
Q. What was the date of the first fire you set?
A. I do not remember.
Q. How many years ago?
A. About two years ago.
Q. You have set over fifty fires, haven't you?

A. Around that.

Q. All kinds of houses and stores?

A. Yes, sir.

Q. Some of these fires were set at night?

A. They were.

Q. Most of them at night?

A. No, sir, not almost all.

Q. And you did it because you were paid?

A. Yes, sir.

Q. In other words, you are a professional fire-bug?

A. Whatever you may call it.

THE "BRAINS"

The "brains" or leader of a well-organized arson ring may be from any walk of life and of either sex. The head of an arson ring in Chicago was a grandmother. Among the hundreds of fires set by this ring was one in which a crippled child was so badly burned that he died. This ring was broken up by the apprehension of two torches in the act of setting fire to a printing plant. Confessing shortly after their arrest, these two men involved the grandmother and eventually led to the return of sixty indictments resulting in over twenty convictions.

Another case involved an attorney as the brains of a ring that not only preyed upon insurance companies but that also defied law enforcement authorities for months. Working through several salesmen and intermediaries, a chain of command involving his son, this master criminal never had any actual contact with an insured concerning a fire. The authorities broke this ring by first convicting what might be termed the advance salesman—his duty was to find and bring to the attention of others in the ring any prospects who might be persuaded to have fires. Then several of the insureds who had hired the services of the ring were picked up, placed on trial, and also convicted. All of a sudden the dam of silence broke and evidence sufficient to convict the "brains," his son, and the torch of the ring was soon secured.

In one case in Pennsylvania an insurance agent was convicted of a conspiracy to commit a crime along with several of his associates in a loosely organized arson ring. This man had long been suspected of supplying insurance and counseling policy-holders to have fires, but evidence of arson was difficult to secure. Another "insurance man," unlicensed but working on commission for a legitimate agent, sold a great deal of insurance because he "guaranteed a fire with every policy."

During the depression of 1930 to 1935, corrupt public adjusters were frequently found at the head of arson rings. A public adjuster is an individual who represents an insured in pressing his claim against an insurance company for a loss suffered by the insured. For his services the public adjuster is paid a percentage of the money the insured collects from the insurance company. The fee is generally 10 per cent. The insurance company pays the public adjuster, who in turn deducts his percentage and then pays the insured.

The public adjuster operates in a crowded, highly competitive field. There are a great number of them, several usually grouping together into a partnership, all pooling their resources of friends and "connections" to secure "losses"—claims upon insurance companies resulting from losses sustained as a result of damage incident to a fire.

Public adjusters solicit business immediately after a fire. For instance, each day at 6:00 A.M. a list of fires for the previous day is posted in the Fire Patrol offices in New York City as reported by the Fire Department. Before the normal business world sits down to their desks the adjusters are waiting outside the homes and offices of an insured whose home or place of business was burned out the previous night.

A few of the more enterprising seek information about fires before they occur. Initial contacts with torches soon lead to the development by the adjuster of customers who might want fires and hence increased business for the torch. Naturally, the public adjuster wants all of a torch's "business"—wants to handle each "loss"—and soon some kind of partnership is established. (The details of an arson ring headed by a public adjuster will be set forth later in this chapter.)

SALESMEN AND INTERMEDIARIES

The salesmen of an arson ring sell a service—the setting of fires. Usually their customers come to them, seeking them out, but sometimes the field men of an arson ring seek out prospective customers and offer the services of their ring and, like any salesman, picture the advantages of a "good fire" in glowing terms.

An arson ring depends almost solely upon word of mouth advertising—one satisfied customer telling another. Once an insured enters into a conspiracy to set a fire with an arson ring, every device at the command of members of the ring is brought into play to utilize the new client as a salesman: "Do any of your friends want fires? . . . We did a good job for you, now try to help us. We'll do a good job for your friends. . . . You can make a little money with us, and no risks. Just tell us who might want a fire. We'll do the rest, and pay you a commission. . . . If it's a friend you can trust, tell him to call me up. I'll help him out if he wants a fire."

These "satisfied customers" become the intermediaries of an arson ring, really salesmen on a commission basis. They are the initial contact between the business man who wants a fire and the arson ring. Sometimes an intermediary never had an incendiary fire of his own, but is acquainted with the operations of the ring through friendship with a ring

member or one of its customers. Sometimes he may be a
supposedly reputable citizen. In Nebraska the president of
a large lumber company, well thought of in his home city,
hired an arson ring to set two fires in the yards of his firm.
The intermediary in this case was one of the top five men
in the city.

A case that is indicative of the character of these salesmen
and intermediaries concerned a large furniture concern.
Agents of the arson ring secured information concerning the
financial condition of the company. The proprietors were
immediately contacted but apparently resisted the suggestion that they have a "business" fire. Negotiations covered a
considerable period of time but were finally successful—a
disastrous fire involving the loss of many thousands of dollars resulted. However, the two members of the arson ring
who were most active in overcoming objections to the above
fire were picked up for violations of other laws and bargained with authorities shortly after their arrest.

Among their former associates against whom they informed were the proprietors of the furniture store, whose
reluctance to have a fire was overcome by their assurances:
"Nothing to it, leave it to us."

Investigators must remember that a salesman or intermediary for an arson ring may be found among the most reputable groups of citizens in any city. Investigators need not
drop a line of investigation merely because it points to a
man with a good reputation and an apparently blameless
record.

"CUSTOMERS"

The same line of reasoning is also true in regard to the
customers of an arson ring. They may be any business men
in any field whatsoever. There is even one case on record
of a minister hiring members of an arson ring to burn

Ignition device set by a professional torch in the kitchen of an apartment in Port Richmond, Staten Island.

Close-up shows inflammable materials and method of ignition. It was intended that cigarette burn down, ignite matches, burn toilet paper, and thus set off kerosene in containers. This is a fairly common method because of the mistaken belief that all the materials will burn and thus leave no trace of arson, but the metal containers holding the kerosene are not destroyed, and lab analysis may reveal traces of kerosene.

Three of four simple ignition devices served to burn down three New York bungalows while the owner was absent. The fourth one (*pictured above*) failed to burn and clearly pointed to arson.

down an ancient church in order to collect the insurance to build a new one.

Aside from the torch, the ideal source of information about an arson ring is one of its customers. Prosecutors are usually alert to this fact, because they can readily promise immunity to an insured in return for his testimony about the ring, whereas public policy does not favor complete immunity for a callous criminal such as the torch.

Testifying under immunity, the customer spells out the operation of each member of the ring known to him. Such members can be picked up and evidence secured sufficient for conviction in this specific case. This was the technique which secured the break in the arson ring headed by the attorney and his son, just described under the section dealing with the "brains" of a ring.

AN ARSON RING IN ACTION

Possibly the greatest challenge to any arson investigator will occur when he is confronted with a series of fires set by an organized ring of arsonists. Knowledge of their organization, their standard operating procedure, and the type of men and women who make up the ring will be invaluable to the investigator when he seeks to solve such crimes. Only by some study of the ramifications of such rings can an investigator be equipped to cope with them effectively.

The case of Sammy the Torch and his public adjuster bosses which was investigated and tried during the depression era is indicative of the manner in which arson rings operate when the economic climate is favorable. The ring was headed by a firm of public adjusters. Two of the top men were convicted of charges arising out of the operation of this ring, but one won a reversal on appeal because of a technicality relating to a point of law. In any event, the following picture of an arson ring's operation was developed through the testimony of several members of the ring who seized the opportunity of saving themselves from long terms in prison by aiding in sending their co-conspirators to jail. Their testimony is a graphic illustration of an arson ring in action.

Sammy had been setting fires for himself, a few relatives, and a customer or two before he came to the attention of the adjusters. A meeting was arranged and one of the public adjusters told Sammy: "I know all about it; I should like you to do work for my office. If you have any fires, turn them over to me; if I have any fire trade, I'll turn them over to you."

Sammy asked his new friend what he meant. The adjuster explained: "You know, we are in the business. Certain agents come around our office and ask us if somebody wants fires and then I recommend you; I will give you all the business." He then added something to the effect that he expected Sammy to turn over his own fires to him but would pay a commission on them.

Later a salaried employee who worked for the public adjusting firm testified that his boss told him in the presence of another member of the firm: "Listen, Jack, if you know anybody that wants to make a fire in their building we have the proper man to do that kind of work."

Another witness, a former telephone operator for the adjustment firm, testified that she knew Sammy the Torch as "Sam," that he visited the office quite frequently, "*Sometimes twice a day*," and that she kept his telephone number listed under "Sam" in a book containing names and telephone number of persons frequently called. She also testified that she had called Sammy the Torch several times at the request of her employers, who merely asked her to call "Sam."

The first known fire involving this ring was set for a woman "client." An individual we will call Sol Solomon, formerly in partnership with Sammy the Torch in a legitimate business, was the contact man. Sol testified that one of the public adjusters called him in and said he'd been looking for either Sammy or himself. The adjuster then gave Sol an address and told him, "See a woman by the name of Rose, she wants a fire made." Sol visited Rose and presented the business card of the public adjuster. He left with a check for $200 and a "contract." He promptly reported back to the adjuster's office and asked him to cash the check, but he was instructed to leave it. Sol made several attempts to secure the cash, but finally was told that the check had been given to Sammy.

Apparently Sammy had made a satisfied customer of Rose because the ring's next recorded fire resulted from her efforts. A woman storekeeper testified that she had conducted a dairy which Sammy burned out for her after Rose arranged a meeting. She told the court that Rose called at her home and talked with her. She told Rose that business was bad in the dairy and Rose said she would "fix her up." At the end of the conversation Rose called someone on the telephone. Whoever she talked to seemed satisfied with a few descriptive details of the storekeeper and her business, because Rose gave the woman one of the business cards of the public adjusting firm with the name Rose written on it and directed her to go to the address listed on the card and ask for a certain partner.

This woman went to the office as directed and talked to this man. He said he knew all about it and what she wanted and wrote her first name, "Bertha," upon one of his cards and put it in his pocket. He then told her he'd send over a dark man with glasses and she'd know it was the right man because he'd give her the card with her name on it. (Sammy was dark and wore glasses.)

The next day Sammy called at Bertha's home, gave her the card, and told her that the public adjuster had sent him over to make a fire for her. After some bargaining the price of $200 was agreed upon and $50 in cash was handed over as a down-payment.

On the evening of the fire Sammy arrived at the store with a candle and a package of celluloid scraps, went into the rear of the store while his "customer" waited in the front section, set his lighted candle close to the celluloid, and then helped Bertha lock up the store for the night. The two then went around the corner to her home where the woman paid Sammy the remaining $150.

She too apparently went on the satisfied customer list because the fire was a "good" one, the company paying a loss of $1937.

The next fire concerned a physician who insisted on the stand that one of the partners in the adjusting firm "sold" him the idea of a fraud fire, testifying as follows:

Q. Did you ever have any conversation with the defendant concerning fires?

A. I came up to his office from time to time, during the time I knew him . . . he took me into his confidence, more or less, and he told me that no fire, regardless of how it is made, could be a perfect fire unless it has been by a so-called professional . . . two weeks prior to the time my residence was burned, we got to talking about policies and fires again, and he asked me how much insurance I carried. I said I had a six-thousand-dollar policy and my father had a four-thousand one.

Q. What was your father's insurance?

A. My father carries a policy for his own furniture . . . I had my own furniture besides my equipment, which I had insured . . . About two weeks before the fire took place we discussed my policy. He said, "Here is a chance for you to make a little money, I know you have not got an awful lot of money, and I suppose a couple of thousand dollars would help you considerably." Well, it came as a shock to me at the time; I no more dreamed of any such idea than I would about the man in the moon at the present time . . . he harped on it for two weeks before the fire. About three or four times he said, "You are very foolish if you don't do something like that. It is being done every day in the week. People are making money on it."

Q. Did he at any time tell you whether or not he had a firebug?

A. He told me they had. The way he expressed it, he said, "It is impossible to set a fire to any building without a firebug, because you would not be able to really burn down the place before the fire engines came, and you have got to have firebugs." He said, "Every adjuster has his own firebug."

Q. Coming again to the proposed firing of your place, when did he start talking about that?

A. Two weeks prior . . . and then he told me about three or four times before . . . four days before the fire—four days before the fire he said, "Well, have you made up your mind?" Four days before the fire . . . I decided I would have the fire performed.

Q. In the meantime, did you meet a person named Sam?

A. That was four days before the fire I met him for the first time.

Q. Where did you meet him?

A. In the adjuster's office, on Court St.

Q. Who introduced you?

A. The adjuster . . . When I had acquiesced to having the building set on fire, he said, "All right, I will introduce you to a man who is going to set your building on fire." He introduced me, he said, "Sam, I want you to meet the Doctor. Go on over to his office. I want you to look around and see what you can do for him."

Q. Was there any conversation then concerning the price, at that time?

A. Yes; just this: When I spoke to the adjuster at first, he said, "This man is charging an awful lot to set buildings on fire, but being as I know you so well," he said, "I am going to see I get the best possible break for you." So he said, "In your particular case a fire they should charge at least $1000 for, I am going to have this done for about $200 for your sake." I said, "All right, it is perfectly satisfactory with me."

Q. Coming back to when Sam looked over your place, did you go back to the public adjuster again?

A. I came back the following day and he told me to bring my policies.

Q. This was all before the fire?

A. Yes, sir. I brought my policies.

Since everything was apparently in order—Sammy the Torch had looked over the site of his proposed fire, the price had been arranged, and the crooked adjuster had the policies—the fire was set as planned and a good settlement secured for the Doctor.

Another member of the ring previously convicted of first degree arson and awaiting sentence in Raymond Street Jail was then called as a witness. He was the unlicensed insurance broker who was alleged to have solicited business with the novel guarantee of "a fire with every policy."

Q. Do you know this defendant?

A. I do.

Q. Did you see his partner and have a talk with him?

A. I did.

Q. As a result of something the partner said to you, did you go somewhere?

A. Yes, sir. I went to a certain doctor's residence.

Q. And there was a fire there?

A. Yes, sir.

Q. Did you see the defendant there?

A. I did . . . I was introduced to a fellow named Sam, which the partner said I should meet him there . . . I asked the defendant, "Is this the man that your partner told me I shall meet here—Sam—that had this fire made here?" He said, "Well, that is the man, I suppose." He answered me in this kind of a way—that this is Sam, this is the one that made the job, he is the man who is the mechanic."

After some questioning it was brought out that the insurance broker was interested in securing the services of Sammy the Torch for his own clients. One of the known fires concerned an insured named Brown. The questioning progressed as follows:

Q. Mrs. Brown's fire was set later?
A. Yes.
Q. You solicited the fire?
A. Yes, sir.
Q. And you were paid $200?
A. Sammy got $200, he gave me $50.
Q. You were the broker?
A. Yes, sir.
Q. In arranging between Sammy and Mrs. Brown?
A. Yes, sir.

In all a total of twenty-six individuals were brought to justice as a result of their participation in the activities of this ring whose moving force was a firm of supposedly reputable businessmen, aided and abetted by such "satisfied customers" as Rose acting as intermediaries and such men as the crooked broker acting as salesmen.

The pattern seldom changes.

FAMILY GROUPS

Many torches initiate their fire-setting careers by a little arson for relatives. Others never progress to full-fledged arson ring operations but will continue to set fires for relatives. Sammy the Torch admitted in court that his first few fires were for relatives. In fact, an arson ring may be formed of persons closely related to one another. A ring in New York's Westchester County was found to be closely related, and another ring in Chicago was composed of five members of the same family.

A few years ago thirteen persons, both men and women, nearly all related by blood or marriage, introduced a new modus operandi in the field of arson rings. Two of them would move into a town, renting a small house on the outskirts, buying furniture on credit, securing insurance, and then setting a fire.

They would pay as little cash as possible for the furniture. Others in the gang removed the furniture from the house prior to the fire, substituting some old pieces of junk. This gang kept a truck for this purpose and sometimes used the furniture as the basis for insurance in a new location, or at other times sold it in another town.

Because of their extensive fire preparations, an elaborate plant, and several separate fires, as well as the location of their "homes" on the outskirts of towns and villages, most of the fires resulted in total destruction.

Whenever any suspicions seemed to have been aroused and pointed questions were put to them, the group would abandon their claim. They had little to lose—the rental on the house, the initial premiums, and the cash down-payment on the furniture being all they risked. Their method of operation permitted them to set fires in at least fifteen different states before being apprehended. Once alerted, however, authorities sent all thirteen to prison.

"IMPROMPTU" ARSON RINGS

An impromptu arson ring may be termed a group of two or more persons who do not normally set fires but who are banded together in other criminal activities such as burglary, buying and receiving stolen property, and like crimes, and who are willing to set a fire now and then.

An impromptu arson ring was only recently exposed in New York City. Jacob (Little Jake) Weiss and Morris (Moishe) Shapiro were both burglars. Jake Mayron was the third man in this group, hired to do the heavy work of car rying the necessary arson materials. The limited activity of this ring was curtailed almost at the outset by the alertness of several members of the New York Police Department's Safe and Loft Squad.

A "stool" reported to this police unit that two old time burglars appeared to be back in business. They were doing a great deal of riding around and consulting with strangers. These were no youngsters. Little Jake was sixty-seven, Moishe was seventy, and Jake Mayron was fifty-nine. While Mayron had no record, Moishe's record of sixteen arrests was mostly concerned with safe cracking, and Little Jake's record listed kidnaping and robbery along with burglary in an extensive "sheet" of seventeen arrests. One old-time detective had remarked, "He'd do anything for a dollar." Turning to arson seemed to be in character for Little Jake, who seemed to be the moving force behind the entire activity.

It was Little Jake who bargained with the customer, a run-of-the-mill business man who wanted his small garment factory burned out for the insurance. It was Little Jake who took the down-payment for the job and Little Jake who hired Mayron. But it was Moishe who bungled the actual fire-setting and killed himself, Little Jake, and one of the Safe and Loft Squad's crack detectives.

One of the surviving detectives, who interrupted these criminals in their fire-setting after following them for several weeks in the belief they were planning another burglary or safe cracking, told the story at the trial of Jake Mayron and the customer, Al Keshner, for murder during the course of a felony.

"We heard them slopping gasoline around the floor," Detective Howard J. Phelan testified. "The place was saturated with gasoline. The floor and tables were wet with it."

He and his partner, John Daggett, seized Weiss and Shapiro and asked them, "Is it ready to go off?" Little Jake denied it was due to "go" but Phelan told them, "We better get out of here. This place is loaded."

"I came to on the floor," Phelan continued from the stand. "My clothes were on fire. I heard two voices screaming inside the loft. I crawled down to between the first and second floors. I saw a body hanging in the elevator shaft. I thought it was Daggett. I yelled to him, but he didn't answer."

It was a trial that highlighted the damage and death that an incendiary fire can cause—three dead and between a half a million and a million dollars' property damage.

While the jury acquitted Mayron, they found against Keshner, not recommending mercy and thus forcing a mandatory sentence of death in the electric chair. However, the sentence was commuted by Governor Dewey upon application of the District Attorney in the spring of 1953. It seemed a harsh application of New York's felony murder statute, but in the final analysis anyone who sets a fire must face the possibility of being responsible for the death of a human being.

Investigators should realize that such impromptu rings will continue to operate in the arson field if they find it more profitable then burglary or other crimes, and it is the duty of the investigator to make fire-setting as unprofitable as possible and thus, at the very least, curtail some of their operations.

KNOW YOUR LOCAL TORCHES

An arson investigator must know persons in his locality who might set fires for any reason whatsoever. Newly arrived residents with a previous history of fire-setting should be noted on a file of known torches. In one Chicago case an investigator recognized the modus operandi as that commonly employed by most of the real old-time professionals who had operated in that city many years before. Investigation showed an old-timer had recently been released from prison and had returned to his old trade.

The extreme value of such knowledge is clearly demonstrated in a case which occurred toward the end of the depression years when professional fire-setters were experiencing a slump in their "business." A torch who in years gone by had set a good many fires in New York City traveled over the river to New Jersey to set a fire for a small grocer in Newark. Apparently rusty from lack of activity, the torch was severely burned as he set the blaze. He managed to make his get-a-way but a "stool" heard of his injuries and told two New York investigators of them. An examination of fires in the New York area failed to reveal a fire with the earmarks of this professional, but when the quest was extended to outside the metropolitan area the grocery fire in Newark was discovered. An arrest was made and a confession implicating the grocer and an intermediary was secured.

SPECIAL TECHNIQUES OF INVESTIGATION

A man setting one fire for some real or imagined reason doesn't let anyone know of his act if at all possible. On the other hand an arson ring must let others know of their willingness to set fires; otherwise they'd have to go out of business.

Aside from their customers a great many individuals on what might be termed the fringe of the underworld hear of their activity and, seeking to ingratiate themselves with police or to secure pay for their information, will inform authorities or interested agencies such as the National Board of Fire Underwriters of the activities of the arson ring. This happened in the middle of the undercover investigation of the Brooklyn Arson Ring. A "stool" approached Mr. Bruce Bielaski, top man in the National Board's Arson

Department, with valuable information about two members of the ring.

Many law enforcement agencies employ undercover men who also operate in this underworld fringe, and they may obtain knowledge of arson rings in addition to other criminal activities. Only recently one undercover man prevented a fire in the Bronx by giving the fire marshal information secured during an undercover investigation of some other crime.

Another undercover technique is that of tapping wires. First the law enforcement agency concerned must secure some evidence of criminal activity other than mere suspicion and on this basis apply for a court order giving them permission to intercept telephone conversations. Intercepted phone calls permit the shaping of a picture concerning members of the ring—who they are and with whom they associate.

Surveillances of members, friends, and contacts aid in developing the full picture. These surveillances may be plants at homes or offices, or they may be mobile if sufficient investigators are available to tail the suspects.

"Roping"—the planting of an undercover man to gain the confidence of some member of the arson ring or to appear as a prospective customer—is of little value in court upon trial because it smacks of entrapment. However, it will uncover the ring.

In one case the undercover agent was "wired for sound" and conversations in which members of the arson ring described their previous fires and the extent and manner of their operations were recorded electrically. Thirty such recorded conversations were later admitted in evidence and played in open court—with devastating effect.

The information gleaned from the "stool," explored and supported by information secured through the interception of telephone messages and the surveillance of members of an arson ring, will permit the investigator to decide as to the best method of "roping." Surprisingly enough, but pinpointing the manner in which these criminal groups seek out new business, is the technique of setting out as bait what appears to be an ordinary business man in search of someone to set a "good" fire.

COOPERATION OF THE PROSECUTOR

It is an absolute necessity to secure the active cooperation of the local prosecutor as he alone can present the case to the grand jury, can secure adequate personnel, and can promise the necessary immunity or mitigation of punishment.

In fact, it is the belief of many experienced arson investigators that only with the active cooperation of prosecutors can arson rings be fully exposed. When the prosecuting attorney takes a sincere interest in arson cases, familiarizing himself with such prosecutions by actually trying them, it almost invariably happens that the difficulty of the cases and the opportunity for real service to his community appeals increasingly to the prosecutor and soon results in a marked decline in arson within his jurisdiction. Any arson ring can be apprehended and successfully prosecuted whenever special attention is given to it by a prosecutor.

CHAPTER FOURTEEN

RESPONSIBILITY FOR DETECTING ARSON

THERE has always been considerable confusion as to whether the police or fire department should bear the responsibility for detecting and investigating arson. In some cities the fire department is charged with such duties; in others the arson squad is a unit of the police department; while in still others the responsibility is so poorly delineated that either can conveniently wait for action by the other.

Human nature being what it is, the reader can understand police reaction to an arson unit of fire-fighters and the firemen's reaction to a police arson unit. "They know all about fires," the cops will say of the fire squad. "Let them catch the firebug, if they can." The firemen may not refuse to cooperate with the police arson unit, but as one police officer was told in a large Eastern city, "You're supposed to be a detective. Well, do a little detecting."

Firemen may qualify as arson investigators because they are well grounded in the techniques of fire-fighting and can readily learn the necessary rudiments of police work. They are particularly competent in determining the causes of fires and in ascertaining the point of origin. Police officers, on the other hand, may also become able arson investigators by acquiring a knowledge of the modus operandi of arsonists, some experience in determining the causes of fires, and some practice in learning how to isolate points of origin.

THE LOS ANGELES FIRE DEPARTMENT'S ARSON BUREAU

No better example of a fire department unit can be found than the precision unit of the Los Angeles Fire Department. The Arson Bureau is staffed by a captain serving as commanding officer, nine full time investigators, each holding the rank of firemen, and one stenographer. All of them are qualified under the Los Angeles civil service rules and are regularly assigned to the Fire Department. The investigators are selected from the fire service ranks on the basis of merit and qualification by the Chief Engineer of the Department.

The working chart of this unit is based on three crews of two men each performing their duties on a twenty-four-hour basis. Additional investigators are also assigned to duty from 8:00 A.M. to 5:00 P.M. daily, except Sunday. The regular team reports at 4:00 P.M. and works through their twenty-four hours until the following 4:00 P.M. When not occupied by a current investigation, they remain at Fire Department headquarters barracks subject to call. Daytime personnel fill in as required, assisting on investigations and thus gaining valuable experience.

The Bureau has a thoroughly equipped office of two rooms in the main fire department headquarters, telephone and radio service, and three two-way radio cars equipped with red lights and sirens, but not marked with any seal or insignia indicating the Fire Department. The men also work in plainclothes rather than in Fire Department uniform.

An interesting feature of this unit, and perhaps a sign of what to expect from the arson squad of the future, is the scope and authority of the unit. The Chief Engineer of the Department has assigned to it the responsibility of investigating the origin of fires within the following categories:

1. All fires in which the fire officer in charge estimates the loss to property (building or contents) to exceed $100.
2. All fires judged to be of incendiary or suspicious origin by the fire officer in charge at the scene.
3. All explosions and all serious burn cases.
4. Any fires in which juveniles are apparently involved.
5. All building fires classified as of "undetermined" origin.
6. All fires in which an investigation is requested for any reason by a fire officer or a responsible citizen.

The express purpose of the Arson Bureau is to *detect* incendiarism through the investigation of fires in the above categories, a grouping based on the experience of years. It is also the belief of responsible officers of this fine department that an increase in the number of incendiary fires detected will increase the arrests and convictions of fire-setters. This should deter potential arsonists and make a major contribution to fire prevention.

Typewritten reports are prepared in about 75 per cent of all the investigations conducted. If the investigation results in an arrest or indicates the need of a conference with the prosecutor, then a summary is prepared for the office of the district attorney, listing the available witnesses and the testimony that can be given by each witness.

Each investigator follows a case from the fire scene through to its conclusion, being responsible for the signing of the complaint, attending all court sessions, and directly assisting the district attorney during the trial.

If a report is not considered necessary, a summary of known facts is made in the Arson Bureau log and on the original fire report. Typewritten reports and this log are both reviewed daily by the Chief Engineer.

This office also maintains a confidential file of all persons involved in fires, date and time of the fire, its cause—if determined—and occupancies. A cross index system makes information readily available, whether it is being sought by name, type of occupancy, or location.

Upon arrival at the scene of a fire the investigators consult with fire personnel and examine the scene. If of incendiary or suspicious origin the investigative crew proceeds to assume complete charge, summoning the official fire department photographer for a picture record. Physical evidence is gathered, appropriately marked and retained in evidence lockers or forwarded to the Police Department's Crime Laboratory.

Prior to arrest the case is discussed with the commanding officer of the Bureau and his oral approval secured before a formal complaint is filed. This insures a thorough review of the case before an arrest is made.

These firemen-investigators carry side-arms and handcuffs by special authority of the Sheriff of Los Angeles County, but several investigators have reported they were handicapped because California law does not classify them as "peace officers" and so cloak them with special powers in regard to arrest and search procedures. The fact that these men have only the powers of a private citizen in making arrests or searches may, at times, be a decided handicap.

The Los Angeles unit and Captain William L. Wiesinger, its commander, deserve a great deal of credit for their honesty in classifying fires. Where there is no direct or indirect evidence of a definite nature as to the exact cause of the fire they classify it as "undetermined." Several times a series of fires which would have otherwise been lost in the files of the department because of hasty or haphazard classification revealed a pattern of fire-setting activity. From time to time this grouping of "undetermined" fires has lead to the uncovering of an arson ring, the arrests of several groups of juveniles, and the pin-pointing of more than one pyromaniac.

The thoroughness of the investigations made by this unit can be gleaned from the statistics of their most recent annual report. A total of 2116 investigations were made, causes determined in 1860 cases, 82 labeled as suspicious, and 174 marked "cause undetermined."

THE BUFFALO N. Y. POLICE ARSON SQUAD

On a smaller scale the city of Buffalo, N. Y., has an arson unit similar to that of Los Angeles. However, it is staffed with police officers.

The two men of this unit are both experienced police officers with many years of investigative experience in the general police field. They are both well acquainted throughout the city and have better-than-average sources of information. One of the men speaks several languages common to segments of Buffalo's population and this, too, is quite an asset.

Presently, the Arson Squad responds to all multiple alarm fires immediately, and responds on the call of the Fire Department Battalion Chief in charge at the scene when a fire is considered to be incendiary, suspicious, or of undetermined origin.

In Buffalo it is believed that the fine cooperation of the Fire Department with the police Arson Squad stems from the fact that fire officials at the scene of a fire are responsible for initially classifying all fires.

As soon as the fire is extinguished the Arson Squad takes over the premises and the scene is kept under police guard until a thorough investigation has been made, photographs taken, and evidence gathered. Any evidence amenable to laboratory analysis is processed through the Police Department Laboratory.

The squad is equipped with a radio car and adequate office space. It maintains extensive fire records by name, location, origin, occupancies, and even a classification of fires resulting from "bad housekeeping" or carelessness.

Detective Sergeant Charles Haggerty, now President of the International Association of Arson Investigators, has developed a pattern of utilization of other personnel of his department that could be put to equally advantageous use in other cities. Whenever a case involves a juvenile the cooperation of the Police Youth Bureau is secured. This not only permits extensive operation with limited personnel, but also brings expertly trained men and women into cases involving juveniles. Whenever a case involves children the Youth Bureau is promptly given the information and the fifteen police officers and four police women of this unit handle the case as a referral from the Arson Squad.

The trained men of the Arson Squad quickly complete the technical aspects of juvenile arson cases and the experts of the Youth Bureau delve into the human relations side of such cases by handling it on an offender-parent-community basis.

Close liaison is also maintained with the Fire Prevention Bureau of the Fire Department. The Battalion Chief in charge of this unit and the inspectors assigned to it work in close cooperation with the Arson Squad and have performed a great deal of valuable work in tracing the course of fires.

THE DETROIT "TEAM" SYSTEM

The arson units of both Los Angeles and Buffalo indicate that either fire or police personnel, when organized into a separate unit with a pin-pointed objective, can adequately cope with the problems of arson. The city of Detroit demonstrates that both fire and police personnel can be combined into one unit.

The Detroit Arson Squad is headed by a Police Department Inspector who maintains the Squad office in the main Fire Department headquarters adjacent to the offices of the City Fire Marshal. The clerical staff is supplied by the Fire Department, which sends copies of all incendiary fire reports to Police as well as Fire Headquarters.

"Teams" are made up of two men, a detective and a "Fire Inspector" who is sworn in as a police officer with full powers of arrest. Teams operate on a five-day week, several teams being on duty at the same time as the exigencies of the service may require. Each team is furnished with a two-way radio car and operate out of Fire Department headquarters.

A fine, top-flight laboratory has been established and is maintained by Fire Department personnel for the analysis of physical evidence brought in by members of the Arson Squad.

These teams of cops and firemen are on the road twenty-four hours a day. They are charged with investigating *every fire where a possibility of crime exists*. They also investigate:

1. Every hotel fire.
2. Every industrial fire.
3. Explosions.
4. Any fire in which any person sustains injuries or a loss of life occurs.
5. Cases in which the Arson Squad did not respond while on the "road," but which were reported on the daily fire bulletin as "cause unknown."

Being "on the road" at the time of an alarm sometimes results in the Arson Squad car arriving at the same time as the fire apparatus. This aids in the preservation of evidence and permits an examination of spectators at a fire for possible pyros.

The entire squad works as a unit in the processing of an arson investigation. Team No. 1 may examine the scene and turn over the final clean-up to Team No. 2 at the expiration of their day's work. Team No. 3 may pick up the interviews of the witnesses in this case from Team No. 2. In this fashion cases do not "lay over" from day to day as investigators finish a day's work and leave for home.

At first glance it may seem that such procedure disperses the work of an investigation a bit too much, but it must also be remembered that to cope with modern arsonists any investigator needs time for rest and relaxation. Over a period of years this system has proved to be more efficient than piling all the work of an investigation upon the original investigating team.

Readers should note the Detroit Team System is a formal extension of the cooperation between police and fire units which has effected remarkable results when both pitch in whole-heartedly and without reservation. A good example is the case of Brooklyn's mentally retarded pyro. As previously noted Fire Marshal Martin Scott and Police Commissioner George Monaghan assigned both fire and detective personnel to the area of this pyro's operations. When Detective Sgt. Frank Weldon made the arrest, Fire Marshal Scott guided the investigation and assigned technical aspects of the case to his own men. This splendid cooperation may have stemmed from the fact that the Police Commissioner served for several years as Fire Commissioner just prior to being named top cop.

It is the joint operation of the Detroit Arson Squad which seems to be the keynote to its success. This system places the full responsibility for arson investigations in the hands of one unit and thereby avoids the shifting of responsibility from one department to another.

Another advantage is the complete harmony which exists between the two departments insofar as the Arson Squad is concerned. The detective gets the complete cooperation of all the services of the Police Department and the fire member of the team gets the same from the Fire Department.

For the first time a large city has recognized the fact that when arson squads are manned solely by one Department, then departmental jealousies are apt to come to the fore. A fire officer may refuse to give the police officer the time of day and vice versa. The joint operation in Detroit overcomes this factor.

PROBLEMS OF RURAL AREAS

A comforting thought to residents of many rural areas is that the fire marshal handles all arson cases, but realistic inquiry develops the cold fact that the force of fire marshals in any state is totally inadequate to investigate the origin of more than a small percentage of fires which may have been arson.

Los Angeles, Buffalo, Detroit, New York, and other cities with top-flight arson squads may be said to deliver close to 100 per cent coverage. In comparison, rural areas are dependent upon the individual training and ability of local police and fire officers and thus receive much more limited coverage.

The general attitude is expressed in one mimeographed instruction sheet of a state fire marshal's office directed to fire officials in his state, which starts off with the words, "If you think an investigation is necessary . . ."

Nine states do not even have state fire marshals, and in some states the commanders of the state police or highway patrol forces act as fire marshals. Even in the states having fire marshals a great deal of the preliminary work must be performed by local fire and police officials. While some of these have worked wonders in view of their limited training and experience, it is unfair to compare their investigations with those of individuals trained for such duty.

Local fire administrators can raise the standards of arson detection in rural areas by training their personnel to be more alert to arson, by making provision for a fireman to be directly responsible for ascertaining the basic facts helpful in initiating an arson investigation, and by insisting upon "honest" classification of fires.

Lectures to fire personnel on the modus operandi of arson has worked wonders in creating interest in detecting fire-setting. The singling out of one man to gather pertinent facts concerning the fire, sometimes pointing to arson, is often a coveted assignment and serves to create additional interest among the men.

This assignment of what might be termed an "arson specialist" among firemen reporting to fires has been utilized by many state fire marshals to alert fire personnel to the detection of arson and also to permit the launching of the initial investigation without loss of time.

Fire Marshal George Clough of New York's Nassau County and former Fire Marshal William Martin of Kentucky are two of these administrators who seek better utilization of fire personnel at the scene of a fire. Fire departments in a great number of states have been circularized on this vital point. The instructions given to the fire units in Kentucky is a good illustration of an attempt to secure the cooperation of men actually at the scene of the fire during its height. In outline form, these instructions cover the following points:

1. At least one fireman, who will respond to every alarm, should be designated as the individual who will obtain certain pieces of vital information. He should be prepared to inform the investigator of the exact time of the alarm, and, if possible, the name of the person giving it.

2. All firemen should note:

    a. Persons or cars leaving the scene or present upon arrival of apparatus;

    b. Whether doors or windows were open, unlocked, or locked when entrance was made;

    c. Any disarrangement of furnishings or contents, drawn shades or the absence of valuable or personal articles or pets which are ordinarily present;

    d. The attitude of owners or occupants and any statements made by them;

    e. Unusual bystanders, particularly those seen at other fires and those who appear unduly excited or interested as to the cause of the fire;

    f. All evidence and preserve it until the arrival of the investigator.

3. The fire officer in charge should:

    a. Have notes made as above facts are reported to him (small details may later become important to the trial of a case); take prompt and proper action when a fire is deemed suspicious, particularly in guarding the scene until the arrival of investigators; entry to the building should be denied to all persons except firemen and police officers until the arrival of investigators.

    b. Seek to determine the exact point of origin, taking particular note if there is any indication of more than one point of origin.

4. Fire-fighting personnel at the scene should *not:*

    a. Move, remove, or handle anything which may be evidence;

    b. Damage the scene in overhauling and cleaning up when a fire is "suspicious";

   c. Open drawers or search to determine the absence of valuables;

   d. Offer public statements as to suspicions of any kind;

   e. Attempt to act as investigators, but give their ideas to the investigators when they arrive.

While the opposite of "honest" classification of fires is dishonest, the word is too harsh. That is why "honest" when used in relation to the classification of fires is bracketed in quotation marks. It's true that some fire officials may be unwilling to classify a fire as of undetermined or unknown origin, but the great percentage of them are willing to do so in the absence of definite evidence pointing to its origin.

However, many fire officials seem to feel the burden of their experience and rank, and think that a prompt judgment as to the cause of the fire is expected of them. These individuals act as if the determination of a fire's origin is a challenge to their ability as fire officers and that to admit they cannot fix the cause of a fire is to admit a serious failing. At times these men give prompt—and misleading—causes of fire solely to feed their own egos. "Careless smoker," "poor wiring," or "overheated stove," are some of the causes ascribed to fires in which no definite proof of such causes was found. These fire officials must be made to realize that there is no reflection on ability when classifying a fire as "unknown" or "undetermined origin." To classify it so is more of a challenge, saying in essence, "I've a lot of experience with fires, but this one stumps me. We'll have to investigate it before we can determine the origin."

State fire marshals are presently doing fine work in utilizing fire personnel and police units in their fight against arson, but a great deal must be accomplished in the training field before top-flight arson detection will exist in rural areas.

PUBLIC APATHY

There's no question that an aroused public has brought into being the fine city units previously described in this chapter. It is equally true that public apathy has failed to provide adequate arson units in many cities and most of the rural areas of the United States.

The complacency of the general public in view of increasing fire losses is difficult to understand. Losses for the first three months of 1953 now total $232,836,000, an increase of 7.6 per cent over the same months of 1952. And in the third month of 1953 the fire losses were the highest on record, amounting to $83,471,000, an increase of 15.5 per cent over the losses reported for March, 1952. Yet no aroused public voiced indignation at such losses, or demanded to know what percentage of these losses resulted from arson.

Even when the people of a locality experience major incendiary fires, there seems to be little concentrated effort to bring about any reform in the method of handling arson cases. Pyros will create a short-lived reign of terror in city after city, but to date little extensive research on the part of public authorities has been directed at the problem of identifying and apprehending these fire-setters.

Fraud fire-setters are known as such to their friends, but are not socially ostracized or brought to summary justice as a murderer would be, for example. They're tolerated, yet Al Keshner, who as the customer of the Little Jakie and Moishe arson ring was responsible for the fire in which Detective Daggett lost his life, can testify that arson is a killer. He was sentenced to die in the electric chair for felony murder. Only a "last ditch" commutation of sentence by Governor Dewey spared his life.

Indicative of the complacency of most people is the fact that the Model Arson Law (See Appendix) drafted by the best brains in the legal field has been adopted by only forty-two states. True, the other six states have "comparable statutes," but this law recommended by the National Board of Fire Underwriters after a great deal of study may plug a few loopholes in these "comparable statutes"—yet six states are still to adopt it.

EDUCATION OF THE PUBLIC

If there is any one thing that can aid arson investigators it would be the education of the public to the truth about arson. The public must realize that arson detection and investigation should be the task of a special unit of either the police or the fire department or, better yet, a joint enterprise. They must realize that arson investigators need their cooperation—need every little bit of help the public can give, particularly when individuals can serve as witnesses in the case of a criminally set fire. And lastly, they must understand that arson is not a crime directed against insurance companies, but is a crime directed against every citizen, against the community—a crime plainly labeled *potential murder.*

APPENDIX

The Model Arson Law now in effect in forty-two states reads as follows:

ARSON—FIRST DEGREE

Burning of Dwellings

Any person who willfully and maliciously sets fire to or burns or causes to be burned or who aids, counsels or procures the burning of any dwelling house, whether occupied, unoccupied or vacant, or any kitchen, shop, barn, stable or other outhouse that is parcel thereof, or belonging to or adjoining thereto, whether the property of himself or of another, shall be guilty of Arson in the first degree, and upon conviction thereof, be sentenced to the penitentiary for not less than two nor more than twenty years.

ARSON—SECOND DEGREE

Burning of Buildings, etc., Other Than Dwellings

Any person who willfully and maliciously sets fire to or burns or causes to be burned, or who aids, counsels or procures the burning of any building or structure of whatsoever class or character, whether the property of himself or of another, not included or described in the preceding section, shall be guilty of Arson in the second degree, and upon conviction thereof, be sentenced to the penitentiary for not less than one nor more than ten years.

ARSON—THIRD DEGREE

Burning of Other Property

Any person who willfully and maliciously sets fire to or burns or causes to be burned or who aids, counsels or procures the burning of any personal property of whatsoever class or character; (such property being of the value of twenty-five dollars and the property of another person), shall be guilty of Arson in the third degree and upon conviction thereof, be sentenced to the penitentiary for not less than one nor more than three years.

ARSON—FOURTH DEGREE

Attempt to Burn Buildings or Property

(a) Any person who willfully and maliciously attempts to set fire to or attempts to burn or to aid, counsel or procure the burning of any of the buildings or property mentioned in the foregoing sections, or who commits any act preliminary thereto, or in furtherance thereof, shall be guilty of Arson in the fourth degree and upon conviction thereof be sentenced to the penitentiary for not less than one nor more than two years or fined not to exceed one thousand dollars.

Definition of an Attempt to Burn

(b) The placing or distributing of any flammable, explosive or combustible material or substance, or any device in any building or property mentioned in the foregoing sections in an arrangement or preparation with intent to eventually willfully and maliciously set fire to or burn same, or to procure the setting fire to or burning of same shall, for the purposes of this act constitute an attempt to burn such building or property.

BURNING TO DEFRAUD INSURER

Any person who willfully and with intent to injure or defraud the insurer sets fire to or burns or attempts so to do or who causes to be burned or who aids, counsels or procures the burning of any building, structure or personal property, of whatsoever class or character, whether the property of himself or of another, which shall at the time be insured by any person, company or corporation against loss or damage by fire, shall be guilty of a felony and upon conviction thereof, be sentenced to the penitentiary for not less than one nor more than five years.

GLOSSARY OF TERMS
USED BY FIREMEN

Apparatus:	Any type of fire fighting equipment such as hook and ladders, pumpers, hose wagons, etc.
Artillery:	Large calibre streams.
Back Draft:	Smoke explosion of pent up gases, heat and smoke suddenly receiving fresh oxygen, thus causing a powerful explosion. Generally due to improper ventilation.
Back Out:	Order given to retreat from a position with a line after it has advanced into a fire building.
Back Stretch:	The stretching of hose lines from a pumper that has passed the fire going into position at a hydrant.
Back Up:	Order given to support a working line in position with an additional line. "Back up that line."
Battering Ram:	A forcible entry tool used to batter down doors, breech brick walls, etc. Generally manned by five men for best results.
Big Bertha:	Large calibre stream apparatus.
Big Guns:	Refers to large calibre streams used at a huge fire.
Big Squirt:	A water tower.
Big Stick:	The serial ladder.
Blow:	A breathing spell, generally a relief by a fresher man or crew to those operating a line in a charged atmosphere. "Take a blow" "Give him a blow."
Blue Lightman:	Generally refers to volunteer firemen,

taken from the fact that most volunteers have blue lights on their private vehicles.

Body Bag: A canvas bag in which bodies of victims are removed from burned premises, etc.

Boloney, Bologna: The small hose carried by most apparatus, the inch and a half hose.

Booster: A small line connected to a tank of water carried on the apparatus.

Bridge Chemical: A special piece of apparatus equipped to fight fires on bridges or in tunnels, highways, etc.

Buff: A civilian interested in firemanics, who frequents fire stations and who responds to alarms.

Bug: Another term used to denote an arsonist or pyromaniac.

Burnout: Term used when the interior of a building, room or apartment is completely gutted by fire.

Butt: The coupling end of the hose (HOSE BUTT). Also designated as the MALE or FEMALE BUTT.

Can: The two and a half gallon Soda and Acid Extinguisher.

Cellar Pipe: Sections of wrought iron that fit together into a long pipe, placed through openings to reach a fire otherwise unapproachable without difficulty.

Charged: Term used to designate a line with water, ready for use (CHARGED LINE); or to designate a room or space filled with pent up smoke, heat and gases.

Coffee Wagon: Hydrant Thawing Apparatus—throws steam into a frozen hydrant to melt the ice.

CO$_2$: The Carbon Dioxide extinguisher carried on apparatus, or to any such extinguishing system.

Coupling: Brass fittings on hose used to connect lengths together.

Darken It Down: Order given to subdue flames to a point

	at which they are under control, though not entirely extinguished.
Dash:	A brief application of water on a small or incipient fire, "Give it a dash."
Deck Pipe:	A large nozzle attached to the deck of apparatus, manned by one man.
Deluge Set:	Equipment setting up a large nozzle into which lines are siamesed to give a heavy stream. Portable and mounted on the street, etc.
Doughnut:	A rolled up length of hose carried on the apparatus.
Exposure:	Any surrounding structures, buildings, materials, etc., subject to fire spread from a central fire.
Fire Lines:	The dividing lines between the scene of operations at a fire and where spectators, etc., are held in check by the Police.
Flying Stretch:	The feeding of hose from a moving apparatus. Most generally used when the fire is met by the pumper before the hydrant is reached.
Fog Nozzle:	A nozzle which discharges water in a fine spray.
Front Piece:	The identification plate on leather helmets which signifies a company by color (Black for Engine Companies, Red for Ladder Companies, Blue for Rescue Companies) on which is large numeral for the company number. Officers wear white face pieces, a large company number as per color above, and a bugle or other device to signify rank.
Give It a Belt:	To hit "showing" fire with a stream to determine its intensity.
Give It a Dash:	To give "showing" or incipient fire a brief application from the hose stream.
Goin' Good:	Term used to signify a fire with an abundance of flame showing upon arrival.
Hanging Ceiling:	A ceiling separated from the floor above

or from the roof by a dead air space. Also called "Cockloft."

Hit It:
Order to direct the stream at "showing" fire.

Hit the Ceiling:
Order to strike the ceiling at an angle with the stream to get better distribution and coverage by deflection of water on the fire.

Hit the Floor:
Order to slide the poles to the street floor, in response to either an alarm, emergency or other reasons.

Hold Fast:
Order to stay where you are, to hold your position with the hose line.

Hold It:
Order to keep the fire where it is at any cost. Also, that the fire can be held in check when a report is being given to headquarters.

Hook:
A tool with a malleable iron head shaped into a point with a hook on the side and varying in length up to thirty feet. Used to rip down ceilings, walls, etc.

Hook-up:
The connecting of lines to pumpers, or pumpers to hydrants.

Hose Change:
Term used when hose is replaced on the apparatus after use, or monthly as per schedule to relieve kinks, etc., periodically.

Hose Jacket:
A brass covering that can be clamped about a burst portion of a length of hose to stop the leak.

Hose Roller:
A metal frame with wooden pulley to fit over a roof or building cornice to allow easy hoisting of a hose or ladder up the face of a building. Also known as a "Ladder Roller."

Hose Strap:
A short length of rope with a metal hook attached; used to fasten a hose line to banisters of a stairway, or on fire escapes, etc., to lessen strain and prevent slipping.

Hose Tag:
Leather slip straps containing a metal

plate or disc bearing a company number and a line number. Used at large fires to identify the lines stretched, one at the source of supply, the other attached at the nozzle.

Hose Test:
Term used to designate scheduled annual or semi-annual testing of hose by companies.

Hose Wagon:
Apparatus designed to carry hose and equipment but not a pump. Used in suburban areas and sections of a city where large amounts of hose might be needed. Hose wagons generally are equipped with a Deck Pipe.

Housewatch:
A type of duty assigned to firemen taking charge of the company watch desk, receiving and recording all alarms, business, etc., in the company journal.

Increaser:
A fitting used to increase a smaller opening to a larger size. The opposite of a Reducer.

In Service:
Term used to designate a unit ready to respond to alarms.

Journal:
Record book in which is kept in chronological order, all alarms, happenings, transactions, etc., of a unit.

Kill It:
The extinguishment of visible fire.

Kink:
Sharp turn, twist or bend which impedes the flow of water through a hose line.

Kink Chaser:
A fireman who lags behind and who generally later excuses himself that he was straightening out the kinks of the hose line for the first few moments.

Ladder Company:
Term used by some departments for hook and ladder companies. In general, apparatus constructed to carry portable and serial ladders, in addition to other equipment.

Locate:
To find the fire. Also when one company is working at a fire for any length of time, another company is sent to Lo-

CATE in the quarters of the absent company, and becomes the absent company
in identity and covers the fire district.

Long Stretch: A stretched hose line consisting of about
eighteen lengths or over.

Medium Stretch: A stretched hose line consisting of about
twelve lengths.

Mushroom: Pent up heat, gases and smoke that have
risen to the highest possible point in a
building, spreading laterally, and then
downward, causing spread of fire and
possible explosion. Relieved by prompt
and proper top ventilation.

Nozzle: The long tapered fitting attached to the
hose line and through which the stream
exits efficiently if sufficient pressure is
maintained at the nozzle. "Controlling
Nozzle" can be shut down at will by the
man on the nozzle. Open nozzle is con-
trolled only at the source. See also "Fog
Nozzle."

Open Up: Order given to forcibly gain entrance
into a building or to have building ventilated to allow pent up heat, smoke and
gases to escape to prevent mushrooming.

Overhaul: Overhauling is the term used to cover
examination, inspection and search to insure no hidden flame or spark which may
rekindle has been overlooked. This operation is performed with the least possible
damage to the building or contents.

Over Your Head
and All Around: Term used in ordering the fireman on
the nozzle in a difficult spot with fire
raging all around to get down on his
knees and whip the stream about in all
directions. This cools off the immediate
vicinity and allows survey of conditions.

Pipe: Nozzle.

Pipeman: The fireman handling the nozzle, or detailed to the nozzle.

Plant: Materials or articles arranged by an arsonist to cause or start a fire. Such evidence can generally be found before it is consumed by fire if the alarm is not delayed. See also SET-UP. Also used to denote investigators stationed at the scene of a probable fire or crime, ready to apprehend the culprit with the evidence and in the act.

Pompier: Also called scaling ladder. Consists of a single wooden spar, reinforced with metal strips running the entire length. The hooks, generally made of a special Swedish steel are of sufficient width to span any sill over which they may be used, provided with teeth to prevent slipping. Made in various lengths of 12, 14, 16 and 18 feet, these ladders are always used in conjunction with a life belt. Rungs usually are fourteen inches long, and the spar has several metal saddles to keep ladder out from the building to protect the hands when in use. Commonly used to reach points higher than the normal reach of other ladders. Sometimes used for opening wire glass windows during ventilation operations.

Pumper: Apparatus equipped to draught and pump water for fire fighting and other uses.

Pumps: The machinery carried on apparatus (and some portable types) that can draught and pump water under pressure.

Push In: The order given to advance a line under trying smoke and heat conditions, to seek out the seat of the fire.

Reducer: A fitting used to reduce a large opening to a smaller size. The opposite of IN-CREASER.

Rekindle: A supposedly extinguished fire that starts up again. This can only be caused by improper overhauling.

Ripe: An especially thick, smoky condition where hot, heavy and rolling fumes are met with at a fire. ("It was really ripe").

Roast: The remains of a person burned to death.

Run: Going to a fire and returning; generally in reference to the apparatus. "We came back from the run about 9:30 P.M."

Salvage: The operation of preventing unnecessary water and smoke damage, protection to stock and property by applying tarpaulins, covers, etc., removal of same to a safe place for reclaiming later. Channeling water via ready made troughs, etc., to stairways and drains.

Scaling Ladder: See POMPIER.

Search: Term used to have a company thoroughly inspect and look for persons or children that may be trapped or overcome in a fire building. Usually conducted by a ladder company while ventilating.

Siamese: A double intake connection which leads into a single outlet, having a clapper valve in each inlet to prevent back flow.

Simultaneous Stretch: Two lines stretched at the same time from the same apparatus.

Set-up: Essentially the same as PLANT.

Short Stretch: A stretched hose line of about six lengths.

Smokie: A condition at a fire where there is little flame but an abundance of smoke.

Snotty: A "smokie" fire that causes the mucus to run down one's nose and face.

Spaghetti: Large quantities of hose stretched at the scene of a fire, in a seemingly hopelessly snarled condition. ("The spaghetti is all over the street.")

Stand Fast: Order given to a company to remain as is until further orders. Generally used to hold a company at the scene of a fire in the event they might be needed.

Still Alarm: An alarm received after a fire has been

extinguished and is merely being reported for record. Requires prompt investigation to ensure it is properly extinguished.

Still Button: The means by which the fire station interior alarm is sounded. ("Hit the still button!")

Stretch: Term meaning to lay out a hose line, or a hose line that has been laid out for use.

Stretches: There are many types of stretches, see under proper heading. (Short, Medium, Long, Flying, Simultaneous, Back, etc.).

Stretch In: Laying of a hoseline into a building or to a fire.

Take Suction: Order to connect a pumper to a water supply other than a hydrant, or when no hydrant is available, or when working adjacent to a river, pond, etc.

Take Up: Term used in ordering a company to pick up hose and equipment and return to quarters. Literally it means cease what you are doing.

Tiller: The steering wheel on the trailer section of hook and ladder trucks, and some water towers, which allows the maneuvering of such long apparatus through traffic and narrow streets.

Tillerman: The fireman assigned to handle the tiller wheel.

Time Out: Time an alarm was received for report purposes, etc.

Torch: Another firemanic term for a fire bug, arsonist, etc.

Truck Company: General firemanic term for a hook and ladder company.

Turnout Coat: A heavy waterproof canvas short coat generally worn by members of a truck company.

Turnouts: The heavy working trousers worn by fireman, wide enough at the bottom to fit over rubber boots, and quickly snapped together at the waist. Term also applies to other fire fighting apparel placed on the apparatus for fire fighting or to the garb worn in quarters when not in uniform.

Turret Gun:
See DECK PIPE, ARTILLERY.

Under Control:
A fire or situation at the stage where it can be easily handled by the available forces. No danger to exposures or of extension.

Ventilate:
To open a building to allow pent up heat, smoke and gases to escape through selected channels to prevent mushrooming and loss of life. This also allows the fire fighters to advance to the seat of the fire by removing the barrier of heat and smoke keeping them back, prevents spread of fire, etc.

Verbal:
A type of alarm received in quarters from a citizen reporting a fire to which the company responds, or a fire discovered through observation which results in the company responding.

Wash Down:
The finishing touches after a fire is out. All debris and wreckage is carefully examined, turned over and wetted, all charred parts left standing given a final brief wetting to insure all fire is extinguished.

Washer:
The rubber grommets which must be in the female couplings to prevent leakage. A good fireman almost automatically feels to see if this washer is present when he handles hose.

Watch Line:
A hose line left at a fire that might break out again in places. (Lumberyards, mattress factories, scenes of large fires, etc.)

Well Charged:
Term to signify a building, or room, in which pent up heat, smoke and gases have been confined for some time before

the arrival of the department. ("It was well charged!")

What's the Exposure: Order for the immediate determination of the possibility of fire spread to other parts of a building, or to adjacent buildings by way of doors, windows, shafts, openings, etc., if fire gains further headway.

"Y" Connection: A connection which allows two lines to run into a single line or vice versa. Differs from the Siamese connection in that it has no clapper valves.

BIBLIOGRAPHY

Annual Reports of The Committee on Incendiarism and Arson of National Board of Fire Underwriters.

Curtis, Arthur F. *The Law of Arson.* Buffalo, New York: Dennis and Co., Inc., 1936.

Kirk, Paul L. *Fire Investigation.* New York, New York: John Wiley and Sons, Inc., 1969.

Lewis and Yarnell. *Pathological Firesetting (Pyromania).* New York: Coolidge Foundation, Publishers, 1951.

Mulcahy, Bernard W., Chief, Fire Prevention Bureau, Cleveland, Ohio. "Arson," *Fire Engineering,* January–May 1953.

Myren, Richard A. *Investigation of Arson and Other Burnings* (Guidebook Series), Chapel Hill, North Carolina: Institute of Government, University of North Carolina, 1952. Prepared for the use of those attending the courses in the investigation of arson and other burnings. Not published. All rights reserved.

News Letters published periodically by International Association of Arson Investigators (restricted to use of Association members).

Rethoret, H. *Fire Investigations.* Printed in Canada by Recording and Statistical Corporation, Ltd., Toronto and Montreal, 1945.

BUREAU OF POLICE

DATE: _____

NAME OF ACCUSED:_____ TIME: _____

I am Detective _____ of the _____ Bureau of Police.

1. You are being interviewed in connection with the alleged commission of the crime of _____.

2. You have an absolute right to remain silent and make no statement to me and your silence will be guarded by the police.

3. Any statement you make with or without counsel can be used as evidence against you.

4. You have a right to the presence of an attorney during this or any further interview the police might have with you. The attorney may be one of your own choosing which you retain, or if you are without funds to employ counsel, the court will appoint one for you.

Do you understand the rights that have been explained to you? _____

You may voluntarily waive the above rights that have been explained to you and make a statement if you so desire.

_____
Signature of Accused

WITNESSES:

_____

_____

(This form, with minor variations, is commonly used by law enforcement agencies.)

BUREAU OF POLICE
INTERVIEW GUIDE

Case No.

Memo by Officer on Statements taken, written or oral:

1. Person interviewed

2. Date and time subject was taken into custody

3. Officer taking subject into custody

4. Location taken into custody

5. Time brought to headquarters————, 19————: ———————— A. M. / P. M.

6. A. Was warrant secured prior to taking statement?
   B. Was warrant served before or after taking statement?

7. Name of interviewing officer
   A. Name (s) of other person (s) present during interview

8. Location of place of interview

9. Exact time interview began———————— A. M. / P. M. ————————, 19——

10. The following advice was given the defendant prior to the interview:
    I am Detective————————of the————————Bureau of Police.
    1. You are being interviewed in connection with the alleged commission of the crime of
    2. You have an absolute right to remain silent and make no statement to me and your silence will be guarded by the police.
    3. Any statement you make with or without counsel can be used as evidence against you.
    4. You have a right to the presence of an attorney during this or any future interview the police might have with you. The attorney may be one of your own choosing which you retain, or if you are without funds to employ counsel, the court will appoint one for you.

11. Do you understand the rights that have been explained to you?————
    You may voluntarily waive the above rights that have been explained to you and make a statement if you so desire.

12. A. Can you read? Answer———— B. Can you write? Answer————————

13. Sobriety (check one)——Sober——Drunk——Drinking——Other (explain)

14. Nervousness (check one)   ——Not nervous ——Slightly ——Extremely

15. Clothing (check one)   ——Neat and orderly——In disorder——Other (explain)

284

16. Physical (check one)   ___Uninjured ___Injured or wounded ___If injured or wounded, explain nature of injury or wound. Did injury or wound appear to impair faculties?

17. Mental (check one)   ___Appeared clear and able to understand questions and their meaning.
___Unable to understand meaning of questions
___Other (explain)

18. Was statement reduced to writing?

19. If reduced to writing, did person interviewed sign it?

20. A. Was it read to him?   B. Did he read it?

21. If he didn't read it, what reason did he give?

22. A. If he did sign it, did he first read it over?
B. If he did sign it, did he request any changes to be made in it?
C. Were such changes made?
D. Initialed?

23. During interview, did person being interviewed complain of being hungry, tired, or sick?
If so, explain nature of complaint and any action taken in response thereto

24. During interview, did accused request to see anyone?
If so, whom?
Action taken reference this request

25. Did accused request to contact anyone by telephone? ___If so, whom?___
_____Action taken reference this request_____

26. Exact time interview ended_____ A. M.
                                             P. M. _____19___

27. For statistical data:
A. Did accused waive rights and make a confession?
B. Did accused request counsel before making a statement?
C. Did the alleged crime in this case become classified as "unsolved" because of the new rules affording certain aforementioned rights to the accused?
D. Was this case brought to a conclusion by the use of a confession?

Witness:

_____

_____

                              _____
                              Signature of Interviewing Officer

285

INDEX